Communications
in Computer and Information Science 2732

Series Editors

Gang Li ⓘ, *School of Information Technology, Deakin University, Burwood, VIC, Australia*

Joaquim Filipe ⓘ, *Polytechnic Institute of Setúbal, Setúbal, Portugal*

Zhiwei Xu, *Chinese Academy of Sciences, Beijing, China*

Rationale
The CCIS series is devoted to the publication of proceedings of computer science conferences. Its aim is to efficiently disseminate original research results in informatics in printed and electronic form. While the focus is on publication of peer-reviewed full papers presenting mature work, inclusion of reviewed short papers reporting on work in progress is welcome, too. Besides globally relevant meetings with internationally representative program committees guaranteeing a strict peer-reviewing and paper selection process, conferences run by societies or of high regional or national relevance are also considered for publication.

Topics
The topical scope of CCIS spans the entire spectrum of informatics ranging from foundational topics in the theory of computing to information and communications science and technology and a broad variety of interdisciplinary application fields.

Information for Volume Editors and Authors
Publication in CCIS is free of charge. No royalties are paid, however, we offer registered conference participants temporary free access to the online version of the conference proceedings on SpringerLink (http://link.springer.comhttp://link.springer.com) by means of an http referrer from the conference website and/or a number of complimentary printed copies, as specified in the official acceptance email of the event.

CCIS proceedings can be published in time for distribution at conferences or as post-proceedings, and delivered in the form of printed books and/or electronically as USBs and/or e-content licenses for accessing proceedings at SpringerLink. Furthermore, CCIS proceedings are included in the CCIS electronic book series hosted in the SpringerLink digital library at http://link.springer.com/bookseries/7899. Conferences publishing in CCIS are allowed to use our online conference service (Meteor) for managing the whole proceedings lifecycle (from submission and reviewing to preparing for publication) free of charge.

Publication process
The language of publication is exclusively English. Authors publishing in CCIS have to sign the Springer CCIS copyright transfer form, however, they are free to use their material published in CCIS for substantially changed, more elaborate subsequent publications elsewhere. For the preparation of the camera-ready papers/files, authors have to strictly adhere to the Springer CCIS Authors' Instructions and are strongly encouraged to use the CCIS LaTeX style files or templates.

Abstracting/Indexing
CCIS is abstracted/indexed in DBLP, Google Scholar, EI-Compendex, Mathematical Reviews, SCImago, Scopus. CCIS volumes are also submitted for the inclusion in ISI Proceedings.

How to start
To start the evaluation of your proposal for inclusion in the CCIS series, please send an e-mail to ccis@springer.com

Petia Radeva · Duc Pham · Stefano Berretti ·
Pascal Lorenz · Latika Kharb · Deepak Chahal
Editors

Information, Communication and Computing Technology

10th International Conference, ICICCT 2025
New Delhi, India, May 24, 2025
Revised Selected Papers

Editors
Petia Radeva
University of Barcelona
Barcelona, Spain

Duc Pham
The University of Birmingham
Birmingham, UK

Stefano Berretti
University of Florence
Florence, Italy

Pascal Lorenz
Université of Haute-Alsace
Haute-Alsace, France

Latika Kharb
Jagan Institute of Management Studies
Rohini, Delhi, India

Deepak Chahal
Jagan Institute of Management Studies
Rohini, Delhi, India

ISSN 1865-0929　　　　　　ISSN 1865-0937　(electronic)
Communications in Computer and Information Science
ISBN 978-3-032-08637-2　　　ISBN 978-3-032-08638-9　(eBook)
https://doi.org/10.1007/978-3-032-08638-9

© The Editor(s) (if applicable) and The Author(s), under exclusive license
to Springer Nature Switzerland AG 2026

This work is subject to copyright. All rights are solely and exclusively licensed by the Publisher, whether the whole or part of the material is concerned, specifically the rights of translation, reprinting, reuse of illustrations, recitation, broadcasting, reproduction on microfilms or in any other physical way, and transmission or information storage and retrieval, electronic adaptation, computer software, or by similar or dissimilar methodology now known or hereafter developed.
The use of general descriptive names, registered names, trademarks, service marks, etc. in this publication does not imply, even in the absence of a specific statement, that such names are exempt from the relevant protective laws and regulations and therefore free for general use.
The publisher, the authors and the editors are safe to assume that the advice and information in this book are believed to be true and accurate at the date of publication. Neither the publisher nor the authors or the editors give a warranty, expressed or implied, with respect to the material contained herein or for any errors or omissions that may have been made. The publisher remains neutral with regard to jurisdictional claims in published maps and institutional affiliations.

This Springer imprint is published by the registered company Springer Nature Switzerland AG
The registered company address is: Gewerbestrasse 11, 6330 Cham, Switzerland

If disposing of this product, please recycle the paper.

Preface

The 10th International Conference on Information, Communication and Computing Technology (ICICCT 2025) was held on May 24, 2025 in New Delhi, India. ICICCT 2025 was organized by the Department of Information Technology, Jagan Institute of Management Studies (JIMS) Rohini, New Delhi, India. The conference received 403 submissions and 60 papers were shortlisted for review and after double-blind reviews and an average of 3 reviews per paper, 17 papers were selected for this volume. The acceptance rate was around 28%. The contributions came from diverse areas of Information technology categorized into two tracks, namely (1) Intelligent Systems and (2) Pattern Recognition.

The aim of ICICCT 2025 was to provide a global platform for researchers, scientists and practitioners from both academia and industry to present their research and development activities in all aspects of communication and network systems and computational intelligence techniques.

We thank all the members of the Organizing Committee and the Program Committee for their hard work. We are very grateful to Pascal Lorenz, University of Haute-Alsace, France as First General Chair, Duc Pham, University of Birmingham, UK as Second General Chair, Petia Radeva, University of Barcelona, Spain as First Program Chair, Stefano Berretti, University of Florence, Italy as Second Program Chair, Parag Kulkarni, Tokyo International University, Japan as Keynote Speaker, Pradeep Singh, National Institute of Technology, Raipur, India as session chair for Track 1, and Ferdous Ahmed Barbhuiya, Indian Institute of Information Technology Guwahati, India as session chair for Track 2.

We thank all the Technical Program Committee members and referees for their constructive and enlightening reviews of the manuscripts. We thank Springer for publishing the proceedings in the Communications in Computer and Information Science (CCIS) series. We thank all the authors and participants for their great contributions that made this conference possible.

July 2025
Latika Kharb
Deepak Chahal

Organization

General Chairs

Pascal Lorenz — University of Haute-Alsace, France
Duc Pham — University of Birmingham, UK

Program Chairs

Petia Radeva — University of Barcelona, Spain
Celestine Iwendi — University of Greater Manchester, UK
Stefano Berretti — University of Florence, Italy

Keynote Speaker

Parag Kulkarni — Tokyo International University, Japan

Conference Secretariat

Praveen Arora — Jagan Institute of Management Studies, India

Program Committee Chairs

Latika Kharb — Jagan Institute of Management Studies, India
Deepak Chahal — Jagan Institute of Management Studies, India

Session Chair for Track 1

Pradeep Singh — National Institute of Technology, Raipur, India

Session Chair for Track 2

Ferdous Ahmed Barbhuiya — Indian Institute of Information Technology Guwahati, India

Technical Program Committee

Gaurav Gupta	Punjabi University, Patiala, India
Sharifah Saon	University Tun Hussein Onn Malaysia, Malaysia
Mohd Adham Isa	Ibnu Sina Institute, Malaysia
Om Prakash Jena	Ravenshaw University, India
Kalpdrum Passi	Laurentian University, Canada
Arshad Ali	National University of Computer & Emerging Sciences, Pakistan
Asma Ahmad	National University of Computer & Emerging Sciences, Pakistan
Shakila Basheer	Princess Nourah bint Abdulrahman University, Saudi Arabia
Sameerchand Pudaruth	University of Mauritius, Mauritius
R. Chithra	K.S. Rangasamy College of Technology, India
Pang Yee Yong	Universiti Teknologi Malaysia, Malaysia
Samir Kumar Bandyopadhyay	University of Calcutta, India
Janmenjoy Nayak	Maharaja Sriram Chandra Bhanja Deo University, India
Ajune Wanis Ismail	Universiti Teknologi Malaysia, Malaysia
Filippo Vella	National Research Council of Italy, Italy
Zuraini Ali Shah	Universiti Teknologi Malaysia, Malaysia
Saylee Gharge	Vivekanand Education Society's Institute of Technology, India
Sharad Saxena	Thapar Institute of Engineering & Technology, India
Surbhi Gupta	Punjab Agricultural University, India
Attila Fazekas	University of Debrecen, Hungary
Ch. Hima Bindu	QIS College of Engineering and Technology, India
Nikhil Marriwala	Kurukshetra University, India
Mohammed Ali Shaik	SR University, India
Ponmagal R. S.	SRM Institute of Science and Technology, India
Nadim Rana	Jazan University, Saudi Arabia
Ali J. Abboud	University of Diyala, Iraq
Chan Weng Howe	Universiti Teknologi Malaysia, Malaysia

Michael Melese	Addis Ababa University, Ethiopia
Aamir Wali	National University of Computer and Emerging Sciences, Pakistan
Nur Haliza Abdul Wahab	Universiti Teknologi Malaysia, Malaysia
Facundo Quiroga	Universidad Nacional de La Plata, Argentina
Nawel Zemmal	University of Souk Ahras, Algeria
Antonio Montieri	University of Naples Federico II, Italy
Latafat Gardashova	Azerbaijan State Oil and Industry University, Azerbaijan
Apostolos Gkamas	University of Ioannina, Greece
Dalibor Dobrilovic	University of Novi Sad, Serbia
A. V. Petrashenko	Igor Sikorsky Kyiv Polytechnic Institute, Ukraine
Abhinav Bhandari	Thapar Institute of Engineering & Technology, India
Kolla Bhanu Prakash	Koneru Lakshmaiah Education Foundation, India
Md. Ali Hussain	Sreenidhi Institute of Science and Technology, India
Mohd Abdul Ahad	Jamia Hamdard University, India
Karamjeet Singh	Thapar Institute of Engineering & Technology, India
Neetu Sardana	Jaypee Institute of Information Technology, India
Anoop V. S.	Thiagarajar School of Management, India
Pratyay Kuila	National Institute of Technology, Sikkim, India
J. Akilandeswari	Sona College of Technology, India
Pradeep Singh	National Institute of Technology Raipur, India
Praveen Kumar Malik	Lovely Professional University, India
Raman Maini	Thapar Institute of Engineering & Technology, India
Suman Madan	ATLAS SkillTech University, India
Rakesh Kumar	Central University of Haryana, India
Khalid Raza	Jamia Millia Islamia, India
Jereesh A. S.	Cochin University of Science and Technology, India
Suraiya Jabin	Jamia Millia Islamia, India
Tarunpreet Bhatia	Thapar Institute of Engineering & Technology, India
Deepika Bansal	Maharaja Agrasen Institute of Technology, India
Varun Malik	Chitkara University, India
Surjeet Dalal	Amity University, Gurugram, India
Martin Puttkammer	North-West University, South Africa
Muhammad Ramzan Malik	University of Sargodha, Pakistan
Pardeep Sangwan	Maharaja Surajmal Institute of Technology, India

Win Pa Pa	Naypyitaw State Polytechnic University, Myanmar
Sudhir Kumar Sharma	Sharda University, India
Pooja Sahgal	Vivekananda Institute of Professional Studies - Technical Campus, India
S. Kalaivani	B. S. Abdur Rahman Crescent Institute of Science & Technology, India
Ashish Sharma	GLA University, India
Suman Mann	Panipat Institute of Engineering and Technology, India
Gowrishankar S.	Dr. Ambedkar Institute of Technology, India

Contents

Track-01 Intelligent Systems

AD-GNN: An Attention-Driven Dynamic Motion-Aware Graph Neural Network for Skeleton-Based Gait Recognition 3
    D. Priyanka and T. Mala

Mixed Reality Portal with Artificial Intelligence Companion 17
    Muhamad Haikal Arman, Ajune Wanis Ismail, and Muhammad Anwar Ahmad

Advancing Indian Vehicle Detection Using YOLO11 and YOLO12 with SAHI Optimization 27
    Aishvi Guleria, Kamya Varshney, Garima, and Shweta Jindal

AI-Driven Secure Vehicle Verification for Smart Transportation: Multi-factor Authentication and Anomaly Detection 45
    Dushmanta M. Kalita, Dilip Kr. Barman, and Abhijit Boruah

MauFish: A Smart Fish Identification App 59
    Shaeez Permessur and Raj Kishen Moloo

ARROW: A New Paradigm for Decentralized Energy-Aware IoT Routing Using Reinforcement Learning and Additive Header Encoding 72
    Mohammadreza Kaghazgaran, Jaafar Gaber, and Pascal Lorenz

The Improvement of Organizational Value Chains Using Distributed Sensor Networks 83
    C. Atsango and J. P. van Deventer

Comparative Analysis of Predictive Models for Analysing Demographics and Academic Features to Predict Student Performance Using Machine Learning Techniques 95
    Harshvardhan Tiwari and Neel Pandey

TRACK-02: Pattern Recognition

Integration of Security Elements into the Honeybee Work Sharing Framework 115
    Sarvesh Chand, Krishneel Sharma, Mansour H. Assaf, and Bibhya Sharma

Origins, Models, Current Status, and Challenges in Textual Emotion Recognition 130
    Abid Hussain Wani and Faezeh Mesrinejad

Deep Learning Approaches for Iris Damage Prediction Using CNN and Image Processing 145
    S. Sangeetha and R. Sujatha

A Novel Computer Vision Method for Measuring Concentration of $KMnO_4$ in Water Treatment Plant 158
    Nityananda Hazarika, Hidam Kumarjit Singh, Ram Kishore Roy, and Tulshi Bezboruah

Medifolio: An Intelligent Medical Portfolio System for Healthcare Management and Consultation 170
    Soham Barve, Shreeya Ranwadkar, Paritosh Gogate, Hemanshu Vaidya, and Aparna Kamble

Compartmental Models for Detecting Fake News Propagation in OSN with Variable Population 185
    V. Nithish Kumar, G. Praneeth Kumar, Sujoy Datta, Santosh Kumar Uppada, and B. Sivaselvan

DermaVLM: Multi-modal Skin Disease Diagnosis 197
    Saket Sultania, Vansh Shah, Rohit Sonawane, and Abhishek Vichare

Predicting Volunteering Commitment Using Machine Learning in South Africa 212
    Sakhiwo Mtwenka, Marie Hattingh, Alex Bignotti, Sonali Das, and Timothy Adeliyi

Robust Image Denoising Using Gradient Seeds, Morphology, and DBSCAN Clustering 224
    Parag Anil Tamhankar and Stephanie Hayden

Author Index 241

Track-01 Intelligent Systems

Funksoft Intelligent Systems

AD-GNN: An Attention-Driven Dynamic Motion-Aware Graph Neural Network for Skeleton-Based Gait Recognition

D. Priyanka[(✉)] [iD] and T. Mala [iD]

College of Engineering Guindy, Anna University, Chennai 600 025, India
priyankasekard2511@gmail.com, mala@auist.net

Abstract. Gait recognition is a biometric identifier that distinguishes individuals based on their walking patterns. Unlike other biometrics, gait recognition operates from a distance, requires no active cooperation, and is challenging to disguise. Traditional approaches predominantly utilize silhouette sequences to extract gait features, yet these methods are vulnerable to occlusions and fail to preserve fine-grained spatial details. To address these limitations, model-based methods utilize pose-estimation techniques to effectively capture spatial and temporal joint information, establishing skeleton-based recognition as a powerful alternative. However, existing skeleton-based methods often neglect the importance of different body parts and overlook the dynamic motion characteristics inherent in gait sequences. To address these challenges, this study proposes an Attention-Driven Dynamic Motion-Aware Graph Neural Network (AD-GNN), which integrates an Attention-Driven Graph Convolutional Network (AGCN) and a Dynamic Motion Network (DMN) module. AGCN facilitates selective focus on critical joint relationships across spatial and temporal dimensions, while DMN captures intricate local and global motion dynamics, enabling a richer feature representation of gait sequences. By aggregating the strengths of AGCN and DMN, the proposed model extracts discriminative features that significantly enhance gait recognition performance. Evaluations of the CASIA-B dataset demonstrate that the AD-GNN model achieves superior accuracy compared to state-of-the-art skeleton-based approaches, establishing its effectiveness and robustness for real-world gait recognition tasks.

Keywords: Gait Recognition · Biometric Authentication · Graph Neural Network · Pose Estimation · Model-based Approach · Attention Mechanism

1 Introduction

Biometrics involves identifying or verifying individuals based on their physiological or behavioral traits. Physiological biometrics use features like fingerprints, iris scans, and facial recognition, while behavioral biometrics rely on characteristics such as gait and signature to differentiate individuals [1]. Gait-based biometric recognition offers a significant advantage as it allows identification from a distance without user cooperation, making it challenging to replicate. However, gait biometrics face difficulties due to variations in clothing, objects carried, viewing angles, and other factors that can alter a person's gait pattern [2]. Consequently, a robust gait recognition system must address these challenges to extract consistent and distinctive gait features uninfluenced by external factors.

Approaches to gait recognition are broadly categorized into appearance-based and model-based techniques. Appearance-based methods use silhouettes to extract gait features [3]. However, existing systems often overlook the complexity and rapid changes in environments when extracting silhouettes [4]. Moreover, silhouettes retain appearance-related information such as clothing and carrying conditions, making them susceptible to variations in appearance. With advancements in pose estimation techniques, model-based approaches have gained prominence in gait recognition. Pose estimation models generate skeletal joint key points, providing gait features independent of appearance compared to appearance-based methods [5]. The skeleton representation of the human body portrays posture and dynamic movements over time.

Graph Convolutional Networks (GCNs) [6] play a pivotal role in comprehending skeleton-based gait representations by encapsulating both spatial and temporal nuances of joint movements [5]. By structuring gait data as graphs, these networks facilitate the analysis of correlations among joints and frames, which is essential for understanding an individual's distinct gait pattern. The primary challenge in gait recognition lies in accurately distinguishing an individual's gait among variations and similarities between multiple gaits. This necessitates the extraction of fine-grained gait features that capture intricate details in joint movements, thereby enabling robust identification [7]. The graph-based approach offers an advantage by capturing local and global relationships between joints and frames, yet real-world challenges such as clothing variations, viewing angles, and environmental factors pose significant hurdles.

In this paper, an Attention-Driven Dynamic Motion-Aware Graph Neural Network (AD-GNN) is proposed for processing skeleton-based gait sequences by extracting spatial and temporal movement features. Each layer within AD-GNN integrates three distinct pathways: spatio-temporal, dynamic, and residual. The spatio-temporal pathway employs graph-based techniques to extract joint features by modeling spatial and temporal relationships in gait sequences. The dynamic pathway enhances motion modeling by leveraging local and global mechanisms to capture sequential information. The residual pathway facilitates effective gradient propagation and preserves essential features from previous layers. This hierarchical structure enables AD-GNN to capture both spatial and temporal dependencies efficiently. Fusion steps at the end of each pathway aggregate the extracted spatio-temporal and dynamic features before passing them to subsequent layers for higher-level abstraction. Additionally, the model incorporates affine transformations, rescaling, and alignment to ensure a unified pose representation across different subjects and viewing conditions.

By stacking multiple AD-GNN layers, the model effectively learns fine-grained motion characteristics and constructs a discriminative gait representation. The extracted features undergo global average pooling and are then passed through a fully connected layer to generate a robust gait embedding for recognition. This approach enables precise identification of individuals based on their gait patterns.

The contributions of the paper are as follows:

- The proposed AD-GNN model integrates an Attention-Driven Graph Convolutional Network (AGCN) and a Dynamic Motion Network (DMN) to extract both spatial and temporal movement features for skeleton-based gait recognition.
- Design of a multi-path architecture within each AD-GNN layer, comprising spatio-temporal, dynamic, and residual pathways, to model diverse aspects of gait sequences effectively.
- Incorporation of transformation techniques (affine transformation, rescaling, and alignment) to establish a unified pose representation and enhance gait feature consistency.
- Comprehensive evaluation of AD-GNN using the CASIA-B dataset, demonstrating its effectiveness across different covariate conditions, including variations in viewpoint, clothing, and carrying conditions.

The paper is structured as follows: Sect. 2 reviews existing studies on gait recognition based on skeleton representation. Section 3 details the proposed AD-GNN architecture and its submodules. Section 4 provides comprehensive information on the dataset and implementation details. Section 5 presents the analysis of the obtained results. Finally, Sect. 6 concludes the paper by summarizing the findings and suggesting future research directions.

2 Related Work

Model-based approaches in gait recognition leverage simulated models or skeletal representations to capture human structure and movement dynamics. Recent advancements in deep learning have facilitated the development of accurate pose estimation models. Works such as PoseGait [2] and CNNpose [8] utilized skeleton sequences as matrices and employed CNN models for analysis. Similarly, PTSN [9] and its 3D variant PTSN-3D [10] combined CNN and LSTM models to extract static and dynamic features from 2D and 3D skeleton coordinates. Moreover, Yao et al. [11] introduced the Skeleton Gait Energy Image (SGEI), which aggregates the skeleton positions over frames. The skeleton features are first processed using a decomposition technique and then combined with model-free features to extract gait features. However, this model does not capture the correlations between joints.

Recently, transformer-based models have been explored for gait recognition, effectively capturing spatial and temporal dependencies. For instance, the authors in [12] employed a spatial transformer network to extract skeletal features, but its reliance on long frame sequences posed challenges for real-time applications. Similarly, Gait-TR [13] used self-attention mechanisms to dynamically learn spatial gait patterns, but its effectiveness in modeling temporal relationships was limited due to the lack of explicit temporal modeling strategies. GaitPT [14] addressed these challenges by introducing a pyramid transformer architecture designed to extract spatial and temporal features in an anatomically coherent manner using skeleton-based inputs. By hierarchically aggregating joint-level movements from fine to coarse levels, the model learns comprehensive full-body motion representations. Although transformers offer powerful feature extraction capabilities, their high computational cost and extensive data requirements often hinder practical deployment in real-world gait recognition scenarios.

Additionally, Graph Convolutional Networks (GCNs) have gained attention for learning joint correlations and improving global context modeling. For example, Shopon et al. [7] used a residual connection-based GCN model to identify discriminative features and mitigate overfitting. Methods such as JointsGait [15], GaitGraph [16], GaitGraph2 [17], GaitDLF [18] and SFG-Net [19] leveraged GCN-based architectures to extract gait representations, but they primarily focused on spatial relationships while overlooking fine-grained temporal motion patterns. Furthermore, existing GCN-based methods do not explicitly model local and global motion dynamics, which are crucial for robust gait recognition. To address these limitations, this study introduces AD-GNN, which combines AGCN for selective joint correlations and DMN for capturing fine-grained motion dynamics. By incorporating both spatial and temporal awareness, the proposed AD-GNN model enables a more comprehensive and discriminative representation of gait sequences, significantly improving recognition performance.

3 Proposed Model

In this section, the basic concepts and proposed network architecture with its modules are discussed in detail.

3.1 Preliminaries

A human skeleton is modeled as a graph $G = (V, E)$, where $V = \{v_1, \ldots, v_N\}$ represents N joints, and E defines the connectivity between them [16]. The structure of the skeleton is encoded by an adjacency matrix $A \in \mathbb{R}^{N \times N}$, where $A_{ij} = 1$ if an edge connects joint v_i to v_j, and $A_{ij} = 0$ otherwise. Since the skeleton graph is undirected, A is symmetric [16].

A gait sequence is represented as a series of graphs, where each joint v_n at time t has a feature vector $x_{t,n} \in \mathbb{R}^C$, forming a feature tensor $X \in \mathbb{R}^{T \times N \times C}$. Here, T represents the number of frames in the sequence, N is the number of joints, and C denotes the feature dimension (e.g., 2D coordinates and confidence scores). The pose at time t is expressed as $X_t \in \mathbb{R}^{N \times C}$. A learnable weight matrix $\Theta^{(l)} \in \mathbb{R}^{C^l \times C^{l+1}}$ is used in each layer l of the model to transform node features.

3.2 Proposed AD-GNN Model

Figure 1 illustrates the proposed Attention-Driven Dynamic Motion-Aware Graph Neural Network (AD-GNN) model, designed to capture both spatial and temporal features for accurate gait recognition. The input skeleton sequences undergo preprocessing through batch normalization, followed by transformations such as affine transform, rescaling, and alignment, ensuring uniform pose representation across subjects and viewing conditions.

Initial features are extracted using the Spatial-Temporal Graph Convolutional Network (ST-GCN) model [20], which effectively captures the spatial and temporal relationships in the gait sequences. These extracted features are then processed by two subsequent modules: the Attention-Driven Graph Convolutional Network (AGCN) and the Dynamic Motion Network (DMN). The AGCN module emphasizes selective focus on critical joint relationships by incorporating attention mechanisms across spatial and temporal dimensions. Meanwhile, the DMN module leverages both local and global motion mechanisms to capture intricate motion dynamics in the gait sequences, enriching the feature representation.

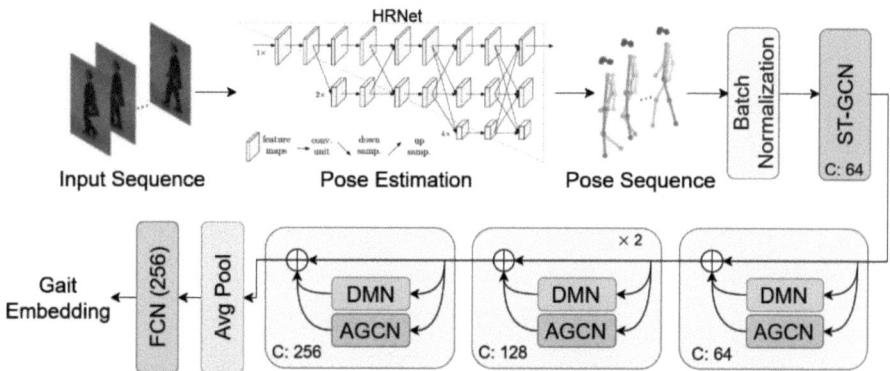

Fig. 1. Framework of Attention-driven Dynamic Motion-aware GNN (AD-GNN) for Skeleton-based Gait Recognition

Each pathway's features are added, and a residual connection is included to preserve essential information. The relevant features are then passed to the next layers for further processing, enabling the model to retain the most important information for subsequent abstractions. By stacking multiple AD-GNN layers, the model effectively learns fine-grained dynamic motion characteristics and constructs a robust gait representation. Finally, global average pooling is applied to the extracted features, followed by a fully connected layer, which generates discriminative gait embedding for gait recognition.

3.3 Attention-Driven Graph Convolutional Network (AGCN)

As shown in Fig. 2, the AGCN model is designed to process skeleton-based gait sequences by efficiently extracting both spatial and temporal features. The module builds upon the ST-GCN while incorporating attention mechanisms to enhance the representation of critical joint relationships. By integrating hierarchical feature extraction with adaptive attention mechanisms, AGCN efficiently captures the intricate motion patterns essential for gait recognition.

ST-GCN. Given a sequence of skeleton graphs, ST-GCN applies graph convolution to extract spatial features and temporal convolution to capture motion dynamics. For a gait sequence represented by the feature tensor $X \in \mathbb{R}^{T \times N \times C}$ and adjacency matrix A, the spatial graph convolution operation [16] is defined as:

$$X_t^{(l+1)} = \sigma(\tilde{D}^{-\frac{1}{2}} \overline{A} \tilde{D}^{-\frac{1}{2}} X_t^{(l)} \theta^{(l)}) \quad (1)$$

where $\overline{A} = A + I$ includes self-loops to retain individual joint features, $\tilde{D}$ is the diagonal degree matrix of $\overline{A}$, and $\theta^{(l)}$ is a learnable weight matrix. The activation function $\sigma(\cdot)$ introduces non-linearity to enhance feature learning.

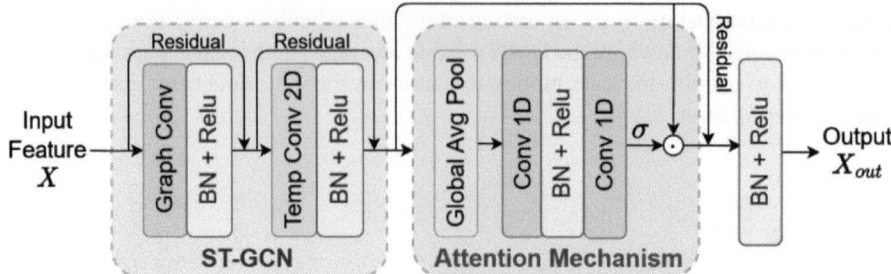

Fig. 2. Structure of AGCN Model

To capture temporal dependencies, ST-GCN applies a 2D convolution along the temporal axis:

$$X'_t = ReLU(BN(Conv2D(X_t))) \qquad (2)$$

where *Conv2D* denotes a temporal convolutional layer, *BN* represents batch normalization, and *ReLU* is the activation function. This operation extracts motion-related information by learning temporal transitions across frames.

Attention Mechanism. To refine spatial feature learning, AGCN integrates an attention mechanism that dynamically reweights the importance of different body regions. This mechanism enhances discriminative feature extraction by prioritizing informative joints. Given a feature tensor X', the attention scores are computed as:

$$X_{att} = \sigma\left(W_2 \cdot ReLU\left(BN\left(W_1 \cdot GAP(X')\right)\right)\right) \qquad (3)$$

where *GAP* denotes global average pooling, W_1 and W_2 are learnable weight matrices, and σ represents softmax normalization. This attention mechanism selectively enhances the most relevant joints while suppressing less informative ones.

To preserve the original information, the computed attention weights X_{att} are used to scale the input features, followed by a residual connection:

$$X_{out} = ReLU(BN(X_{att} \odot X') + X')) \qquad (4)$$

where $\odot$ denotes element-wise multiplication. This formulation ensures that essential joint features are emphasized while maintaining the integrity of the original representation.

3.4 Dynamic Motion Network (DMN)

As shown in Fig. 3, Dynamic Motion Network (DMN) model employs two primary components: a Local Feature Extractor (LFE) and a Global Feature Extractor (GFE), both based on ST-GCN to capture both short-term (local) and long-term (global) dependencies in gait data. These two outputs are then fused to form a comprehensive representation of dynamic motion.

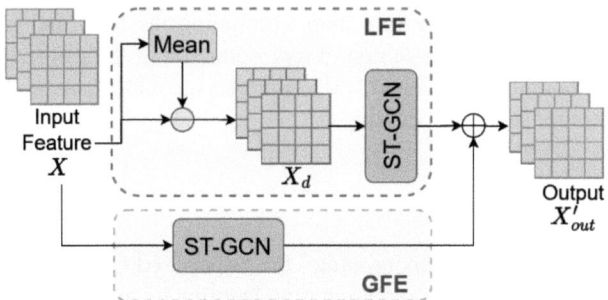

Fig. 3. Structure of DMN Model

Local Feature Extraction. For local feature extraction, the mean feature map across the temporal dimension T is first computed, producing a gait template that captures the average appearance of the gait over time. This is done by computing:

$$X_m = \frac{1}{T}\sum_{t=1}^{T} X_t \quad (5)$$

where $X_m \in \mathbb{R}^{N \times C}$ represents the gait template, which aggregates the joint features across all time steps. The dynamic feature map X_d is then obtained by subtracting the gait template X_m from each frame in the sequence:

$$X_d = \{X_t - X_m | t = 1, 2, \ldots, T\} \quad (6)$$

where $X_d \in \mathbb{R}^{T \times N \times C}$ represents the dynamic features, capturing the deviations from the mean gait template over time. The local feature extractor uses ST-GCN model to learn the spatial-temporal features from the dynamic gait data:

$$X'_{LFE} = STGCN(X_d) \quad (7)$$

Here, X_{LFE}' represents the output of the LFE, which is the learned representation of the dynamic gait features.

Global Feature Extraction. For global feature extraction, ST-GCN is applied directly to the original input sequence X, capturing the long-term dependencies and global features across the entire sequence:

$$X'_{GFE} = STGCN(X) \quad (8)$$

where X_{GFE}' represents the global feature map that captures the overall motion of the gait over time. The outputs from both the local and global feature extractors are then fused to create the final representation:

$$X'_{out} = X'_{LFE} + X'_{GFE} \quad (9)$$

where X_{out}' is the final fused feature map, combining the local and global dynamic features to provide a rich spatial-temporal representation of the gait sequence. Finally, the outputs from both the AGCN and DMN modules are added and passed through the subsequent layers for further processing.

3.5 Loss Function

The proposed AD-GNN model incorporates the Supervised Contrastive (SupCon) loss function [21], which encourages representation learning by attracting features from the same class while moving distinct classes apart in the embedding space. Given a batch of N samples, each with an anchor-positive pair, the loss is computed as:

$$\mathcal{L}_{\text{SupCon}} = \sum_{i \in I} \frac{1}{|P(i)|} \sum_{p \in P(i)} \log \frac{\exp(z_i \cdot z_p / \tau)}{\sum_{a \in A(i)} \exp(z_i \cdot z_a / \tau)} \qquad (10)$$

where z_i and z_p are normalized feature vectors, $P(i)$ denotes the set of positive samples for anchor i, $A(i)$ includes all samples except i, and τ is a temperature scaling factor.

4 Dataset and Implementation Details

The CASIA-B dataset is a widely used public dataset that contains walking data from 124 subjects, recorded under various conditions such as different viewpoints, clothing, and carrying items [22]. It includes 11 distinct viewpoints and covers three walking conditions: normal (NM), bag (BG), and cloth (CL). Each subject has 10 sequences per view: 6 for the normal condition and 2 for each of the bag and cloth conditions.

For evaluation, a training-testing split is employed where 74 subjects are used for training, and the remaining 50 subjects are designated for testing. In the testing phase, the first 4 NM sequences are selected as the gallery, while the remaining sequences are divided into three probe subsets: 2 NM, 2 BG, and 2 CL sequences [17]. Initially, the dataset provides silhouette images, from which skeleton sequences are extracted for further processing.

Pose estimation is performed using the HRNet model, pre-trained on the COCO dataset, to detect skeleton keypoints [16]. The AD-GNN model, utilized for feature extraction, consists of four layers with 1, 1, 2, and 1 building blocks, and output channels of 64, 64, 128, and 256, respectively. Each block is followed by batch normalization and ReLU activation to extract key features. The final layer is a fully connected layer with 256 nodes for feature representation. The model's performance is optimized using the supervised contrastive loss function.

Data augmentation techniques, such as sequence order flipping, sequence mirroring, and the addition of Gaussian noise to both individual joints and across the sequence, are applied during training. The model is trained on sequences of 60 frames with a batch size of 64 for 300 epochs. The loss temperature is set to 0.01, and the Adam optimizer is used.

During the testing phase, the Euclidean distance is calculated to identify the most suitable match in the gallery, enabling robust comparison and recognition of gait patterns.

5 Result Analysis

The study evaluates the AD-GNN model in comparison with existing appearance-based and model-based approaches, analyzing their performance under various conditions, including normal walking, clothing variations, and bag-carrying scenarios. The assessment focuses on the CASIA-B dataset, reporting the average rank-1 accuracy across different probe angles while excluding identical view cases. The evaluation highlights performance variations due to view changes and walking conditions.

Table 1. Comparison of the proposed AD-GNN model with skeleton-based methods on the CASIA-B dataset under normal walking condition (NM) using averaged Rank-1 accuracy (%), excluding cases with identical views.

Probe Angle NM# 5–6	Gallery NM # 1–4					
	PoseGait [2]	PSTN [9]	JointsGait [15]	GaitGraph2 [17]	GaitDLF [18]	Proposed
0°	55.3	49.3	68.1	78.5	80.1	**81.2**
18°	69.6	61.5	73.6	82.9	**87.1**	86.5
36°	73.9	64.4	77.9	85.8	87.7	**88.9**
54°	75	63.6	76.4	85.6	89.2	**89.7**
72°	68	63.7	77.5	83.1	84.4	**87.4**
90°	68.2	58.1	79.1	81.5	84.4	**89.9**
108°	71.1	59.9	78.4	84.3	84.2	**87.2**
126°	72.9	66.5	76	83.2	85.2	**86.3**
144°	76.1	64.8	69.5	84.2	85.2	**86**
162°	70.4	56.9	71.9	81.6	85.4	**86.2**
180°	55.4	44	70.1	71.8	**80.6**	77.4
Mean	68.72	59.3	74.4	82.05	84.86	**86.06**

Table 1, 2 and 3 presents a comparative analysis of the proposed AD-GNN model against state-of-the-art skeleton-based gait recognition methods on the CASIA-B dataset under normal walking (NM), walking with a bag (BG), and walking with a coat (CL) condition, respectively. The results indicate that the proposed model achieves superior performance across all three conditions, demonstrating its robustness in handling diverse gait variations.

Under the NM condition, the proposed model attains an average Rank-1 accuracy of 86.06%, outperforming GaitDLF [18] (84.86%) and GaitGraph2 [17] (82.05%), highlighting its ability to effectively capture discriminative gait features. Similarly, in the BG condition, the proposed model achieves 73.89%, surpassing GaitDLF [18] (70.74%) and GaitGraph2 [17] (73.19%). Even in the CL condition, which presents significant occlusions, the model maintains the highest accuracy of 68.21%, outperforming GaitDLF [18] (67.95%) and GaitGraph2 [17] (63.57%).

Table 2. Comparison of the proposed AD-GNN model with skeleton-based methods on the CASIA-B dataset under bag carrying condition (BG) using averaged Rank-1 accuracy (%), excluding cases with identical views.

Probe Angle BG# 1–2	Gallery NM # 1–4					
	PoseGait [2]	PSTN [9]	JointsGait [15]	GaitGraph2 [17]	GaitDLF [18]	Proposed
0°	35.3	29.8	54.3	69.9	68.2	**70.1**
18°	47.2	37.7	59.1	**75.9**	71	72.5
36°	52.4	39.2	60.6	78.1	74.2	**78.6**
54°	46.9	40.5	59.7	**79.3**	75.8	73.6
72°	45.5	43.8	63	71.4	69	**75.3**
90°	43.9	37.5	65.7	71.7	71.2	**78.9**
108°	46.1	43	62.4	74.3	71.5	**74.5**
126°	48.1	42.7	59	**76.2**	71.2	75
144°	49.4	36.3	58.1	73.2	72	**74.8**
162°	43.6	30.6	58.6	73.4	70.5	**73.9**
180°	31.1	28.5	50.1	61.7	63.5	**65.6**
Mean	44.5	37.2	59.1	73.19	70.74	**73.89**

These improvements are attributed to the AGCN, which enhances spatial feature learning by capturing significant joint relationships, and the DMN, which refines temporal motion patterns by leveraging both local and global ST-GCN. These components enable a more comprehensive understanding of gait dynamics, leading to state-of-the-art performance across all conditions.

Table 4 presents a comparative analysis of appearance-based and model-based gait recognition methods on the CASIA-B dataset. Appearance-based models, such as GaitSet [3], GaitPart [23] and IGaitSet [24], exhibit the highest accuracy across all conditions due to their ability to leverage silhouette-based representations. GaitPart [23] achieves the best overall performance, with an accuracy of 96.2% (NM), 91.5% (BG), and 78.7% (CL), and a lower standard deviation (SD = 9.06), indicating stable performance across varying conditions.

Among model-based approaches, skeleton-based methods such as PoseGait [2] and PSN [9] show significantly lower accuracy, particularly under BG and CL conditions, reflecting the challenges of modeling occluded or altered gait patterns. In contrast, GaitGraph [16] and the proposed AD-GNN demonstrate superior performance in learning spatial-temporal gait dynamics. AD-GNN achieves 86.1% (NM), 73.89% (BG), and 68.21% (CL), outperforming GaitGraph [16] in the CL condition. Furthermore, AD-GNN exhibits a lower standard deviation (SD = 9.12) compared to GaitGraph [16] (SD = 10.78), highlighting its greater consistency across conditions. The lower SD of AD-GNN suggests its enhanced robustness to gait variations, making it a promising approach for skeleton-based gait recognition in challenging real-world scenarios.

Table 3. Comparison of the proposed AD-GNN model with skeleton-based methods on the CASIA-B dataset under cloth varying condition (CL) using averaged Rank-1 accuracy (%), excluding cases with identical views.

Probe Angle CL# 1–2	Gallery NM # 1–4					
	PoseGait [2]	PSTN [9]	JointsGait [15]	GaitGraph2 [17]	GaitDLF [18]	Proposed
0°	24.3	18.7	8.1	57.1	67	**68.4**
18°	29.7	21	46.9	61.1	**68.1**	67.5
36°	41.3	25	49.6	68.9	69.1	**72.1**
54°	38.8	25.1	50.5	66	68.9	**69.6**
72°	38.2	25	51	67.8	64.4	**70.6**
90°	38.5	26.3	52.3	65.4	68	**70.3**
108°	41.6	28.7	49	68.1	**69.2**	68.9
126°	44.9	30	46	67.2	**71.3**	68.5
144°	42.2	23.6	48.7	63.7	**69.3**	65.6
162°	33.4	23.4	53.6	63.6	**70.1**	65.8
180°	22.5	19	52	50.4	62.1	**63**
Mean	35.95	24.2	49.8	63.57	67.95	**68.21**

Table 4. Average Rank-1 accuracy and Standard Deviation (SD) for CASIA-B dataset compared with appearance-based models.

Type	Method	NM	BG	CL	SD
Appearance-based	GaitSet [3]	95.0	87.2	70.4	12.57
	GaitPart [23]	**96.2**	**91.5**	**78.7**	**9.06**
	IGaitSet [24]	95.5	90.5	73.0	11.8
Model-based	PoseGait [2]	68.7	44.5	36	16.97
	PSN [9]	69.8	43.5	33.2	18.87
	GaitGraph [16]	**87.7**	**74.8**	66.3	10.78
	Proposed	86.1	73.89	**68.21**	**9.12**

Figure 4 presents a t-SNE visualization of the learned feature embedding, showcasing the separability of gait representations across different subjects and covariate conditions (NM, BG, CL). Each color corresponds to a distinct subject ID, while different marker shapes represent gait variations under different covariates.

The visualization reveals well-clustered subject-specific embedding, indicating that the proposed AD-GNN model effectively captures discriminative gait features. Notably, the embedding within each subject exhibit a degree of separation based on covariate conditions, reflecting the model's sensitivity to external gait variations. However, the preserved intra-subject compactness suggests that despite these variations, the model maintains identity consistency across covariate changes. The distinct cluster boundaries indicate the model's effectiveness in capturing both spatial and temporal gait patterns, ensuring enhanced feature discrimination. These findings reinforce the model's capability to learn compact, discriminative gait embedding, effectively mitigating covariate influences and improving gait recognition performance.

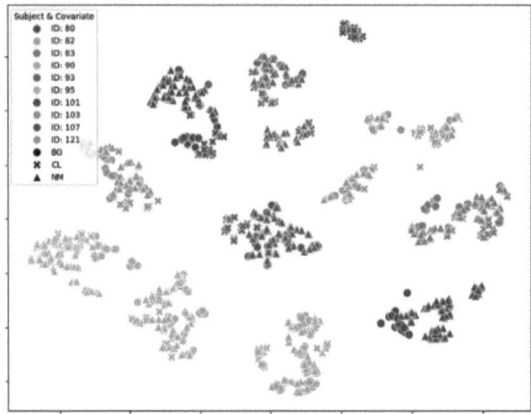

Fig. 4. t-SNE visualization of the feature distribution learned by the proposed AD-GNN model for 10 randomly selected subjects.

In summary, the analysis of results suggests potential areas for enhancement in the proposed model. Future directions may involve exploring bottleneck architecture, experimenting with diverse loss functions, and incorporating a wider range of datasets for improved performance and robustness.

6 Conclusion

In this work, the gait recognition system shifts from traditional silhouette-based methods to skeleton sequences, driven by advancements in pose estimation techniques. The introduction of the AD-GNN model and its submodules, such as AGCN and DMN, demonstrates the effectiveness of model-based approaches in capturing detailed gait features, focusing on both spatial and temporal joint motion. AGCN captures inter-joint dependencies through graph convolutions, while DMN improves feature extraction by employing ST-GCN for dynamic and global features.

Empirical evaluation on the CASIA-B dataset, considering factors like viewpoint variations, clothing changes, and carrying conditions, highlights the robustness and flexibility of the AD-GNN-based approach. The AGCN and DMN submodels each contribute distinct advantages, showing the model's ability to handle various gait patterns. The results validate the potential of this model for real-world gait recognition tasks, improving accuracy in diverse conditions.

The findings of this study open new avenues for enhancing gait recognition, offering opportunities to refine model architectures, develop new loss functions, and incorporate more diverse datasets. As gait recognition advances, the use of skeleton-based approaches like AD-GNN, shows great promise for improving the accuracy and reliability of individual identification based on unique walking patterns.

References

1. Minaee, S., Abdolrashidi, A., Su, H., Bennamoun, M., Zhang, D.: Biometrics recognition using deep learning: a survey. Artif. Intell. Rev. **56**(8), 8647–8695 (2023)
2. Liao, R., Yu, S., An, W., Huang, Y.: A model-based gait recognition method with body pose and human prior knowledge. Pattern Recogn. **98**, 107069 (2020)
3. Chao, H., He, Y., Zhang, J., Feng, J.: Gaitset: Regarding gait as a set for cross-view gait recognition. In Proceedings of the AAAI conference on artificial intelligence. **33**(01), 8126–8133 (2019)
4. Song, X., Wang, Y., Huang, Y., Shan, C.: Gait recognition via view-aware part-wise attention and multi-scale dilated temporal extractor. Image Vis. Comput. **156**, 105464 (2025)
5. Teepe, T., Khan, A., Gilg, J., Herzog, F., Hörmann, S., Rigoll, G.: Gaitgraph: graph convolutional network for skeleton-based gait recognition. In 2021 IEEE International Conference on Image Processing (ICIP), pp. 2314–2318. IEEE (2021)
6. Lakshmi, P. R., Geetha, A. V., Priyanka, D., Mala, T.: PRISM: Predicting student performance using integrated similarity modeling with graph convolutional networks. In: 2023 12th International Conference on Advanced Computing (ICoAC), pp. 1–7. IEEE (2023)
7. Shopon, M., Bari, A.H., Gavrilova, M.L.: Residual connection-based graph convolutional neural networks for gait recognition. Vis. Comput. **37**, 2713–2724 (2021)
8. An, W., et al.: Performance evaluation of model-based gait on multi-view very large population database with pose sequences. IEEE Trans. Biomet. Behav. Identity Sci. **2**(4), 421–430 (2020)
9. Liao, R., Cao, C., Garcia, E.B., Yu, S., Huang, Y.: Pose-based temporal-spatial network (PTSN) for gait recognition with carrying and clothing variations. In: Zhou, J., et al. (eds.) Biometric Recognition. CCBR 2017. LNCS, vol 10568. Springer, Cham (2017). https://doi.org/10.1007/978-3-319-69923-3_51
10. An, W., Liao, R., Yu, S., Huang, Y., Yuen, P.C.: Improving gait recognition with 3D pose estimation. In: Zhou, J., et al. (eds.) Biometric Recognition. CCBR 2018. LNCS, vol. 10996. Springer, Cham (2018). https://doi.org/10.1007/978-3-319-97909-0_15
11. Yao, L., Kusakunniran, W., Wu, Q., Zhang, J., Tang, Z., Yang, W.: Robust gait recognition using hybrid descriptors based on skeleton gait energy image. Pattern Recogn. Lett. **150**, 289–296 (2021)
12. Zhang, C., Chen, X.P., Han, G.Q., Liu, X.J.: Spatial transformer network on skeleton-based gait recognition. Expert Syst., e13244 (2023)
13. Xu, C., Makihara, Y., Li, X., Yagi, Y., Lu, J.: Cross-view gait recognition using pairwise spatial transformer networks. IEEE Trans. Circuits Syst. Video Technol. **31**(1), 260–274 (2020)
14. Catruna, A., Cosma, A., Radoi, E.: Gaitpt: skeletons are all you need for gait recognition. In 2024 IEEE 18th International Conference on Automatic Face and Gesture Recognition (FG), pp. 1–10. IEEE (2024)
15. Li, N., Zhao, X., Ma, C.: JointsGait: A model-based gait recognition method based on gait graph convolutional networks and joints relationship pyramid mapping. arXiv preprint arXiv:2005.08625 (2020)
16. Teepe, T., Khan, A., Gilg, J., Herzog, F., Hörmann, S., Rigoll, G.: Gaitgraph: graph convolutional network for skeleton-based gait recognition. In 2021 IEEE International Conference on Image Processing (ICIP), pp. 2314–2318. IEEE (2021)

17. Teepe, T., Gilg, J., Herzog, F., Hörmann, S., Rigoll, G.: Towards a deeper understanding of skeleton-based gait recognition. In Proceedings of the IEEE/CVF Conference on Computer Vision and Pattern Recognition, pp. 1569–1577 (2022)
18. Wei, S., Liu, W., Wei, F., Wang, C., Xiong, N. N.: Gaitdlf: global and local fusion for skeleton-based gait recognition in the wild. J. Supercomput., 1–27 (2024)
19. Priyanka, D., Mala, T.: SFG-Net: Semantic relationship and hierarchical Fusion-based Graph Network for enhanced skeleton-based gait recognition. Eng. Appl. Artif. Intell. **148**, 110399 (2025)
20. Hang, R., Li, M.: Spatial-temporal adaptive graph convolutional network for skeleton-based action recognition. In: Proceedings of the Asian Conference on Computer Vision, pp. 1265–1281 (2022)
21. Khosla, P., et al.: Supervised contrastive learning. Adv. Neural. Inf. Process. Syst. **33**, 18661–18673 (2020)
22. Yu, S., Tan, D., Tan, T.A.: framework for evaluating the effect of view angle, clothing and carrying condition on gait recognition. In 18th International Conference on Pattern Recognition (ICPR 2006), vol. 4, pp. 441–444. IEEE (2006)
23. Fan, C., et al.: Gaitpart: Temporal part-based model for gait recognition. In Proceedings of the IEEE/CVF Conference on Computer Vision and Pattern Recognition, pp. 14225–14233 (2020)
24. Yang, D., Bai, Y., Wang, H., Zhang, X.: A fine-grained human gait recognition algorithm based on unordered video sequences. In 2024 13th International Conference of Information and Communication Technology (ICTech), pp. 6–10. IEEE (2024)

Mixed Reality Portal with Artificial Intelligence Companion

Muhamad Haikal Arman(✉) [id], Ajune Wanis Ismail [id], and Muhammad Anwar Ahmad [id]

Universiti Teknologi Malaysia, Skudai, Malaysia
muhamad.haikal@graduate.utm.my, {ajune,muhammad.anwar}@utm.my

Abstract. In this study, we describe the design of a Mixed Reality (MR) portal system with an AI companion. Our system allows the user to enter various virtual portals that are placed in the real world via an MR headset. Each portal contains a virtual world with a different theme and settings. The user can explore and perform activities relating to the virtual world theme. The AI companion will accompany the user and provide guidance. We use Natural Language Processing (NLP) for the AI companion to provide conversational between the user and the AI companion. The user can ask the AI companion about the specific virtual world. In addition, the AI companion is also able to interact with certain objects inside the virtual world. The goal of this MR portal system is to provide an educational application that is interactive and immersive. We provide the initial proof of concept implementation of the system. This study also highlights the technical challenges and solutions in integrating the AI companion that understands the context of each virtual world.

Keywords: Mixed Reality · Artificial intelligence Companion · Natural Language Processing

1 Introduction

A mixed reality (MR) environment is defined as an immersive space in which the physical and virtual worlds combine. According to Milgram and Kishino (1994), MR is an immersive environment in which the physical and virtual worlds merge to provide users with a unified experience [1]. It exists on a continuum which ranges from a completely real environment, which contains solely real objects, to a fully virtual environment, in which users interact with purely synthetic worlds. MR encompasses both Augmented Reality (AR), which overlays digital content on the actual world, and Augmented Virtuality (AV), which incorporates real-world aspects into a virtual environment [2]. In recent years, MR has been further defined as an environment where physical and digital objects coexist and can be interacted in real time [3]. Furthermore, an MR system also possesses spatial understanding capabilities. It enables MR devices to have spatial awareness functionalities such as occlusion handling, collision detection and lighting, which is essential for creating interactive experiences that feel natural and intuitive [4, 5].

Artificial Intelligence (AI) companions simulate human-like interaction and companionship. AI companions are effective in fostering social connections and reducing feelings of loneliness. In addition, it also helps users feel understood and supported by providing individualized interactions and responding to the requirements. AI companions are increasingly acknowledged for their ability to improve social connectivity and emotional well-being. These digital companions, often in the form of chatbots or robots, offer ongoing, non-judgmental emotional support and companionship. Research indicates that friendship artificial intelligence chatbots (FAIC) have gained popularity during periods of social isolation, such as during the COVID-19 pandemic, as they offer a semblance of social interaction and emotional connection [6]. The emotional engagement provided by these chatbots is not merely reactive; they are designed to exhibit emotional intelligence, thereby enhancing user satisfaction and fostering a sense of belonging [7, 8]. AI companions are effective at encouraging social engagement and minimizing feelings of loneliness [9]. AI companions make users feel understood and supported by providing personalized interactions and responding to their needs. This can have a substantial impact on mental health and overall quality of life.

The integration of MR and AI is paving the way for innovative applications across various domains, including education, healthcare, and social interaction. An MR portal enhanced with an AI companion can significantly improve user engagement and learning outcomes by providing personalized experiences and interactive environments. Therefore, in this study, we describe the design of an MR portal system with an integrated AI companion. We provide the system design as well as the initial prototype of the MR portal system.

2 Related Works

Mixed reality (MR) plays a significant role in merging digital and physical environments, allowing users to interact with both seamlessly. This technology represents a transformative approach to blend digital and physical experiences. MR portals combine AR and virtual reality (VR) to provide engaging and interactive experiences. A key aspect of MR is its reliance on spatial understanding, which enables the integration of virtual objects into real-world settings. This capability is particularly beneficial in medical training, where MR tools like HoloLens 2 have been shown to improve clinical evaluation skills among medical students by providing an immersive learning experience that combines the benefits of VR and AR [10, 11]. Moreover, MR technology has been recognized for its potential to revolutionize educational methodologies. By creating immersive and interactive learning environments, MR can enhance student engagement and facilitate experiential learning [12, 13].

This study focuses on the development of an MR portal system integrated with an AI companion. One of the applications of MR portals includes the digitalization of cultural heritage and tourism. It was demonstrated that virtual portals can enable individuals to "time travel" between realities, enriching their understanding of historical contexts by overlaying virtual information onto real-world locations [14]. This feature not only improves the experience of visitors but also works to establish a stronger relationship with cultural heritage sites, making them more accessible and appealing to a larger demographic. Research has shown that AI adaptivity significantly improves learning outcomes, particularly in inquiry-based science learning contexts [15]. By tailoring interactions to the preferences and learning styles of users, AI companions can provide personalized support, making the educational experience more effective and engaging [16]. Thus, by integrating AI companions and leveraging the strengths of both mixed reality and artificial intelligence, such systems can provide personalized, engaging, and effective interactions that cater to the diverse needs of users across various domains.

Previously, an AR-based portal allowed 3D objects to overlay the real world environment. This markerless AR scans real-world environments and can place the portal on the floor of the real world in real-time. AR portals connect virtual reality with deep immersion and mobile AR with device ubiquity [17]. The external side of an AR portal must be transparent while blocking the visualization of models behind it. Users can see a "doorway" that leads into a virtual world using a smartphone's camera. Users can wander freely and explore the scene as if it were in a "real" setting. AR portals can feature lifelike 360 spheres of real-world sites or be digitally built into a variety of imagined realms [17]. For this study, we chose Meta Quest 3 to develop the MR portal system experience [18]. We utilized the Head-Mounted Display's (HMD) color passthrough feature, which allows users to view the real world in full color while wearing the headset. This technology enhances immersion by combining virtual and physical environments. The HMD also includes depth sensors to measure object distance, improve spatial awareness, and accurately position the portal within the user's surroundings.

AI represents the other crucial component in developing the MR portal system with an integrated AI companion. The AI character utilized in this study is Convai NPC conversational dialogue system [19]. As noted in [20], when a technology with a personal consultant knows the user well, it holds the potential to affect our lives in ways we cannot even imagine. The virtual companion provides intelligent software or application that offers support, assistance, and companionship across various aspects of users' lives [21]. Moreover, the integration with voice recognition and intelligent assistants can enhance the user engagement and accessibility [22].

3 System Design

3.1 Mixed Reality Portal

MR portal in this study is a door, so the user can teleport to another world. A portal has been defined as a gateway or door in the game, the experience of moving from one reality to another via a tunnel, door, aperture, hole, or the like. Figure 1 displays the MR portal, as a gateway to the virtual world, that overlays the real-world environment. The real environment is our laboratory, the 3D avatar is present in our lab and while we are talking to the 3D avatar, the conversational panel will display the texts. This study proposes using an MR headset Quest 3 and enabling passthrough features so we can see the portal appear in the real world.

Based on Fig. 2, the full application once we start with the HMD's color passthrough allows the user to view the surrounding real world. Then, the life-size avatar stands AI companion to the user. Once the user has selected a portal, he/she can step into the portal

Fig. 1. MR portal

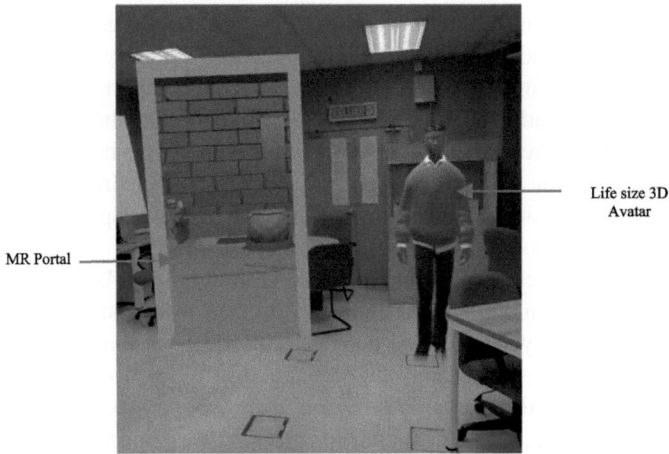

Fig. 2. A full view of the MR portal overlays in our real world

and enter the virtual environment. In the virtual environment, the user can interact with certain objects and perform 3D object manipulation.

3.2 AI Companion with NLP

Conversational Artificial Intelligence (Convai) [23] is dedicated to creating lifelike, interactive, and customizable AI characters for virtual worlds and MR applications. It uses advanced natural language processing (NLP) and emotion modelling to help characters understand and respond in human-like ways, allowing for natural, context-aware conversations. Additionally, NLP provide significant interactivity and connection with the AI companion [20]. The platform seamlessly integrates with major Unity development environments, ensuring real-time performance. Convai's characters can be tailored to a variety of personalities, from cheerful to sad, as well as moods, from happy to angry, providing scalable characteristics. Figure 3. Illustrates the flowchart for the interaction between the user and the AI companion and is further explained below.

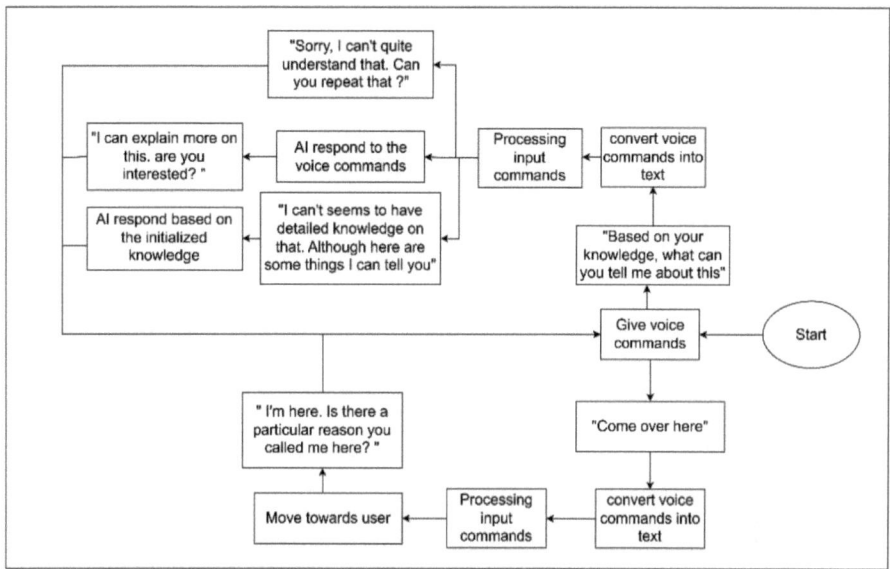

Fig. 3. Flowchart for interaction between user and AI companion

Voice commands are used as the interaction between the user and the AI companion. The potential for development along with integration with voice recognition and AI companion can be beneficial within the MR [21]. Users initiated the conversations using voice commands, prompting the AI companion to respond in dialogue. Other than that, the user can request assistance or information from the AI companion. Furthermore, the user-controlled AI companion actions and behaviours with voice commands to perform specific tasks or actions. Voice commands that are utilized for AI companions are calling and asking. Calling voice is used for changing the position of the AI companion. Ask voice command utilized to ask AI companion questions, although the knowledge of AI companion is limited to what has been initialized during the creation of AI companion.

3.3 Integrating MR Portal with AI Companion

Integration of the MR portal application with AI companion is done after the development of both elements is complete. The integration is significant to enable interaction between AI companions with the virtual environment of the MR portal application. Furthermore, the application is designed to be compatible with the Meta Quest 3 HMD, allowing it to run and execute efficiently within the Meta Quest 3's MR environment. This compatibility is important because it takes advantage of the HMD's colour passthrough to provide high-quality MR experience, with the AI companion improving user interactions and overall experience in the virtual world. Figure 4. Shows the application system flow of this project and further explained below.

Firstly, the user will wear and activate the HMD, then activate it along with initializing passthrough. When the passthrough has been initialized, then the user needs to go through the tutorial first. In the tutorial session, the user will learn to select and manipulate 3D

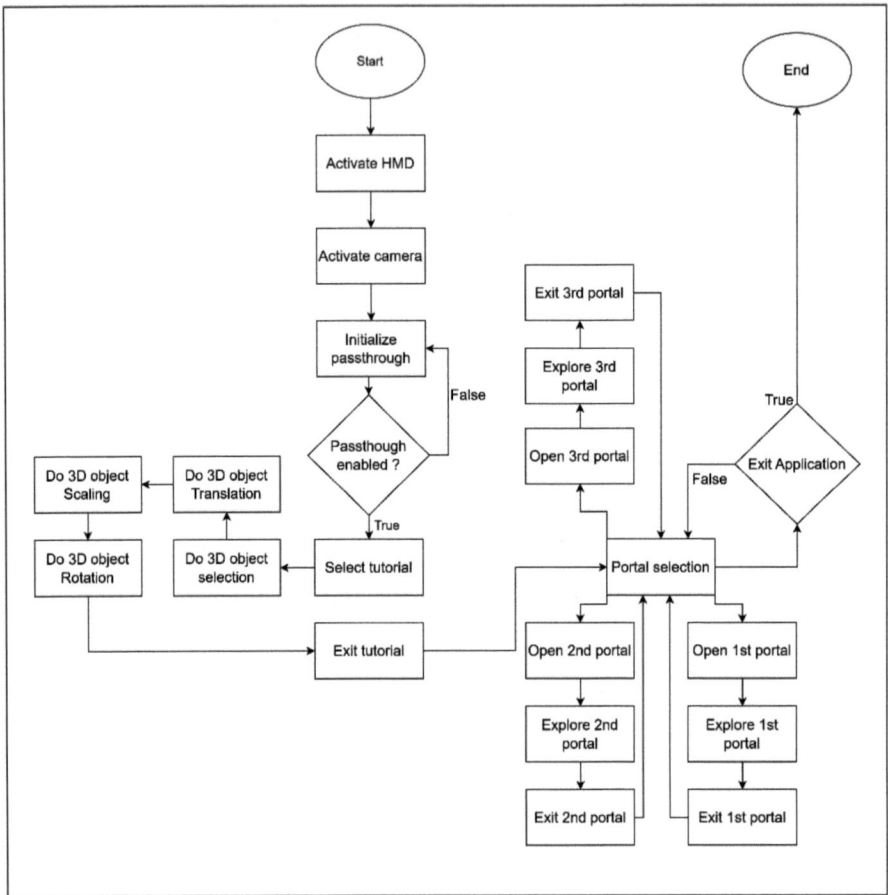

Fig. 4. Application system flow

objects. The user will do 3D object translation, scaling, and rotation before ending the tutorial session. After finishing the tutorial, the user either the first, second, or third portal to explore. The application will terminate when the user confirms on exiting the application. During the exploration, the AI companion will accompany the user and guide the user through each of the portal's virtual environments. If the user has any questions regarding the particular portal, the user can ask the AI companion and it will answer if the question is within its knowledge-base.

4 Results

This section discusses the initial results of the implementation of the MR portal with an AI companion. Figure 5. Shows the workspace for the MR user and the hardware and equipment utilized, which consist of a computer to handle the computationally intensive tasks required to run the MR application smoothly, Meta Quest 3 HMD that allows users to experience MR and Met Quest 3 controller that allows users to interact with the MR environment. The setting shows a computer and monitor have been placed on a physical table. The user should stand once they wore the Meta Quest 3 HMD and hold the controller.

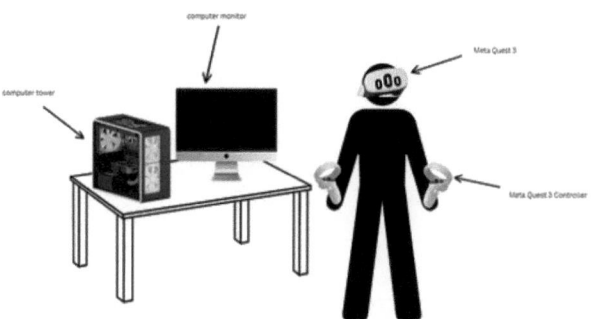

Fig. 5. MR workspace setting

The portal acts as a transitional interface. Users can look through it to see the virtual environment while still being aware of their real-world surroundings. Through this, users can explore and experience worlds they are not able to access in real life, such as fantastical landscapes, historical settings, or future cities. In addition to being useful for education, entertainment, and even therapy, this would be a great tool. The user could have the ability to control what they experience in the new world, from choosing landscapes to interacting with objects and characters. It might even allow people to "create" their own worlds with limitless possibilities. Figure 6(a) shows the user was outside the MR portal while in Fig. 6(b) the user has entered inside the VR environment. Both Fig. 6(a) and Fig. 6(b) illustrate the initial result of the MR portal and AI companion in a real-world environment.

As for adding an AI companion, this study explores whether the user is exploring a fantasy world, studying in a historical setting, or working in a professional environment, the AI could provide advice, and tutorials, or even help them navigate the world, making the experience smoother and more enjoyable. In a complex MR world, the AI companion could help with decision-making and solve problems in real-time. For example, in a virtual escape room, the AI might give hints or guide the user through tricky puzzles. If someone is exploring a new virtual environment, the AI could provide relevant information about the surroundings or even help with navigation.

Figure 7. Shows the conversation between the user and the AI companion where the user asks about the content of the portal and the AI companion explains in detail along with a friendly invitation. Figure 8. Shows how the AI companion responds to the user's command when the user gives the command to the AI companion to come closer. The AI companion responds and follows the user's order.

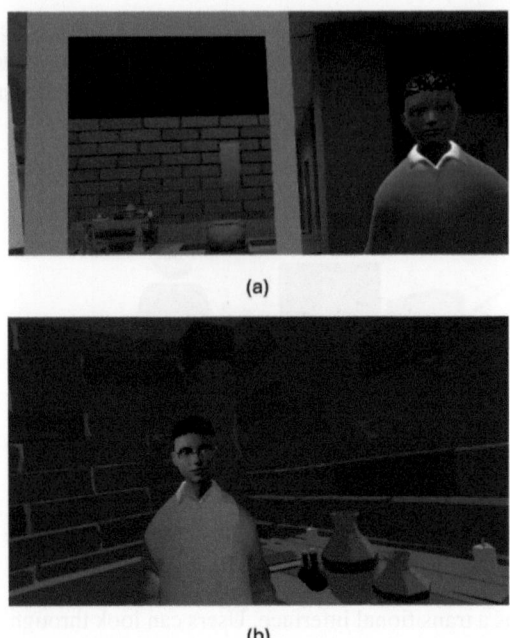

Fig. 6. (a) Outside the portal environment (b) Inside the portal environment

Fig. 7. Conversation between user and AI companion

5 Conclusion

MR portal that can transport users to another world is captivating. It blends both AR and VR to create an immersive experience that feels real, while also allowing people to "step" into entirely different environments. Adding an AI companion as an assistant to an MR portal would enhance the experience by offering personalized guidance, real-time problem-solving, and emotional support, making the virtual world more interactive and engaging. The AI could help users navigate environments, provide educational support, and even serve as a dynamic companion in adventures or social interactions.

Based on the experiment, we can summarize that by utilizing the capacity of Quest 3 HMD as an enabler for MR technology, the real feeling of entering a portal into another place could be achieved. MR enable 3D objects to interact with the real world environment further increasing the immersivity of having a portal in the real world environment. This quality of immersion is supported by the presence of AI companions that replicate real life humans that are able to have a conversation and awareness of their surroundings. In future works, we will improve the design of the virtual environment and the AI companion's knowledge-based. Additionally, we will conduct user evaluation through usability testing and user feedback The primary data elements to be collected after testing encompass user behavioral metrics such as engagement time, session duration, and task completion rate while the user interacts with the application.

Acknowledgement. We would like to extend our heartfelt gratitude to the Ministry of Higher Education for the financial support under the Fundamental Research Grant Scheme (FRGS), UTM, FRGS/1/2023/ICT10/UTM/02/2. Thanks to ViCubeLab at Universiti Teknologi Malaysia for their invaluable support and facilities.

References

1. Milgram, P., Kishino, F.: A taxonomy of mixed reality visual displays. IEICE Trans. Inf. Syst. **77**(12), 1321–1329 (1994)
2. Milgram, P., Takemura, H., Utsumi, A., Kishino, F.: Augmented reality: a class of displays on the reality-virtuality continuum. In: Das, H. (ed.) Telemanipulator and Telepresence Technologies, pp. 282 – 292. SPIE (1994). https://doi.org/10.1117/12.197321
3. Shenoy, R., Intiaz, C., Tiwari, S., Krishnan, G.: Design and development of a mixed reality application for aphasia rehabilitation: the ICMR-MiRAR project. Technol. Disabil. **36**(1–2), 1–15 (2024). https://doi.org/10.3233/tad-230008
4. Delmerico, J., et al.: Spatial Computing and Intuitive Interaction: Bringing Mixed Reality and Robotics Together (2022). https://doi.org/10.48550/arxiv.2202.01493
5. Ahmad, M.A., Suaib, N.M., Ismail, A.W., Asari, M.K.S.M.: RGBD Depth Sensor Frame Data Streaming to Handheld Device Using WebRTC-Based Framework. In: 2024 IEEE International Symposium on Consumer Technology (ISCT), pp. 220–224 (2024). https://doi.org/10.1109/ISCT62336.2024.10791163
6. Li, B., Yao, R., Nan, Y.: How do friendship artificial intelligence chatbots (FAIC) benefit the continuance using intention and customer engagement? J. Consum. Behav. **22**(6), 1376–1398 (2023). https://doi.org/10.1002/cb.2218
7. Indrayani, L.M., Amalia, R.M., Hakim, F.Z.M.: Emotive expressions on social chatbot. Jurnal Sosioteknologi **18**(3), 509–516 (2020). https://doi.org/10.5614/sostek.itbj.2019.18.3.17
8. Bilquise, G., Ibrahim, S., Shaalan, K.: Emotionally Intelligent chatbots: a systematic literature review. Hum. Behav. Emerg. Technol. **2022**, 1–23 (2022). https://doi.org/10.1155/2022/9601630
9. Broadbent, E., Billinghurst, M., Boardman, S.G., Doraiswamy, P.M.: Enhancing social connectedness with companion robots using AI. Sci. Robot **8**(80), eadi6347 (2025). https://doi.org/10.1126/scirobotics.adi6347

10. Ganeshkumar, A., et al.: Innovations in craniovertebral junction training: harnessing the power of mixed reality and head-mounted displays. Neurosurg. Focus **56**(1), E13 (2024). https://doi.org/10.3171/2023.10.focus23613
11. Zhang, C., Gao, H., Liu, Z., Huang, H.: The Potential value of mixed reality in neurosurgery. J. Craniofacial Surgery **32**(3), 940–943 (2020). https://doi.org/10.1097/scs.0000000000007317
12. Alizadeh, M., Figueroa, R.B.: MAVR in the Metaverse, pp. 26–27. Ascilite Publications (2024). https://doi.org/10.14742/apubs.2024.1185
13. Allcoat, D., Hatchard, T.D., Azmat, F., Stansfield, K.E., Watson, D.G., von Mühlenen, A.: Education in the digital age: learning experience in virtual and mixed realities. J. Educ. Comput. Res. **59**(5), 795–816 (2021). https://doi.org/10.1177/0735633120985120
14. Evagelou, A., Kleftodimos, A., Lappas, G.: Creating location-based mobile applications for tourism: a virtual AR guide for Western Macedonia. Digital **4**(1), 271–301 (2024). https://doi.org/10.3390/digital4010014
15. Yannier, N., Hudson, S.E., Chang, H.L., Koedinger, K.R.: AI adaptivity in a mixed-reality system improves learning. Int. J. Artif. Intell. Educ. **34**(4), 1541–1558 (2024). https://doi.org/10.1007/s40593-023-00388-5
16. Spirig, J., García, K., Mayer, S.: An Expert Digital Companion for Working Environments, pp. 25–32 (2021). https://doi.org/10.1145/3494322.3494326
17. Permana, R., Tosida, E., Suriansyah, M.: Development of augmented reality portal for medicininal plants introduction. Inter. J. Global Operat. Res. **3**, 52–63 (2022). https://doi.org/10.47194/ijgor.v3i2.141
18. Meta Platforms Inc, Meta for Developers. https://developers.meta.com/horizon/develop/unity, Accessed 11 Feb 2025
19. Convai, Convai - Conversational AI for Virtual Worlds. https://www.convai.com/, Accessed 11 Feb. 2025
20. Ishigaki, S.A.K., Ismail, A.W., Halim, N.A.A., Suaib, N.M.: Voice commands with virtual assistant in mixed reality telepresence. In: Ortis, A., Hameed, A.A., Jamil, A. (eds.) Advanced Engineering, Technology and Applications. ICAETA 2023. CCIS, vol. 1983. Springer, Cham (2024). https://doi.org/10.1007/978-3-031-50920-9_12
21. Fadzli, F.E., Ismail, A.W., Taliba, J., Mohd Hashim, S.Z.: Intelligent Holo-assistant avatar with lip-syncing. In: Thampi, S.M., Hu, J., Das, A.K., Mathew, J., Tripathi, S. (eds.) Applied Soft Computing and Communication Networks. ACN 2023. LNNs, vol. 966. Springer, Singapore (2024). https://doi.org/10.1007/978-981-97-2004-0_3

Advancing Indian Vehicle Detection Using YOLO11 and YOLO12 with SAHI Optimization

Aishvi Guleria(✉) [ID], Kamya Varshney [ID], Garima [ID], and Shweta Jindal [ID]

Indira Gandhi Delhi Technical University for Women, New Delhi, Delhi 110006, India
aishviguleria@gmail.com

Abstract. Vehicle detection and surveillance of traffic are important areas of city planning, especially in highly populous countries with heavy road traffic like India. This study focused on training YOLO11 and YOLO12 to enhance the vehicle detection for the Indian traffic scenario and incorporating SAHI inference technique for improved detection of small-sized vehicles. Since Indian traffic is composed of diverse vehicles types like two-wheelers, auto-rickshaws, trucks, buses, tempos and cars, this research aims to achieve high accuracy and efficiency in vehicle detection. Performance of both the models was compared based on metrics like precision, recall, f1-score and speeds of inference, preprocessing and postprocessing. Experiments demonstrated how SAHI inference enhanced the small-size vehicle detection accuracy. Comparing both models showcased the performance trade-offs where YOLO12 performed better in terms of accuracy, whereas YOLO11 came out to be a more efficient model. While YOLO11 recorded minor misclassifications, YOLO12 showed no such hallucinations. These findings demonstrated the robustness of YOLO models when applied for complex challenges like Indian Traffic Vehicle detection.

Keywords: Indian Vehicles · Indian Traffic · YOLO · YOLO11 · YOLO12 · SAHI · Object Dejection

1 Introduction

Object Detection is a significant application of the computer vision domain and plays a role in various real-world scenarios, including surveillance, traffic monitoring, robotics, assistive technology, and medical imaging. Different models like FasterRegion-Convolutional Neural Network (RCNN)[1], Detection Transformer (DETR) [2], and You Only Look Once (YOLO) [3] have been released to support object detection. Among these state-of-the-art models, YOLO models have been perceived as prominent choices due to their ease of deployment, low computational cost, high speed, and efficiency. These factors account for the active utilization of YOLO models for traffic monitoring and vehicle identification. They can handle complex real-world traffic scenarios, making them a good choice for the given use case.

1.1 YOLO Family Models for Object Detection

YOLO family models range from YOLOv1 [3] to YOLO12[4], with some other variants like YOLO-NAS [5], PP-YOLO[6], YOLOR[7], YOLOS[8], YOLOX [9] and Scaled-YOLOv4 [10]. Originally proposed by Redmon et al. in 2015, YOLOv1 viewed object detection using a combination of bounding box and class probabilities. YOLOv2 [11] and YOLOv3 [12] released in 2016 and 2018 respectively mainly noted architecture differences in terms of backbone. Later YOLO development and improvement became a community effort, releasing YOLOv4 [13], YOLOv5 [14], PP-YOLO, and Scaled-YOLOv4 in the same year, i.e. 2020, followed by YOLOR, YOLOS, YOLOX in 2021. These models showed an iterative improvement due to changes in architecture, improvement in the anchor finding algorithm, and optimization of the hyperparameters. 2022 witnessed release of YOLOv6 [15] and YOLOv7 [16] which further improved the efficiency and speed. In 2023 YOLO-NAS and YOLOv8 [17] were released, while YOLOv8 significantly optimized the speed-accuracy via integrating an anchor-free split head, YOLO-NAS employed quantization for optimizing the performance. 2024 saw the release of YOLOv9 [18], YOLOv10 [19], and YOLO11 [20], each of which proposed a groundbreaking technique to improve model performance and efficiency, which is discussed in the related work section of this paper. Later advancement, YOLO12 released in February 2025, proposed an attention-centric object detection model.

YOLO11 employed architectural changes to improve performance while maintaining speed. It used significantly fewer parameters than its older version, helping it to achieve an optimized performance. On the other hand, YOLO12 employed an attention-centric architecture for a better understanding of the surroundings in the image. Thus, both of these latest models will be considered for this study.

1.2 Need to Study the Indian Traffic Scenario of Vehicles

Indian traffic scenarios are far unlike Western traffic scenarios. Unlike orderly highways with well-defined lanes, Indian roads are very dynamic, unstructured, and congested. The reasons why Indian traffic detection is highly challenging are (i) Heterogeneous Vehicle Population: Indian roads accommodate a variety of vehicles like two-wheelers, three-wheelers (autos), buses, tractors, and tempos and trucks with different shapes, sizes, and motion characteristics. Heterogeneity prevents baseline object detection models trained on conventional datasets (like COCO [21] or Pascal VOC [22]) from generalizing. (ii) Unpredictable Road Behavior: Lane discipline is not strictly adhered to; cars change lanes suddenly, and two-wheelers make sharp turns in small gaps between buses and cars, making detection difficult. (iii) Dense and Congested Traffic: Indian roads are highly congested, and the cars move very close to one another. These types of occlusions, like a car occluding a partially or fully another car, are more difficult to detect. (iv) Vehicle-specific speed limits: Various vehicle types—two-wheelers, cars, buses, and trucks—have different speed regulations based on the type of road thereby using vehicle-based classification can improve compliance with road safety rules (v) Variable Road Infrastructure: Road quality and development vary significantly from place to place in India ranging from high-speed highways to narrow city roads and rural mud roads, making models robust in various terrains.

1.3 Small Object Detection

One of the significant drawbacks of traditional object detection models such as YOLO is that they do not detect small objects, particularly in high-resolution images. This is a gigantic issue in Indian traffic because two-wheelers account for more than 70% of Indian vehicles [23], and three-wheelers (autos) are a common mode of public transport. Missing these vehicles in identification results in inaccuracies in autonomous vehicle systems, traffic modeling, and accident-avoidance models. Also, two-wheelers and automobiles are more susceptible to accidents as they are small and in continuous transit between bigger entities. Such a model that fails to detect them may miss out on critical locations of near collisions or violations. Thus, a technique compatible with YOLO11 and YOLO12 is needed such that it supports small object detection. This study will discuss Slicing Aided Hyper (SAHI) Inference [24] to improve small object detection.

1.4 Contribution

This paper introduces a new method of enhancing Indian vehicle detection with the power of YOLO11 and YOLO12, with SAHI inference [24]. The major contributions of this paper are:

1. Training YOLO11 and YOLO12 on an Indian vehicle dataset with multiple vehicle classes such as two-wheelers, autos, cars, buses, tempos, tractors, and trucks.
2. Applying SAHI inference in the interest of improving detection of small vehicles, beyond the capability of YOLO.
3. Testing the performance of the model over actual Indian road traffic environments and comparing against the baseline YOLO11 and YOLO12 results to exemplify the competence of SAHI in small object detection.

2 Related Work

2.1 Evolution of YOLO

Object detection model YOLO is extensively utilized throughout the globe because of its ability to process information in real-time. Its use is in traffic monitoring systems, security systems, agriculture, and medical applications. YOLO is increasingly being utilized in India to solve region-specific problems. Datasets used in India provide incredibly diverse datasets compared to the world. Issues such as heavy traffic flow, varied vehicles, complex rural and urban environments, public places with congestion, and poor-quality surveillance videos are contributing to the poor quality of images. To illustrate traffic monitoring, YOLO is capable of detecting vehicles, pedestrians, and even vehicle plates. It is, however, struggling to detect occluded and small objects on heavily congested roads, a common trait of Indian cities. In agriculture, YOLO assists in crop tracking to detect pests, but the detection of small pests or diseases at an early stage is an open problem. Similarly, the resolution vs. accuracy relationship is a behemoth problem when using YOLO-based security systems to crowd surveillance and event detection in Indian roads and markets, where there is limited illumination, occlusion, and wearing of the face mask seriously impacts detection scores. However, with the introduction of other newer YOLO models, attention technology, vision transformers [25] [26], and multi-scale detection [27], these issues are being resolved in Indian datasets.

The YOLO object detection series has evolved significantly, introducing various architectural improvements and optimization techniques to enhance speed and accuracy. YOLOv1 [3], introduced in 2016, laid the foundation with its single-pass detection approach, offering real-time performance but at the cost of lower accuracy. YOLOv2 [11], released in 2017, introduced anchor boxes and multi-scale detection, improving localization precision. YOLOv3 [12] in 2018 further enhanced real-time object detection with improved feature extraction. YOLOv4 [13], introduced in 2020, focused on better performance and speed trade-offs, while YOLOv5 [39], also from 2020, transitioned to a PyTorch-based implementation for greater efficiency and lightweight deployment. Subsequent advancements introduced alternative architectures and optimizations. PP-YOLO [6], developed in 2020, integrated Path Aggregation Networks (PAN) and optimized loss functions for improved accuracy, while Scaled-YOLOv4 [10] incorporated Cross Stage Partial Networks (CSPNet) into the PAN architecture for better efficiency. YOLOR [7] (2021) focused on multi-task learning to handle various vision tasks within a single model. YOLOX [9] introduced an anchor-free architecture the same year, simplifying bounding box detection.

In 2022, YOLOv6 [15] adopted an EfficientRep Backbone for improved feature extraction, and YOLOv7 [16] emphasized higher accuracy through advanced techniques. YOLOv8 [17] (2023) introduced a CSPDarknet backbone with a PAFPN neck to improve feature fusion and detection precision. YOLOv9 [18] (2024) implemented Programmable Gradient Information (PGI) for better model training and accuracy, while YOLOv10 [19] introduced a dual-head architecture for reduced latency and state-of-the-art performance. Further advancements in 2024 and 2025 focused on refining efficiency and detection accuracy. YOLO-NAS [5] leveraged Neural Architecture Search (NAS) to create quantization-friendly blocks and optimize model training. YOLOv11 [20] introduced the C3K2 block, which employs smaller 3×3 convolutional kernels to enhance feature extraction. Finally, YOLOv12 [4] adopted an attention-centric architecture to improve speed and accuracy, solidifying its position as a cutting-edge real-time object detection framework.

2.2 Models Used for Object Detection in the Indian Scenario

The major issue with object detection models on India's roadways is the multidimensionality of traffic, high congestion, and randomness on the roads. Compared to Western nations, where traffic is strictly orderly and lane-based, Indian traffic consists of uncontrolled two-wheeler, three-wheeler, bus, truck, and even walking movement. Vehicle detection becomes challenging on Indian roads because of the diversity, poor visibility, frequent obstruction of view and low-resolution CCTV cameras. Due to these problems, sophisticated Deep Learning models tailored explicitly for Indian datasets have been created that perform well in high-density and disorganized traffic conditions. The second half discusses the models used for traffic detection in India, how they differ from Western methods, and the challenges of attempting to detect bikes and auto rickshaws. Table 1 describes the available Indian vehicle object detection studies, which are limited in number, and indicates the need for work in this area and how this problem can be investigated with different techniques.

Table 1. A literature review of existing studies for Indian Traffic Vehicle Detection

Title	Year	Dataset used	Model Used	Results
[28]	2010	Video snapshots from roadside surveillance cameras (India)	Adaptive background subtraction	Identified 92% of the infringing vehicles at the stop-line during red signals in real-world test scenarios successfully
[29]	2020	Government CCTV footage (India)	Select-Detector, Image Quality Enhancer, Image Transformer, Smart Recognizer	Achieved 87% accuracy in stolen/suspicious vehicle detection using an automatic traffic monitoring system with deep learning
[30]	2022	TrafficCAM dataset (Indian cities)	DeepLabV3 + (ResNet-101), Mask R-CNN, SOLOv2, and Mask2Former	Provides TrafficCAM with 4,402 labeled images and 59,944 unlabeled frames which support traffic flow analysis and supervised and semi-supervised learning
[31]	2022	Indian Roads Dataset (IRD)	Inception_v3 model with a Single Shot Detector (SSD)	Constructed IRD with over 8,000 annotations from 3,000 + images to enhance traffic light detection in Indian urban scenes
[32]	2023	FGVD and IRUVD datasets (Indian datasets)	Enhanced YOLO-NAS	Achieved 84.51% accuracy for FGVD and 96.61% accuracy for IRUVD, which outperforms baseline models for vehicle detection on Indian traffic
[33]	2023	Indian Traffic Dataset (ITD)	YOLOv8s object detection model	Trained ITD, representing varying vehicle makeup at various Indian stations, facilitating training of resilient traffic management models

2.3 Small Object Detection Techniques

Small object detection in images is extremely difficult due to their comparatively smaller size with fewer characteristic features. Various approaches have been introduced to overcome such difficulties, some of which are Feature pyramid networks (FPN) [34], which enhance multi-scale detection by building a multi-scale feature representation of an image. The method tends to enable better small-sized object detection by fusing features that are both high-resolution and semantically rich. The combination of the FPNs with attention mechanisms has been found in research to enhance significantly small object detection with applicability to some features. This is preceded by Attention Mechanisms [35] that enable dynamic adjustments on the weights of the features so the model can concentrate on the most crucial parts of an image. Adding attention modules enables the detection of small objects and thus can enhance detection performance. One area where this is implemented is the S-Feature Pyramid Network; it utilizes shallow feature pyramids with the addition of attention modules for enhanced accuracy in the object detection of small objects. Another technique is SAHI [24], an open-source library that was constructed for the enhancement of small-object detection. Small objects are poorly detected because standard object detectors fail due to their low pixel representation. SAHI attempts to overcome this by breaking down the image into overlapping patches (referred to as slices) and executing the inference on the patches individually. Utilizing such a model, maximum resolution points for every patch for small objects. Post-processing, outputs from all the slices are concatenated to achieve the final detection output.

3 Methodology

3.1 Dataset Selection

This study uses the Indian Vehicle Dataset [36] available on Kaggle. This dataset was proposed by Data Cluster Labs. The authors compiled a set of 50,000 + images of real-life vehicles on Indian roads, captured using mobile phones from 2020–22 and crowdsourced from more than 1000 + areas of rural and urban settings. The professionals at Data Cluster Labs manually reviewed and verified every image. The dataset included images captured under multiple conditions, like in daylight, night, and varied distances, making it an optimum choice for the use case of this study. However, only a smaller portion of the dataset is available for free, which includes about 750 images which doesn't require advanced setup. Figure 1 represents the number of instances of every class of vehicles that occurs in the training set. The dataset included 7 classes of vehicles:-

- Indian Auto
- Bus
- Truck
- Tempo
- Tractor
- Car
- Two Wheelers

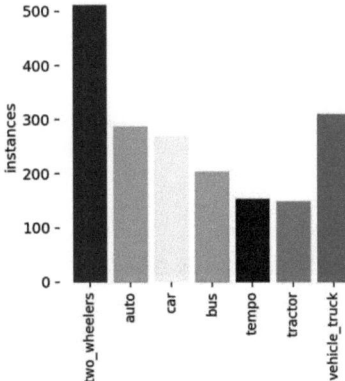

Fig. 1. Count of instances of every class of vehicles

3.2 Dataset Preparation

The available dataset provides the images and corresponding annotation files in XML format. However, YOLO models follow a different format for annotation. Thus, a script was devised for automating the conversion of annotation XML files to the YOLO accepted format (Fig. 2) which includes 4 parameters: (i) class_id is an index of object class helps in mapping the object class to object class title (ii) x_center and y_center represent the normalized x and y coordinates of the bounding box center respectively (iii) width and height represent the normalized width and height of the bounding box respectively. < x_center >, < y_center >, < width > and < height > lies in the range of 0 to 1. Since this study involves training a YOLO model for a custom dataset, a new YAML is needed for referring training, validation data, and testing data along with declaring the object classes.

<class_id> <x_center> <y_center> <width> <height>

Fig. 2. YOLO accepted format for label annotations

3.3 SAHI Inference Implementation

Fig. 3. Tile inference in SAHI technique

SAHI is a technique proposed by Ultralytics [37] to improve small object detection for YOLO models. Since YOLO models only scan the image once, small objects are often overlooked, especially when spanning a few pixels. Thus, SAHI tackles this by splitting an image into small tiles (patches), as illustrated in Fig. 3, performing inference on each tile, and finally fusing the outputs. The inference stage of SAHI involves three essential steps. One, the input image is broken into overlapping tiles of smaller size so that each area of the image is processed adequately. Two, inference is independently performed on each of these tiles using YOLO as if each was a separate input. Three, all the objects detected across the tiles are mapped back to the original image space, and overlapping detections are handled with Non-Maximum Suppression (NMS) [19] to remove duplicates.

One of the strongest capabilities of SAHI is that it helps models like YOLO identify small details that otherwise get lost in the process of downscaling. It is particularly useful for tasks like aerial imagery, satellite imagery, and medical imagery, where objects of interest are small compared to the size of the entire image. SAHI is also useful with high-resolution images because inferring the entire image at once can be computationally expensive and can be taxing for GPU memory limits. Although it does have its perks, SAHI does have some trade-offs. Because it makes inferences on multiple tiles rather than the entire image, it takes longer to infer and consumes more computational resources. The trade-off is usually worth it, however, when dealing with datasets where small object detection is paramount. Overall, SAHI significantly enhances the ability of YOLO to detect small-sized objects in large images by introducing high-fidelity analysis via tiled inference.

4 Results and Findings

4.1 Experimentation Setup and Training

Training, validation, and testing of YOLO models were conducted using the Ultralytics YOLOv8 library (version 8.3.78), which provides an optimized solution for object detection tasks. Training of the models was conducted in a CPU-only setup without any GPU usage. The hardware setup was an Intel Xeon processor running at 2.20GHz, and the software setup was Python 3.11.11 and PyTorch 2.5.1 + cu124 as the deep learning framework. Training was conducted on this setup, using multi-threading and data loading optimization to achieve the best performance. The images are resized to 640 X 640 pixels and both models are trained for 30 epochs using the custom YAML file prepared for the Indian Vehicle Dataset [31]. The training data employed in YOLO model training was split into 80:10:10 to provide an equal proportion for model learning and testing. 80% (593 images) of the data was utilized for training to allow the model to learn effectively. 10% (73 images) was used for validation to allow the adjustment of hyperparameters and prevention of overfitting. 10% (78 images) was reserved for testing to allow unbiased evaluation of the actual-world performance of the model. Figure 4 and Fig. 5 illustrate the training and validation loss over 30 epochs for YOLO11 and YOLO12 respectively.

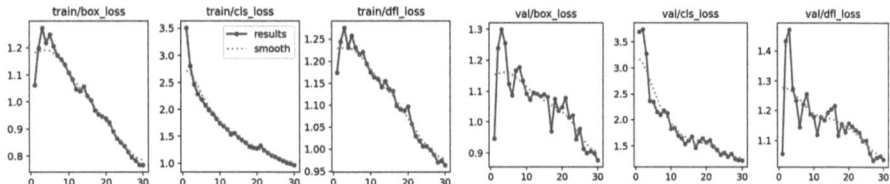

Fig. 4. Training and Validation loss for YOLO11

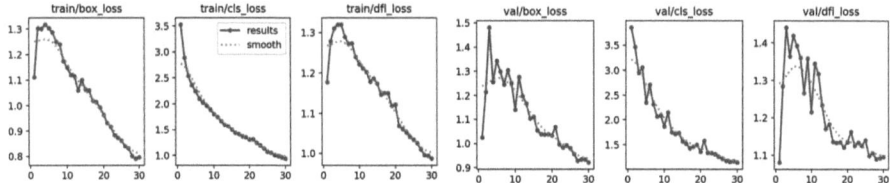

Fig. 5. Training and Validation loss for YOLO12

4.2 Evaluation Metrics and Results

The model was evaluated for a validation dataset to understand the performance of the model and how it performed in aspects of accuracy and efficiency. The evaluation metrics include precision [38], recall [38], F1-score [38], mAP (mean average precision) [39][39] and speed for pre-processing, inference and post processing. "Precision or Confidence (as it is called in Data Mining) denotes the proportion of Predicted Positive cases that are correctly Real Positives." [38] Eq. 5 represents the formula for evaluating the precision. It measures how accurately the model correctly identifies the positive instances. "Recall or Sensitivity (as it is called in Psychology) is the proportion of Real Positive cases that are correctly Predicted Positive." [33] Eq. 6 represents the formula for evaluating the recall. It measures the model's ability to identify relevant objects. The F1-score relates precision and recall, as seen in Eq. 3. "The F1-measure effectively references the True Positives to the Arithmetic Mean of Predicted Positives and Real Positives, being a constructed rate normalized to an idealized value." [38]

$$Precision = \frac{TP}{TP+FP} \quad (1)$$

$$Recall = \frac{TP}{TP+FN} \quad (2)$$

$$F1 = 2 \times \frac{Precision \times Recall}{Precision + Recall} \quad (3)$$

Another important evaluation metric for object detection is mAP. "Mean Average Precision (mAP) is computed as the mean of the average precision scores for each class, where average precision is the area under the precision-recall curve." [39] mAP50 uses an IOU (Intersection Over Union) threshold of 0.5 [39]. mAP 50–95 was defined by *Lin et al.* as "We report mean average precision (mAP) at IoU thresholds ranging from 0.5 to 0.95, denoted as mAP@[0.5:0.95]. This metric provides a more comprehensive evaluation of object detection performance." [40] Eq. 4 and Eq. 5 represent the mathematical formula for the calculation of mAP50 and mAP 50–95 respectively.

$$mAP_{50} = \frac{1}{N} \sum_{i=1}^{N} AP_i^{IOU=0.50} \quad (4)$$

$$mAP_{50-95} = \frac{1}{10} \sum_{j=0}^{9} mAP_{50+j\times 5} \quad (5)$$

Table 2. Results of Evaluation metrics for YOLO11 and YOLO12

Model	mAP50	mAP50–95	Precision	Recall	F1 Score	Preprocess speed (ms)	Inference speed (ms)	Postprocess speed (ms)
YOLO11	0.651	0.487	0.679	0.649	0.664	6.8	213.5	1.2
YOLO12	0.718	0.554	0.766	0.662	0.71	6.7	329.3	3.0

Table 2 summarizes the results obtained for every metric. YOLO12 records a higher precision (0.766) as compared to YOLO 11 (0.679) which means YOLO12 has fewer cases of false positives as compared to YOLO11. A similar pattern can be seen for the recall metric. The recall value for YOLO 12 is higher than the recall value for YOLO11. As the F1-score depends on recall and precision, thus YOLO12 has a better F1-score. Figure 6 graphically represents these metrics, showcasing YOLO12 beating YOLO11 in terms of performance.

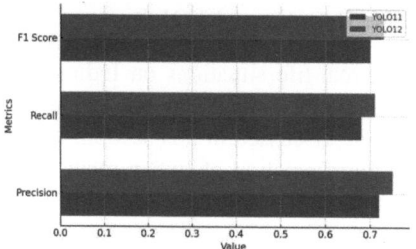

Fig. 6. Comparing Precision, Recall, and F1-score of values

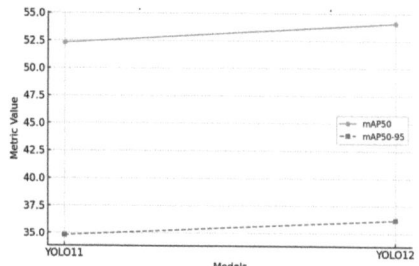

Fig. 7. Comparing YOLO11 AND YOLO12 for mAP YOLO models

Figure 7 shows the graphically plotted values of mAP50 and mAP50–95. An evident rise can be seen for both mAP50 and mAP50–95 from YOLO11 to YOLO12. The mAP50 value increases by 10.29% for YOLO12 (0.718) from YOLO11 (0.651). Similarly, the mAP50–95 value shows an improvement of 13.76% for YOLO12 (0.556) from YOLO11 (0.487). Another interesting parameter of comparison is the speed in terms of pre-processing, inference, and post-processing, i.e. time taken by the model for pre-processing, inference, and post-processing of the image. Thus, a better model will have lesser speed. From Fig. 8, it can be observed that both models have similar pre-processing speeds, 6.8ms (YOLO11) and 6.8ms (YOLO12), but the post-processing speed for YOLO12 (3ms) is higher than YOLO11 (1.2ms). The inference speed for YOLO12 (329.3ms) is 54.24% higher than YOLO11 (213.5ms), which means YOLO12 takes more time to infer an image as compared to YOLO11, as illustrated in Fig. 9.

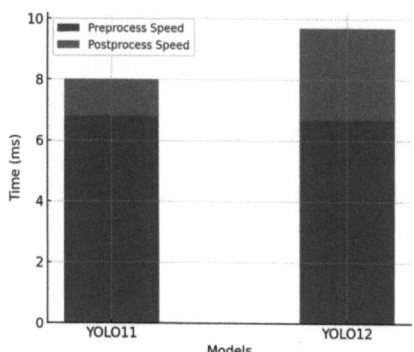

Fig. 8. Comparing preprocess and post-process and YOLO12

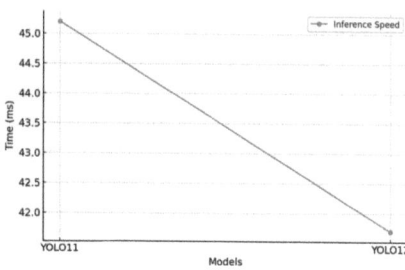

Fig. 9. Comparing inferencing speed of YOLO11 speed of YOLO11 and YOLO12

4.3 Baseline YOLO vs. Trained YOLO vs. SAHI-Enhanced YOLO

To test the understanding of YOLO models for real-life situations on Indian roads, the authors took real images of Indian traffic, available on the Internet and inferred the results. The results for two such images will be discussed in this section. Image 1 (sourced from Dreamstime [41]) was a classic representation of Indian roads packed with heavy traffic and highly occluded vehicles. YOLO 11 baseline model identified a few cars and some people, missing out on vehicles like an auto or any two-wheeler, detecting a total of 8 vehicles (in Fig. 10a). However, the YOLO11 model trained on the Indian Vehicle Dataset detected multiple two-wheelers and even autos, approximately 33 vehicles (in Fig. 10b) i.e. about 4.1 times more than baseline YOLO11, but these results show misclassification of rickshaws as two-wheelers (the vehicle class it was not trained for). Implementing SAHI inference with this model (in Fig. 10c), improved the detection by approximately 7.6 times (61 vehicles) than the baseline YOLO11, continuing the slight cases of misclassification. In the case of YOLO12, the baseline model (in Fig. 10d) detects 3 more vehicles (total of 11 vehicles) than baseline YOLO11 but shows few cases of false positives like detecting an auto as a car. The trained variant overcomes this, as it detects 19 vehicles (in Fig. 10e) and doesn't classify any vehicle, showing the improvement brought by training the model, which is further improved ~ 2.7 times using the SAHI inferencing (52 vehicles), i.e. about 4.7 times more vehicles (in Fig. 10f) as compared to baseline YOLO12. Table 3 shows the number of vehicles detected by every model. On comparing YOLO11 (trained) and YOLO12 (trained), it can be seen that YOLO 11 has detected a higher number of two-wheelers even though they have low confidence scores and misclassified autos as cars, whereas YOLO12 doesn't show any such error. SAHI inferencing helped YOLO12 (trained) and YOLO11 (trained) to detect small far-away objects, but YOLO11 still carried the previously discussed flaws.

For Image 2 sourced from Financial Express [42], representing heavy metropolitan traffic, YOLO11 (trained) demonstrated a similar pattern of hits and misses as it did for Image 1. The vehicle detection was enhanced by about 1.38 times (33 vehicles) and 1.25 times (30 vehicles) respectively with SAHI (in Fig. 11c) and without SAHI (in Fig. 11b) as compared to baseline YOLO11(in Fig. 11a). Trained YOLO12 (in Fig. 11f) showed a slight improvement of about 1.1 times (20 vehicles) than baseline YOLO12 (18 vehicles) but it did not record any false positives like the baseline variant. Even for this image, SAHI inferencing with trained YOLO12 (in Fig. 11f) gave the most balanced results, detecting ~ 1.9 times more vehicles (35 vehicles) than baseline YOLO12 (in Fig. 11e) without any hallucinations. These results can be attributed to the complexity of traffic in both images. On one hand, Image 1 consists of overlapping vehicles, diverse in vehicle types whereas Image 2 shows heavy traffic but with better vehicle boundaries.

Table 3. Inference results for image 1 and image 2 for different YOLO variants and inferencing techniques

Inference Type			IMAGE 1		IMAGE 2	
Model	Training	SAHI	Inference time	Identified objects	Inference time	Identified objects
YOLO11	No	No	182.4ms	5 persons, 7 cars, 1 bus, 1 umbrella	148.7ms	3 persons, 11 cars, 10 buses, 3 trucks
YOLO11	Yes	No	182.5ms	21 two-wheelers, 2 autos, 9 cars, 1 tempo	166.3ms	7 two-wheelers, 18 autos, 4 cars, 1 tempo
YOLO11	Yes	Yes	1.18s	30 two-wheelers, 11 autos, 14 cars, 3 tempos, 3 vehicle trucks	0.56s	7 two-wheelers, 20 autos, 4 cars, 2 tempo
YOLO12	No	No	219.5ms	4 persons, 9 cars, 1 bus, 1 truck, 1 umbrella	169.7ms	2 persons, 12 cars, 4 buses, 2 trucks
YOLO12	Yes	No	276.6ms	10 two-wheelers, 2 autos, 6 cars, 1 tempo	198.6ms	5 two-wheelers, 12 autos, 3 cars
YOLO12	Yes	Yes	1.39s	24 two-wheelers, 7 autos, 16 cars, 3 tempo, 2 vehicle trucks	0.65s	11 two-wheelers, 16 autos, 6 cars, 2 tempos

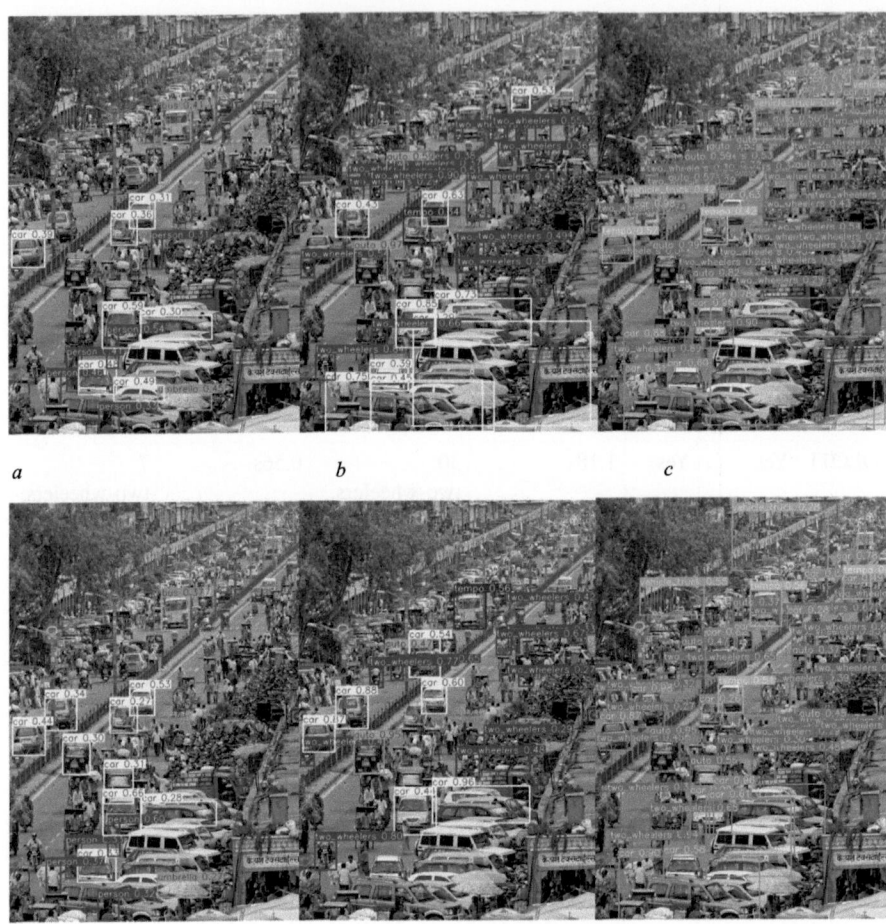

Fig. 10. YOLO11 (Baseline) – Image (b): YOLO11 (Trained) – Image 1 (c): YOLO11 (Trained + SAHI) – Image 1 (d): YOLO12 (Baseline) – Image 1 (e): YOLO12 (Trained) – Image 1 (f): YOLO12 (Trained + SAHI) – Image 1

Another interesting thing to note is the Inference time for both images. For image 1, baseline YOLO 11 (182.4ms) and trained YOLO11 (182.5ms) took almost the same time, and the inferencing time for the same image using the SAHI technique was increased by 546.58% (1.18s). For the same image, baseline YOLO 12 (219.5ms) took 20.34% more time than baseline YOLO 11 (182.4ms). Similarly, trained YOLO12 (276.6ms) took approximately 51.56% more time than trained YOLO11 (182.5ms). The best detection algorithm so far, SAHI inference on trained YOLO12, took about 1.39s which is about 17.80% more than trained YOLO11 with SAHI (1.18s) and 533.26% higher than baseline YOLO12 (219.5ms). A similar trend continues for image 2, baseline YOLO 12 (169.7ms) needed 14.12% time for inferencing as compared to baseline YOLO11 (148.7ms). Trained YOLO12 (198.6ms) took approximately 19.45% more time than trained YOLO11 (166.3ms) and SAHI inference on trained YOLO12 took about 0.65s, which is about 16.07% more than trained YOLO11 with SAHI (0.56s).

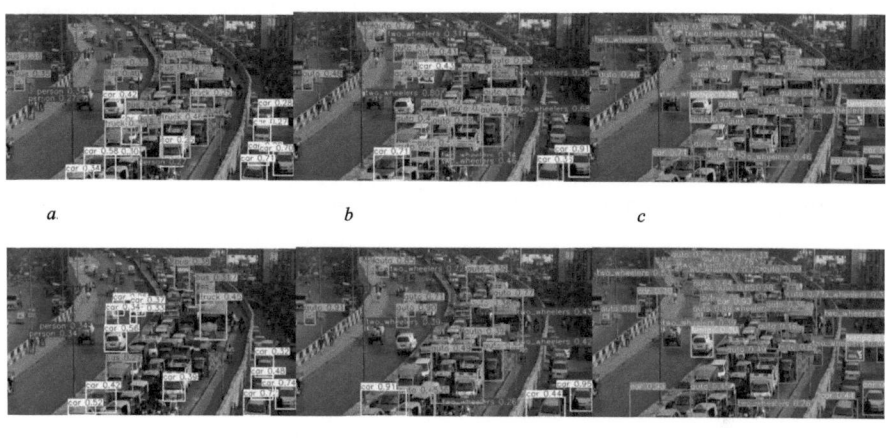

Fig. 11. YOLO11 (Baseline) – Image 2 (b): YOLO11 (Trained) – Image 2 (c): YOLO11 (Trained + SAHI) – Image 2 (d): YOLO12 (Baseline) – Image 2 (e): YOLO12 (Trained) – Image 2 (f): YOLO12 (Trained + SAHI) – Image 2

5 Conclusion

Indian vehicle detection is especially difficult because of the vast variability in vehicle shapes, road surfaces, and vehicle types, combined with dense traffic. Indian traffic, as opposed to typical object detection datasets, has novel vehicle classes like loaded trucks, tempos, and auto-rickshaws, which need to be classified precisely for autonomous driving, traffic control, and road safety surveillance. This paper emphasizes the need for specially crafted detection models trained on Indian road scenes to provide consistent performance. Thus, this study compared YOLO11 and YOLO12 performances on Indian vehicle detection in dense traffic conditions. From the results, authors observed that YOLO11 improved with training, as it detected about 4 times more vehicles in high occlusion Indian traffic settings and 1.25 times more vehicles in low complexity traffic settings with clearer vehicle boundaries. However, it still had issues with misclassification for certain vehicle classes, e.g., the discrimination of similar classes of vehicles like tempos and auto-rickshaws. YOLO12, on the other hand, recorded better performance in all the major measures like mAP, precision, and recall. It detected approximately 1.7 times more vehicles post-training for a complex Indian traffic scenario with overlapping vehicles and about 1.1 times more vehicles when low occlusion occurs among the vehicles, without any cases of false positives or misclassifications. At the expense, however, was increased inference time for YOLO12, which could become a bottleneck in real-time applications.

Use of the SAHI method was useful in enhancing the detection of small vehicles, a matter of extreme importance in Indian road conditions with high-density, heterogeneous traffic. The YOLO11 detected approximately 7.6 more vehicles in complex traffic with overlapping vehicles and about 1.4 times more vehicles in low-complexity traffic scenarios, with this technique, but with the downside of very few misclassifications. Whereas SAHI-enhanced YOLO12 saw its detection capabilities improve by about 5 times for a high-occlusion Indian traffic scenario and about 2 times for a low-occlusion Indian traffic scenario. Thus, YOLO12 outperformed YOLO11 in terms of accuracy. However, using SAHI with YOLO increased the inference time significantly, proving to be a notable trade-off. Even with such advances, finding an optimal balance between inference speed and accuracy continues to be challenging. The findings of this study can be used for further developing vehicle detection systems with potential in traffic monitoring, autonomous driving, and smart city infrastructure.

References

1. Girshick, R.: Fast r-cnn. In: Proceedings of the IEEE International Conference on Computer Vision, pp. 1440–1448 (2015)
2. Zhu, X., Su, W., Lu, L., Li, B., Wang, X., Dai, J.: Deformable detr: deformable transformers for end-to-end object detection. arXiv preprint arXiv:2010.04159(2020)
3. Redmon, J., Divvala, S., Girshick, R., Farhadi, A.: You only look once: unified, real-time object detection. In: Proceedings of the IEEE Conference on Computer Vision and Pattern Recognition, pp. 779–788 (2016)
4. Tian, Y., Ye, Q., Doermann, D.: YOLOv12: Attention-Centric Real-Time Object Detectors (2025)
5. Aharon, S., et al.: Super-Gradients. GitHub. Zenodo (2021). https://zenodo.org/record/7789328
6. Long, X., et al.: PP-YOLO: An effective and efficient implementation of object detector (2020). arXiv preprint arXiv:2007.12099
7. Wang, C.-Y., Yeh, I.-H., Liao, H.-Y. M.: You Only Learn One Representation: Unified Network for Multiple Tasks. arXiv preprint arXiv:2105.04206(2021)
8. Fang, Y., et al.: You Only Look at One Sequence: Rethinking Transformer in Vision through Object Detection. arXiv preprint arXiv:2106.00666(2021)
9. Ge, Z., Liu, S., Wang, F., Li, Z., Sun, J.: Yolox: Exceeding yolo series in 2021. arXiv preprint arXiv:2107.08430(2021)
10. Wang, C. Y., Bochkovskiy, A., Liao, H.Y.M.: Scaled-yolov4: Scaling cross stage partial network. In: Proceedings of the IEEE/CVF Conference on Computer Vision and Pattern Recognition, pp. 13029–13038 (2021)
11. Redmon, J., Farhadi, A.: YOLO9000: Better, faster, stronger. In: Proceedings of the IEEE Conference on Computer Vision and Pattern Recognition, pp. 7263–7271 (2017)
12. Redmon, J., Farhadi, A.: Yolov3: An incremental improvement. arXiv preprint arXiv:1804.02767(2018)
13. Bochkovskiy, A., Wang, C.Y., Liao, H.Y.M.: Yolov4: Optimal speed and accuracy of object detection. arXiv preprint arXiv:2004.10934(2020)
14. Jocher, G., et al.: ultralytics/yolov5: v3. 0. Zenodo (2020)
15. Li, C., et al.: YOLOv6: A single-stage object detection framework for industrial applications. arXiv preprint arXiv:2209.02976(2022)
16. Wang, C.Y., Bochkovskiy, A., Liao, H.Y.M.:YOLOv7: Trainable bag-of-freebies sets new state-of-the-art for real-time object detectors. In: Proceedings of the IEEE/CVF Conference on Computer Vision and Pattern Recognition, pp. 7464–7475 (2023)

17. Varghese, R., Sambath, M.: Yolov8: a novel object detection algorithm with enhanced performance and robustness. In: 2024 International Conference on Advances in Data Engineering and Intelligent Computing Systems (ADICS), pp. 1–6. IEEE (April 2024)
18. Wang, C.Y., Yeh, I.H., Mark Liao, H.Y.: Yolov9: learning what you want to learn using programmable gradient information. In European conference on computer vision, pp. 1–21. Springer Nature Switzerland, Cham (September 2024). https://doi.org/10.1007/978-3-031-72751-1_1
19. Wang, A., Chen, H., Liu, L., Chen, K., Lin, Z., Han, J.: Yolov10: Real-time end-to-end object detection. Adv. Neural. Inf. Process. Syst. **37**, 107984–108011 (2025)
20. Khanam, R., Hussain, M.: . Yolov11: An overview of the key architectural enhancements. arXiv preprint arXiv:2410.17725(2024)
21. Lin, T.Y., et al.: Microsoft COCO: common objects in context. In: Fleet, D., Pajdla, T., Schiele, B., Tuytelaars, T. (eds.) Computer Vision – ECCV 2014. ECCV 2014. LNCS, vol. 8693. Springer, Cham (2014). https://doi.org/10.1007/978-3-319-10602-1_48
22. Hoiem, D., Divvala, S.K., Hays, J.H.: Pascal VOC 2008 challenge. World Literature Today **24**(1), 1–4 (2009)
23. Fleury, A.: By the end of this article, one 2-wheeler rider in India will never return home. Zag Daily, December 15 (2023). https://zagdaily.com/content-partner/by-the-end-of-this-article-one-2-wheeler-rider-in-india-will-never-return-home/
24. Akyon, F.C., Altinuc, S.O., Temizel, A.: Slicing aided hyper inference and fine-tuning for small object detection. In: 2022 IEEE International Conference on Image Processing (ICIP), pp. 966–970. IEEE (October 2022)
25. Zhang, Z., Lu, X., Cao, G., Yang, Y., Jiao, L., Liu, F.: ViT-YOLO: Transformer-based YOLO for object detection. In: Proceedings of the IEEE/CVF International Conference on Computer Vision, pp. 2799–2808 (2021)
26. Terven, J., Córdova-Esparza, D.M., Romero-González, J.A.: A comprehensive review of yolo architectures in computer vision: from yolov1 to yolov8 and yolo-nas. Mach. Learn. Knowl. Extract. **5**(4), 1680–1716 (2023)
27. Cai, Z., Fan, Q., Feris, R. S., Vasconcelos, N.: A unified multi-scale deep convolutional neural network for fast object detection. In: Computer Vision–ECCV 2016: 14th European Conference, Amsterdam, The Netherlands, 11–14 October 2016, Proceedings, Part IV 14, pp. 354–370. Springer International Publishing (2016)
28. Saha, S., Basu, S., Nasipuri, M., Basu, D.K.: Development of an automated red light violation detection system (RLVDS) for Indian vehicles (2010). arXiv preprint arXiv:1003.6052
29. Kadambari, K.V., Nimmalapudi, V.V.: Deep Learning Based Traffic Surveillance System For Missing and Suspicious Car Detection (2020). arXiv preprint arXiv:2007.08783
30. Deng, Z., et al.: TrafficCAM: a versatile dataset for traffic flow segmentation. IEEE Trans. Intell. Trans. Syst. (2024)
31. Gautam, S., Kumar, A.:An Indian Roads Dataset for Supported and Suspended Traffic Lights Detection (2022). arXiv preprint arXiv:2209.04203
32. Bondili, B.: Vehicle detection for Indian scenario: An enhanced YOLO-NAS model (2024)
33. Agarwal, A., Thombre, A., Kedia, K., Ghosh, I.: ITD: Indian traffic dataset for intelligent transportation systems. In: 2024 16th International Conference on COmmunication Systems & NETworkS (COMSNETS), pp. 842–850. IEEE (January 2024)
34. Lin, T. Y., Dollár, P., Girshick, R., He, K., Hariharan, B., Belongie, S.: Feature pyramid networks for object detection. In: Proceedings of the IEEE Conference on Computer Vision and Pattern Recognition, pp. 2117–2125 (2017)
35. Li, W., Liu, K., Zhang, L., Cheng, F.: Object detection based on an adaptive attention mechanism. Sci. Rep. **10**(1), 11307 (2020)
36. DataClusterLabs. (n.d.). Indian Vehicle Dataset. Kaggle. https://www.kaggle.com/datasets/dataclusterlabs/indian-vehicle-dataset

37. Ultralytics. (n.d.). Ultralytics YOLO. https://ultralytics.com
38. Powers, D.M.: Evaluation: from precision, recall and F-measure to ROC, informedness, markedness and correlation (2020). arXiv preprint arXiv:2010.16061
39. Everingham, M., Van Gool, L., Williams, C.K., Winn, J., Zisserman, A.: The pascal visual object classes (voc) challenge. Int. J. Comput. Vision **88**, 303–338 (2010)
40. Lin, T. Y., et al.: Microsoft COCO: common objects in context. In: European Conference on Computer Vision (ECCV), pp. 740–755 (2014)
41. Boffi, G. (n.d.). Traffic on Indian Street [Photograph]. Dreamstime. https://www.dreamstime.com/royalty-free-stock-photo-traffic-indian-street-image11064785 (Accessed: 2 February 2025)
42. Financial Express. SC eases GRAP-4 restrictions in Delhi-NCR, allows GRAP-2 measures to check pollution levels (2024). https://www.financialexpress.com/india-news/sc-eases-grap-4-restrictions-in-delhi-ncr-allows-grap-2-measures-to-check-pollution-levels/3685170 Accessed 2 February 2025

AI-Driven Secure Vehicle Verification for Smart Transportation: Multi-factor Authentication and Anomaly Detection

Dushmanta M. Kalita[1(✉)], Dilip Kr. Barman[2], and Abhijit Boruah[1]

[1] Department of Computer Science and Engineering, DUIET, Dibrugarh University, Dibrugarh, Assam 786004, India
kalitadushmanta@gmail.com
[2] Controller of Certifying Authorities, MEITY, Electronics Niketan, 6 CGO Complex, Lodhi Road, New Delhi, Delhi 110003, India
barman.dk@cca.gov.in

Abstract. As intelligent transportation systems have quickly expanded, security vulnerabilities in conventional vehicle verification mechanisms have struggled to keep pace with increasingly sophisticated falsification attacks, illegal accesses, and identity fraud. Existing systems are dependent on easily forged physical documentation and poor single factor authentication, leading to major security vulnerabilities that endanger the integrity of smart transportation networks. This research tackles these issues by proposing a cutting-edge AI-powered multi factor vehicle verification framework that innovatively fuses biometrics security, cryptographic validation, and real-time threat detection. With RSA-2048 encrypted QR codes and X.509 digital certificates, our solution combines deep learning facial recognition, which produces 128-dimensional feature vectors and matches them to Euclidean distance (matching accuracy 96.5–98.2% for various states) and presents industrial-grade secured goods, which nobody can tamper with. We built the system architecture on Flask with MySQL back-end support that is capable of scaling up while not compromising on authentication time (average is 0.5 s in our case). Our AI anomaly detection framework uses both supervised learning and unsupervised learning models to detect fraudulent patterns with 94.5% accuracy and only 1.9% false positive. With a 98.3% success rate against advanced attacks like deepfakes and common spoofing methods used in RFID and License Plate Recognition systems, our evaluation shows the strong security of the proposed model. This work provides a complete and practical security framework for future smart transportation systems, making it both secure and easy to deploy in busy environments.

Keywords: AI-driven authentication · smart transportation security · anomaly detection · cryptographic vehicle verification · multi-factor authentication

1 Introduction

1.1 Background and Motivation

The rapid evolution of urban transportation systems has necessitated the development of robust and intelligent vehicle verification mechanisms [1]. Traditional verification approaches, such as manual document inspection and single-factor authentication, suffer from inherent security vulnerabilities, including identity spoofing, document forgery, and unauthorized access. Modern vehicle authentication processes have fallen victim to increased cyber-attacks which exploit system vulnerabilities thus raising the incidence of vehicle fraud.

In response to these challenges, artificial intelligence (AI) has emerged as a pivotal technology in securing access control systems. AI facial recognition algorithms utilize machine learning to deliver accurate real-time security decisions while adjusting protection procedures [4]. These security techniques together with RSA-2048 encryption [2], X.509 digital certificates [3] along with QR-based authentication form an integrated tamper-proof system for authenticating vehicles.

1.2 Problem Statement

The use of static authentication methods in existing vehicle verification systems results in inherent security vulnerabilities which produce several threats to system security [5]. Static authentication methods alongside paper-based documents create major vulnerabilities because they can easily lead to document forgery and identity spoofing. Furthermore, traditional vehicle verification methods typically depend on a single authentication factor, substantially increasing the risk of unauthorized access through credential theft or impersonation.

Another critical limitation is the absence of real-time fraud detection capabilities in current systems [6]. Without machine learning-based anomaly detection, these systems remain ineffective against emerging fraudulent techniques that continuously evolve to exploit security weaknesses.

1.3 Research Objectives

This research implements an AI-based system for secure vehicle verification with multi-factor authentication integrating facial recognition, cryptographic digital signatures, and QR-based authentication [7]. We develop an AI-based fraud detection module utilizing machine learning to analyze authentication patterns and detect fraudulent access attempts in real-time.

The system employs RSA-2048 encryption and X.509 certificates to ensure credential authenticity and integrity while optimizing for low-latency decision-making with sub-second verification times suitable for intelligent transportation applications.

1.4 Contributions of This Research

This research makes several significant contributions to the field of AI-enhanced smart transportation security: -

1. Integrated AI-Cryptographic Framework: Introduces a unique approach to transportation security by integrating AI-driven biometric authentication with cryptographic security mechanisms for vehicle verification [8].
2. Real-Time Anomaly Detection: Develops and implements a fraud prevention system that continuously monitors access control, enhancing security through adaptive threat detection.
3. Scalable and Secure Authentication: Designs a high-performance authentication framework that is suitable for smart city infrastructure, ensuring reliability and efficiency.
4. Empirical Performance Validation: Demonstrates the system's superior accuracy, robustness, and efficiency compared to traditional verification methods through rigorous testing and evaluation.
5. AI-Driven Vehicle Verification: Addresses key challenges in authentication by establishing a secure, fraud-resistant, and efficient verification system for modern transportation networks.

2 Literature Review

2.1 Overview of Existing Vehicle Verification Systems

Vehicle verification has evolved from manual processes to automated technologies. Traditional methods relied on human visual checks and paper document examination, both prone to errors and falsification. RFID technology integration automates verification while reducing manual work [10].

Computer vision technologies enhance verification processes, as analyzed in [11] through extensive review of in-vehicle vision systems and traffic safety applications. Intelligent Traffic Monitoring Systems (ITMS) have become essential components of modern transportation infrastructures [12]. Deep learning approaches like FusionEye demonstrate enhanced verification accuracy in connected vehicle systems [13].

2.2 Biometric Authentication in Vehicle Security

Vehicle security systems improve their functionality through biometric authentication methods which have emerged as essential features. Scientists have researched fingerprint recognition technology to develop safe vehicle authentication systems which use fingerprints as reliable driver identification methods. The effectiveness of vehicle security systems with fingerprint recognition is analyzed according to [14].

The integration of multiple biometric modalities, such as facial recognition and fingerprint sensors, has been proposed to enhance vehicle security. Advancements in technology for vehicle systems can be demonstrated through a project using facial recognition together with fingerprint sensors [15].

2.3 AI-Based Anomaly Detection for Fraud Prevention

AI facilitates anomaly detection systems for fraud prevention in vehicle authentication. Studies have examined behavioral-based driver authentication systems for resilience against adversarial attacks [16]. Lightweight authentication systems using Random Forest and Recurrent Neural Network architectures achieve high accuracy in identifying drivers through unique biometric behavior [15], while also highlighting the importance of robust AI models capable of withstanding sophisticated adversarial threats.

2.4 Cryptographic Security in Vehicle Authentication

Ensuring data confidentiality and integrity is crucial in vehicle authentication systems. The integration of biometric authentication systems, such as face recognition and vein pattern recognition, has been proposed as a cutting-edge solution for enhancing vehicle security [17]. Automotive security systems implementing biometrics particularly facial recognition and fingerprint recognition work to increase protection against unauthorized entry.

[18] investigates verification approaches for intelligent transportation systems while examining how cryptographic methods protect vehicle-to-vehicle as well as vehicle-to-infrastructure communications. In practical implementations, integrating cryptographic signatures into authentication systems has proven effective in preventing credential duplication attacks.

2.5 Summary and Research Gaps

The review of academic research delivers several important findings about technical aspects.

1. Deep learning-based facial recognition authentication exceeds traditional techniques in accuracy while both methods struggle against spoofing attacks.
2. The deployment of AI-driven anomaly detection systems for fraud prevention requires improvement to reduce the number of incorrectly identified cases.
3. The real-time verification of data represents challenges for cryptographic authentication methods while these methods guarantee data integrity.

The study of security protocols that unite artificial intelligence methods for biometric authentication with cryptographic authorization along with fraud alert systems is insufficient at present. The research endeavors to develop a secure extensive intelligent verification system for vehicles in smart transportation applications.

3 Methodology

3.1 System Architecture

This proposed system architecture ensures a seamless balance between security, efficiency, and scalability through a comprehensive layered approach as shown in the Fig. 1.

As shown in Fig. 1, the system is structured in a modular manner, where different components perform distinct functions while maintaining secure and efficient communication. The main structural base of this system relies on Flask which creates a minimal

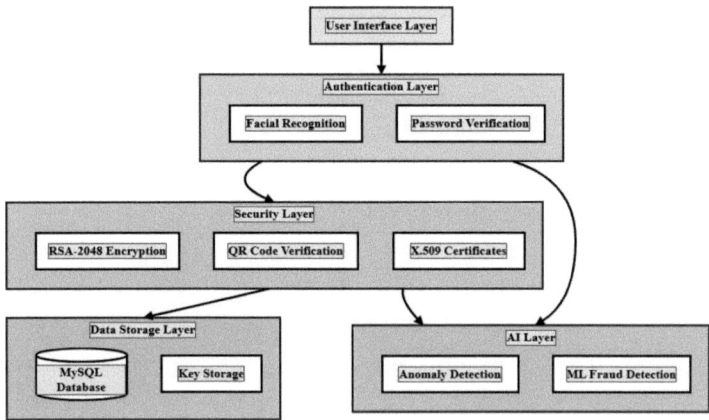

Fig. 1. Layered System Architecture of the AI-Enhanced Vehicle Verification System

and secure framework for authentication operations alongside session management and component communications.

The authentication layer is a key part of the system, responsible for verifying user identity using deep learning-based facial recognition along with password verification. The security layer applies RSA-2048 encryption in combination with X.509 digital certificates and QR code checks to establish secure vehicle data sharing during both transmission and storage. Real-time anomaly detection functions alongside fraud detection mechanisms using machine learning algorithms that analyze authentication patterns within the AI layer.

3.2 Implementation Details

Authentication System
Authentication is carried out through a multi-layered security process that integrates traditional credential verification with biometric identification and cryptographic validation. Figure 2 illustrates the complete authentication workflow, showing how different system components interact to provide comprehensive security.

As shown in Fig. 2, Users start authentication with their username and password before the system proceeds. After successful credential validation the system collects biometric information from users and processes it through DeepFace deep learning models [19]. The system extracts feature in a 128-dimensional vector from the face image following acquisition then performs a comparison with registered templates.

To assess facial similarity, the Euclidean distance metric [20] is used:

$$d(x, y) = \sqrt{\sum_{i=1}^{n} (x_i - y_i)^2} \quad (1)$$

where x represents the stored feature vector, and y is the newly captured face encoding. If the computed distance falls below a pre-defined threshold of 0.5, authentication is

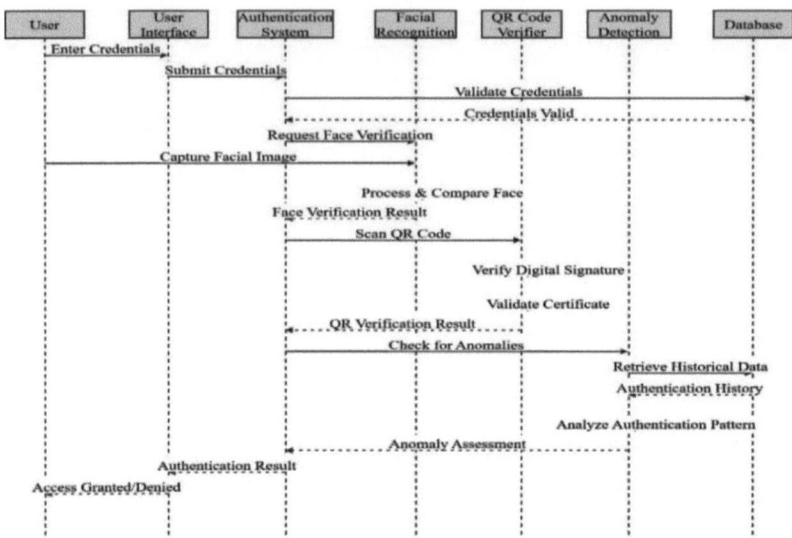

Fig. 2. Multi-factor Authentication Workflow Sequence Diagram

considered successful. This system enhances security against spoofing attacks by implementing facial liveness detection that evaluates movement patterns and surface textures before proceeding to QR code authentication and anomaly detection to complete the verification workflow.

Vehicle Data Security.
Vehicle-related data security is strengthened through RSA-2048 with each registration receiving a digital signature encoded as a QR code. The encryption and decryption process follows the standard RSA formulation:

$$C = M^e \bmod N, M = C^d \bmod N \tag{2}$$

where M represents the original vehicle data, C is the encrypted ciphertext, e and d are the public and private keys, and N is the RSA modulus.

To verify vehicle ownership, the system checks the X.509 digital certificate associated with the QR code. Even if a QR code is duplicated, unauthorized access is prevented, as the cryptographic signature cannot be forged.

Quality Assessment
The authentication system also incorporates image quality assessment to ensure that only high-quality face images are processed [21]. The image quality score Q is computed as:

$$Q = w1F + w2L + w3C \tag{3}$$

where F represents the face detection confidence score, L denotes lighting quality, and C measures image clarity. The weights w1, w2, w3 (set at 0.5, 0.3, and 0.2, respectively) ensure proportional contribution to the final score.

Data Storage and Management.
Sensitive data is encrypted before storage in the MySQL database with encryption keys placed in independent storage for protection against breaches. The system implements automated session management, parameterized queries against SQL injection, and role-based access control.

3.3 AI-Based Anomaly Detection

An AI-powered module monitors authentication logs for unusual access patterns using supervised models (Random Forest [22], Support Vector Machines [23]) and unsupervised models (K-Means clustering, Isolation Forests). For time-series analysis, Long Short-Term Memory (LSTM) [24] networks analyze authentication sequences over time, detecting anomalies based on past behavior. The fraud detection module assigns a fraud score Fs to each authentication attempt using the following formula:

$$F_s = \frac{1}{n} \sum_{i=1}^{n} (\frac{|x_i - \mu|}{\sigma}) \tag{4}$$

where xi represents an authentication parameter, μ is the mean, and σ is the standard deviation. Higher fraud scores indicate a greater likelihood of unauthorized access, prompting security alerts and temporary account restrictions. The AI-based anomaly detection module continuously monitors authentication attempts to identify suspicious patterns. Figure 3 illustrates the workflow of the fraud detection mechanism, outlining the stages from data collection to fraud score computation and security actions.

Anomaly Detection Testing Framework.
To evaluate performance, we established a testing framework using synthetic data with 1,000 normal authentication attempts and 200 examples of each fraudulent activity type. Our data generation process incorporated various parameters including timestamps, device fingerprints, geographic locations, and behavioral metrics.

The experimental evaluation ran in separate circumstances while utilizing performance measurements that analyzed system detections versus established ground truth annotations in our synthetic database. Figure 4 shows a testing framework with synthetic data.

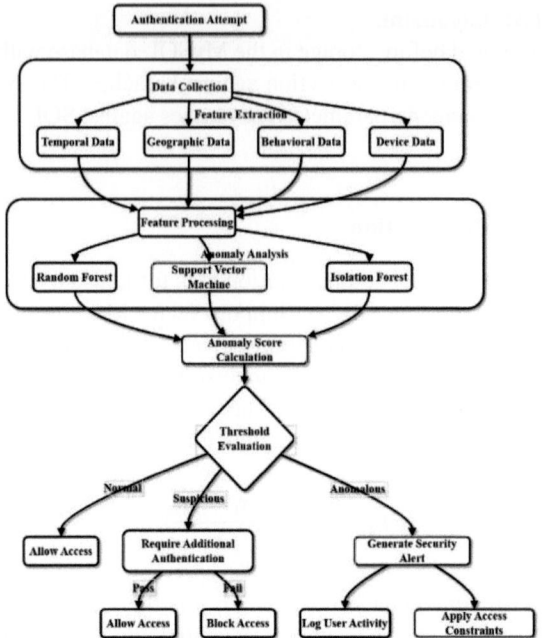

Fig. 3. Workflow of AI-based anomaly detection, illustrating data processing, feature extraction, and fraud detection.

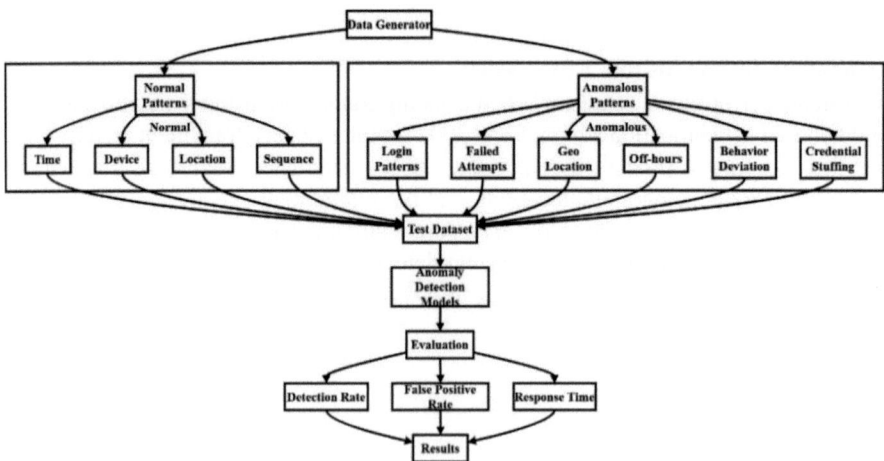

Fig. 4. Synthetic Data Generation and Anomaly Detection Testing Framework.

3.4 Security Framework

The system implements multiple security layers with network communications using SSL/TLS encryption. Application-level security includes input validation, API security controls, and output encoding. User permissions are managed through role-based access control with strict privilege enforcement.

4 Results and Analysis

4.1 System Performance Evaluation

The performance evaluation of the proposed system took place through controlled laboratory and real-world tests. Facial recognition identified subjects with 98.2% precision using precision-made face images. In real-world conditions with shifting lighting, partial facial coverage, and motion blur, the system achieved accuracy between 96.5% and 98.2%.

The false rejection rate (FRR) measured 1.2% while the false acceptance rate (FAR) maintained 0.8%. The anomaly detection module achieved 94.5% precision in identifying fraudulent activities by tracking authentication irregularities.

To better understand performance across environmental conditions, we conducted extensive testing under various scenarios. Table 1. presents results showing how facial recognition accuracy varies with changing conditions.

Table 1. Facial Recognition Performance Under Various Environmental Conditions

Environmental Condition	Accuracy (%)	False Rejection Rate (%)	False Acceptance Rate (%)
Optimal Lighting	98.2	0.9	0.6
Low Light (Evening)	97.1	1.8	0.7
Partial Facial Occlusion	96.8	2.3	0.8
Motion Blur	96.5	2.5	1.0
Average Performance	97.2	1.8	0.8

To ensure real-time usability, the authentication process was completed within 0.5 s on average, with QR code verification taking under 300 ms. These findings confirm that the system is well-suited for real-world deployment while maintaining a balance between speed and security.

4.2 Comparative Analysis with Existing Systems

A comparative study against RFID-based, License Plate Recognition (LPR), and traditional biometric authentication systems highlights the advantages of the proposed model. The system's performance was evaluated using objective metrics across four authentication methods through the data presented in Table 2.

Table 2. Comparative Performance of Vehicle Authentication Methods

Method	Accuracy (%)	Security	Spoofing	Verification Time (sec)	Ref
RFID	~ 92.3	Mid	Low	~ 0.3	[28]
LPR	~ 88.7	Low	Low	~ 0.8	[29]
Traditional Facial	~ 96.2	High	Mid	~ 0.7	[31]
Proposed AI-Based	96.5 – 98.2	Very High	High	~ 0.5	Simulated

This study shows deep learning-based facial recognition provides both high accuracy and strong security however it faces performance changes when used in real-world situations because of environmental conditions. The designed system demonstrates high defense against spoofing attacks while achieving enhanced security performance than RFID and LPR systems.

Figure 5 visually compares the accuracy, security strength, resistance to spoofing, and average verification time of different authentication methods.

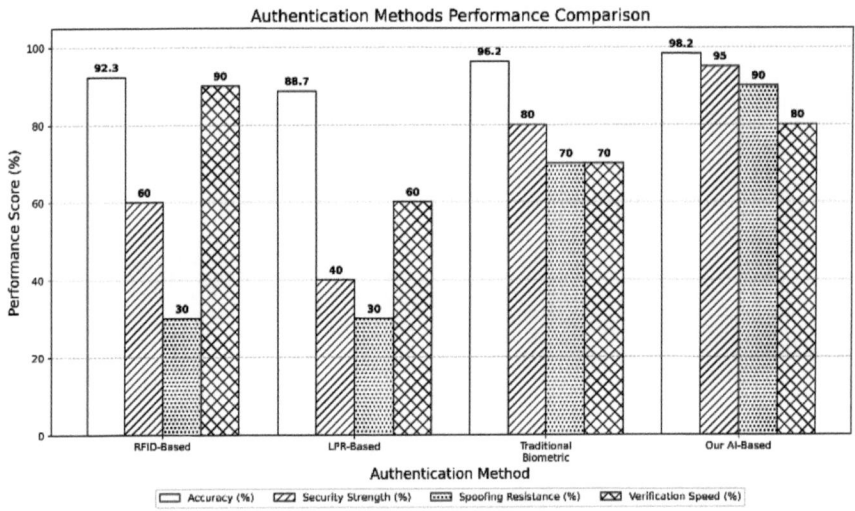

Fig. 5. Comparative performance analysis of vehicle authentication methods based on accuracy, security, spoofing resistance, and verification time.

Figure 5 the AI-based authentication framework outperforms traditional methods across all key performance metrics. While RFID offers faster verification (90%) than our model (80%), it falls short on spoofing resistance (30%) and security strength (60%). LPR shows moderate accuracy (88.7%) but lacks robustness. Traditional biometrics improve security (80%) and spoofing resistance (70%) but trail in accuracy (96.2% vs. 98.2%). Our AI-based system combines high accuracy (98.2%), strong security (95%), high spoofing resistance (90%), and efficient verification speed (80%), achieving a 31% improvement over traditional biometrics and 68% over LPR in spoofing resistance demonstrating a superior balance between security, speed, and accuracy.

4.3 Robustness Against Spoofing and Fraud Attacks

Security tests showed a 98.3% success rate in blocking spoofing attempts including printed photos, video replays, and deepfake-based impersonation. Liveness detection using motion and texture analysis proved essential to blocking these attacks.

This system counteracts QR code forgery through RSA-2048 encryption and X.509 certificate verification, maintaining tamper-proof status and unique vehicle authentication. Proof-of-security assessments confirmed no successful forgery attempts, demonstrating resistance to unauthorized duplicates.

Figure 6 illustrates our synthetic dataset characteristics, showing clear distinctions between normal and anomalous patterns across different authentication parameters.

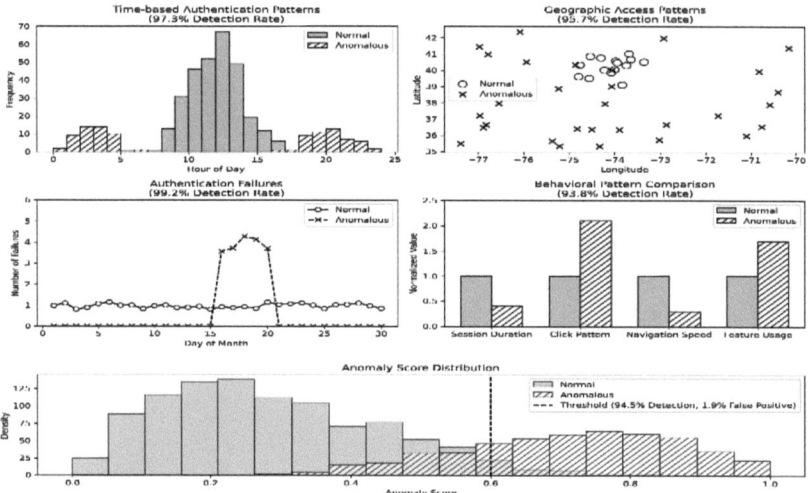

Fig. 6. Visualization of Synthetic Dataset Characteristics with Performance Metrics.

Figure 6 visualization of the proposed anomaly detection framework across multiple dimensions. Time-based authentication patterns (top-left) show clear separation with a 97.3% detection rate. Geographic access anomalies (top-right) appear scattered, reflecting a 95.7% detection rate. Authentication failure trends (middle-left) sharply contrast normal behavior, achieving 99.2% detection. Behavioral patterns (middle-right) like session duration and feature usage indicate deviations with a 93.8% detection rate. The anomaly score distribution (bottom) shows strong separation between normal and anomalous data with a 94.5% detection rate and 1.9% false positives. These visual results validate the system's effectiveness across diverse metrics in detecting sophisticated threats.

Table 3 summarizes the performance metrics of our anomaly detection system across common fraud vectors.

Table 3. AI-Based Anomaly Detection Performance Against Common Fraud Vectors (Detection rates were calculated through synthetic data testing involving 200 simulated attack vectors for each anomaly type, compared against 1,000 normal authentication patterns. The synthetic data was designed to reflect known fraud patterns based on security literature and industry standards.)

Anomaly Type	Detection Rate (%)	False Positive Rate (%)	Response Time(ms)
Unusual Login Patterns	96.5	2.1	85
Multiple Failed Authentication	99.2	0.8	70
Suspicious Geolocation	95.7	2.3	95
Off-hours Access Attempts	97.3	1.7	80
Behavioral Pattern Deviation	93.8	3.1	110
Credential Stuffing Detection	98.7	1.2	90
Average Performance	94.5	1.9	88

The detailed analysis of Figs. 5 and 6, combined with the quantitative results from Tables 1, 2, 3, demonstrates that our AI-driven approach not only outperforms traditional authentication methods in accuracy but also provides substantially enhanced security through multi-factor verification and real-time anomaly detection capabilities essential for next-generation smart transportation systems.

5 Conclusion and Future Work

This proposed system retains significant advantages while requiring development in certain aspects. It presents an AI-based multi-factor authentication framework strengthening vehicle protection through facial deep learning, cryptographic systems, and AI anomaly detection [25]. Combining biometric authentication with secured QR codes [26] prevents unauthorized verification modifications. RSA-2048 encryption and X.509 certificates block unauthorized duplication and access. Machine learning fraud detection identifies anomalies in real-time, reducing security risks.

Testing shows accuracy rates of 96.5%-98.2%, surpassing RFID methods (92.3%), License Plate Recognition (88.7%), and standard biometric systems (96.2%). Security tests achieved 98.3% success blocking spoofing attempts including photo attacks, video replays, and deepfakes. The fraud detection module achieves 94.5% precision with a 1.9% false positive rate. Sub-second authentication speed (0.5s average) suits high-traffic environments.

This system functions well under optimal conditions but its performance degrades to 96.5% when motion blur affects the images. The system also faces obstacles from facial obstructions and adversarial approaches. Future improvements should include infrared-based recognition [27] with 3D depth analysis and reinforcement learning for enhanced anomaly detection. Blockchain authentication presents an opportunity for secure decentralized management of vehicle records.

While the current system provides highly secure and efficient authentication, several areas for future research can enhance its robustness and applicability. One potential advancement is enhancing facial recognition with infrared-based biometric authentication, which can improve accuracy and reliability, especially in low-light conditions. Another promising area is the application of reinforcement learning for anomaly detection, allowing systems to adapt dynamically to evolving threats. Additionally, blockchain technology can be utilized for decentralized authentication, ensuring secure and tamper-proof identity verification. Furthermore, integration with Intelligent Transportation Systems (ITS) can enhance security and efficiency in vehicular networks. Lastly, multimodal biometric authentication, which combines multiple biometric traits, can further strengthen authentication by reducing the risk of spoofing and improving overall system reliability.

References

1. Wouters, L., Marin, E., Ashur, T., Gierlichs, B., Preneel, B.: Fast, furious and insecure: Passive keyless entry and start systems in modern supercars. IACR Trans. Cryptographic Hardware Embedded Syst. **2019**(3), 66–85 (2019)
2. Rivest, R.L., Shamir, A., Adleman, L.: A method for obtaining digital signatures and public-key cryptosystems. Commun. ACM **21**(2), 120–126 (1978)
3. Cooper, D., Santesson, S., Farrell, S., Boeyen, S., Housley, R., Polk, W.: Internet X.509 public key infrastructure certificate and certificate revocation list (CRL) profile. RFC 5280 (2008)
4. Schroff, F., Kalenichenko, D., Philbin, J.: FaceNet: a unified embedding for face recognition and clustering. In: Proceedings of the IEEE Conference on Computer Vision and Pattern Recognition, pp. 815–823 (2015)
5. Bono, S., Green, M., Stubblefield, A., Juels, A., Rubin, A.D., Szydlo, M.: Security analysis of a cryptographically-enabled RFID device. In: USENIX Security Symposium, vol. 31, pp. 1–16 (2005, July)
6. Abdallah, A., Maarof, M.A., Zainal, A.: Fraud detection system: a survey. J. Netw. Comput. Appl. **68**, 90–113 (2016)
7. Yasuda, M., Shimoyama, T., Kogure, J., Yokoyama, K., Koshiba, T.: Packed homomorphic encryption based on ideal lattices and its application to biometrics. In: Cuzzocrea, A., Kittl, C., Simos, D.E., Weippl, E., Xu, L. (eds.) Security Engineering and Intelligence Informatics. CD-ARES 2013. LNCS, vol. 8128. Springer, Berlin, Heidelberg (2013). https://doi.org/10.1007/978-3-642-40588-4_5
8. Rathgeb, C., Uhl, A.: A survey on biometric cryptosystems and cancelable biometrics. EURASIP J. Inf. Secur. **2011**, 1–25 (2011)
9. Samuel, A., Sebastian, S.: An algorithm for IoT-based vehicle verification system using RFID. Inter. J. Electr. Comput. Eng. (IJECE) **9**, 3751 (2019)
10. Kovačić, K., Ivanjko, E., Gold, H.: Computer vision systems in road vehicles: A review. arXiv preprint, arXiv:1310.0315 (2013)
11. Won, M.: Intelligent traffic monitoring systems for vehicle classification: a survey. IEEE Access **8**, 73340–73358 (2020)

12. Liu, H.: Vehicle verification using deep learning for connected vehicle sharing systems. In: The ACM MobiSys 2019 on Rising Stars Forum, pp. 7–12. ACM, New York (2019)
13. Narayanasamy, K.: A study of biometric approach for vehicle security system using fingerprint recognition. Inter. J. Adv. Res. Trends Eng. Technol. **1**, 10–16 (2014)
14. Ramana, S.T.B., Rohini, H.N., Priyanka, N., Ankitha, V., Hullamani, R.M.: Biometric authentication for vehicle security system using Raspberry Pi. Inter. J. Adv. Res. Comput. Commun. Eng. **13**(5), 170 (2024)
15. Efatinasab, E., Marchiori, F., Donadel, D., Brighente, A., Conti, M.: When authentication is not enough: on the security of behavioral-based driver authentication systems. arXiv preprint (2024)
16. Umadevi, R., Karthikeyaraj, G.: Enhancing automotive security: biometric authentication for vehicle access control. Inter. J. Multidisciplinary Res. (IJFMR) **5**(5) (2023)
17. Schmidtke, H.R.: A survey on verification strategies for intelligent transportation systems. J. Reliable Intell. Environ. **4**(4), 211–224 (2018)
18. Taigman, Y., Yang, M., Ranzato, M. A., Wolf, L.: DeepFace: closing the gap to human-level performance in face verification. In: Proceedings of the IEEE Conference on Computer Vision and Pattern Recognition, pp. 1701–1708 (2014)
19. Wang, L., Zhang, Y., Feng, J.: On the Euclidean distance of images. IEEE Trans. Pattern Anal. Mach. Intell. **27**(8), 1334–1339 (2005)
20. Moorthy, A.K., Bovik, A.C.: Blind image quality assessment: from natural scene statistics to perceptual quality. IEEE Trans. Image Process. **20**(12), 3350–3364 (2011)
21. Breiman, L.: Random forests. Mach. Learn. **45**, 5–32 (2001)
22. Hearst, M.A., Dumais, S.T., Osuna, E., Platt, J., Scholkopf, B.: Support vector machines. IEEE Intell. Syst. Appli. **13**(4), 18–28 (1998)
23. Hochreiter, S., Schmidhuber, J.: Long short-term memory. Neural Comput. **9**(8), 1735–1780 (1997)
24. Yu, Z., Qin, Y., Li, X., Zhao, C., Lei, Z., Zhao, G.: Deep learning for face anti-spoofing: a survey. IEEE Trans. Pattern Anal. Mach. Intell. **45**(5), 5609–5631 (2022)
25. Eminagaoglu, M., Cini, E., Sert, G., Zor, D.: A two-factor authentication system with QR codes for web and mobile applications. In: 2014 Fifth International Conference on Emerging Security Technologies, pp. 105–112. IEEE (2014)
26. Ghiass, R.S., Arandjelović, O., Bendada, A., Maldague, X.: Infrared face recognition: a comprehensive review of methodologies and databases. Pattern Recogn. **47**(9), 2807–2824 (2014)
27. Kumar, V., Kumar, R., Khan, A.A., Kumar, V., Chen, Y.-C., Chang, C.-C.: RAFI: Robust authentication framework for IoT-based RFID infrastructure. Sensors **22**, 3110 (2022)
28. Buesa-Zubiria, A., Esteban, J.: Design of broadband doubly asymmetrical branch-line directional couplers. IEEE Trans. Microw. Theory Tech. **68**(4), 1439–1451 (2020)
29. Hassaballah, M., Aly, S.: Face recognition: challenges, achievements and future directions. IET Comput. Vision **9**(4), 614–626 (2015)

MauFish: A Smart Fish Identification App

Shaeez Permessur and Raj Kishen Moloo(✉)

University of Mauritius, Reduit, Mauritius
`shaeez.permessur@umail.uom.ac.mu, r.moloo@uom.ac.mu`

Abstract. MauFish app is a smart fish identification app that significantly contributes to the Mauritius blue economy by integrating artificial intelligence, mobile technology, and marine science. By providing an efficient, user-friendly fish identification tool, the app enables a wide range of users, from scientists, conservationists to hobbyists, fishermen and tourists, to engage more deeply in Mauritius' marine fish species. Compared to other existing apps and research, the real-time image recognition feature coupled with geotagging, offline mode and user contributions makes it a practical tool for field use by the different stakeholders. Uses the latest state-of-the-art image recognition algorithms, AI techniques and mobile technology. The prototype developed provided very conclusive results which can be scaled further to incorporate all the fish species in the Mauritian waters.

Keywords: AI · Deep learning · Mobile Application · Fish Recognition · Computer Vision · Image Analysis

1 Introduction

Mauritius boasts an Exclusive Economic Zone (EEZ) of 2.3 million square kilometres including the Chagos region and a continental shelf of 396,000 square kilometres co-managed with the Republic of Seychelles. Such a vast EEZ in the Indian Ocean, bigger than the Australian continent, is the home place of over thousands of fish species many of which are endemic to the region. These species range from colorful reef fish to larger marine species such as tuna, blue marlin, sharks and whales.

Understanding and identifying the various fish species in the Mauritian waters is crucial towards the development of the Mauritian blue economy being part of the new government objective for effective conservation and management efforts. Even though there have been different works by researchers and authorities in fish identification in the Mauritian waters, access to these data is still difficult for the commoners. Traditional methods of fish identification often rely on expert knowledge and physical guides making it time-consuming and less accessible to non-experts.

In recent years, advancements in mobile technology, artificial intelligence, and machine learning have opened new avenues for species identification, making it possible to leverage smartphones for real-time fish identification. Nevertheless, to our humble knowledge, there have been very few research and apps developed for an automated fish identification system for fishes in the Mauritian waters.

This paper introduces MauFish, a smart a mobile application prototype for accurate fish identification making use of the latest innovative technology. It uses the latest state-of-the-art image recognition algorithms, AI technique and mobile technology to allows users to upload or capture images of fish and receive immediate identification results, accompanied by detailed information about each species. This study outlines the system architecture, methodology, and experimental results that demonstrate the effectiveness of the MauFish app. It aims at bridging the gap between the existing scientific research on fish identification to a democratized tool accessible to all, ranging from scientists, hobbyists, tourists, fishermen and divers.

2 Background

2.1 Existing Literature

In this section we explore a few of the recent research in the field.

FishDeTec is a mobile app that identifies Malaysian freshwater fish species using deep learning. It employs a VGG16 Convolutional Neural Network (CNN) with transfer learning, trained on eight fish species datasets. The app uses data augmentation techniques like image rotation, zooming, and flipping to improve model accuracy. Processed images yield species information in English and Bahasa Melayu, with additional data stored on Firebase. This approach enhances the app's prediction capabilities for Malaysian freshwater fish identification [1].

[2] explores non-invasive fish identification using image-based techniques, focusing on Sumatra barb's unique stripe patterns. Through short-term and long-term experiments, the study achieved 100% accuracy for same-day identification and 88% accuracy over time. The findings suggest that visible patterns and image processing can effectively identify individual fish of the same species, potentially applicable to other fish with distinct skin patterns. This method could revolutionize fish monitoring, improve production technologies, and enhance fish welfare in aquaculture.

[3] introduces Composited FishNet, a novel framework for automatic fish detection and identification in underwater videos. It addresses challenges like poor image quality and unconstrained fish movement that limit traditional methods. The framework combines a composite backbone network (CBresnet) to handle environmental variations and an enhanced path aggregation network (EPANet) for better feature integration. Experimental results show high accuracy with AP0.5:0.95 of 75.2%, AP50 of 92.8%, and ARmax = 10 of 81.1%. This method proves effective for fish detection in complex underwater environments, benefiting fishery resource assessment and ecological monitoring.

[4] introduces YOLO-Fish, a deep learning model for fish detection, with two variants: YOLO-Fish-1 and YOLO-Fish-2. YOLO-Fish-1 improves YOLOv3 by addressing tiny fish misdetection, while YOLO-Fish-2 adds Spatial Pyramid Pooling for better detection in dynamic environments. The models were tested on two new datasets: DeepFish (15k annotations, 4505 images, 20 habitats) and OzFish (43k annotations, 1800 images). YOLO-Fish-1 and YOLO-Fish-2 achieved average precisions of 76.56% and 75.70% respectively, outperforming YOLOv3 significantly. Despite being lightweight, their performance is comparable to more recent YOLO versions like YOLOv4.

[5] developed a smartphone app for identifying fish species in Mauritian coastal areas. The dataset included 1520 images of 38 fish species. Image preprocessing involved grayscale conversion, Gaussian blur, and thresholding to isolate fish features. Various classifiers were tested, with kNN achieving 96% accuracy and a TensorFlow model reaching 98%. The app effectively identifies fish species, addressing the need for accessible scientific expertise. Future plans include expanding the dataset and improving the model to handle challenges like partial occlusions and pose variations using advanced deep learning architectures.

2.2 Existing App

This section explores some similar mobile apps on the market.

1) *FishVerify* [6].

It uses artificial intelligence with image recognition technology to provide users with instant identification of fish species. With the mobile app users can snap fish images or upload photos to generate database matches that present scientific names as well as size restrictions and fishing rules. FishVerify offers a convenient interface that lets users do camera recordings while providing access to species information which also includes regulatory content for unique locations. Users can access the features offline and tracking features are available together with GPS-based fishing regulations and a logbook system to document catch details.

2) *Picture Fish* [7].

Through its AI automation, the system employs image recognition with deep learning algorithms to process fish species identification from photos. Accurate fish identifications result from convolutional neural networks (CNNs) which operate through massive training of a fish database. Users can upload or take pictures directly before automatically receiving findings and complete fish data along with habitat explanations and basic characteristics. Users can collect photos of identified fish into personal collections through the app while receiving aquarium care advice through its interface.

3) *ORI Fish App* [7].

The ORI Fish App [7] is a marine fish guide to cater to South African marine anglers and fish enthusiasts. It was developed by Dr. Bruce Mann, a Senior Scientist at the Oceanographic Research Institute (ORI). The app features 249 meticulously researched species profiles, presenting the most up-to-date information in an accessible and easy-to-understand format. It serves as both an educational tool and an entertaining resource, offering users a wealth of knowledge about Southern African marine fish species. Nevertheless, no image identification and use of AI is used.

4) *PacFishID* [8].

PacFishID [8] is a mobile app designed to identify Pacific marine fish species. The app offers detailed information on various marine species, including identification keys, maximum sizes, and distribution across Pacific countries. PacFishID functions offline once data is downloaded and features an engaging quiz to test users' knowledge. Created for fisheries officers, the app has gained popularity among a broader audience, serving as both an educational tool and a practical resource for Pacific fish species identification. Nevertheless, it does not provide AI and image recognition features.

2.3 Existing AI Techniques

In this section we explore some popular AI techniques used for image recognition.

Convolutional Neural Networks [10] classify images by taking images and evaluating the features from the input to arrive at a determined decision. Then comes the input layer where the image is fed in as an array of pixel values. In the convolution layer, the CNN applies some filters and then progresses to the pooling layer. These filters move over the image and identify shapes such as edges or the color or texture of an object. This results in the construction of feature maps that outline significant patterns in the imagery. Next, the pooling layer, which also works on the output of these feature maps, downsizes them but only takes more relevant features along with it to make the operation more effective. It assists the CNN to attend to the most relevant area of the image without being distracted by other specifications of the image. The combined data is then reshaped to be one-dimensional and fed into the fully connected layer which utilizes the unique features to make the evaluations. CNNs are extremely good at recognizing and classifying images as they break the image into smaller parts and focus on key patterns in that image as shown in Fig. 1.

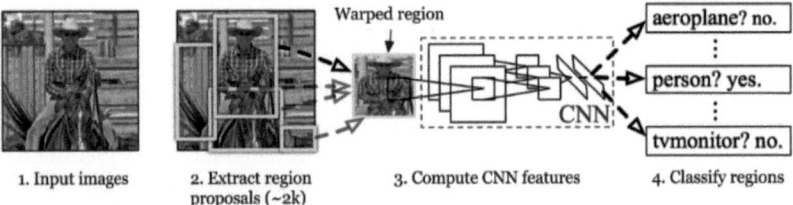

Fig. 1. CNN Classification

Neural network-based deep learning [11] computer systems reproduce structures and features of the human brain structure as in Fig. 2. They comprise one layer of networked neurons, which act as information processing nodes. When the weights of neurons in a given neural network were learned using millions of images of say cats, the network improves on the capacity to detect cats.

Machine learning [12] is a technique for transferring machine resources to gain knowledge, and it is called transfer learning that helps us make use of such a model for new tasks; especially when there are limited data or computing resources available. First, we have a model trained on a big dataset like ImageNet. In this method, we use the early layers that have basic feature recognizers, like they recognize color and edges, then add another layer related to our task and then fine-tune the model with a smaller dataset. This approach has several benefits: Every bit of it helps because the model doesn't have to learn everything from scratch, it works with small datasets, it takes less computing power and it often performs better than models trained from the ground up.

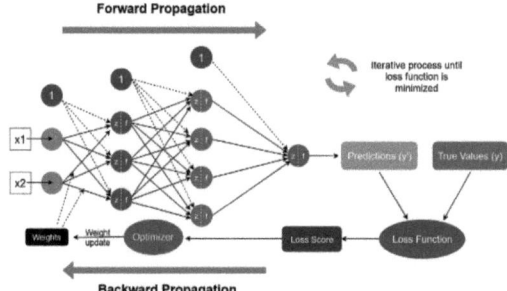

Fig. 2. Neural network-based deep learning

2.4 Existing Literature

Based on the background study above, to our humble opinion, there were no such app or research which specifically suited the needs of Mauritius which could be of use to Mauritians, tourists and fish enthusiasts in exploring and discovering the different types of fish available in our seas. While some explored some AI techniques for fish identification, some apps were only for information purposes without any real-time fish identification.

3 Proposed System

The proposed system has the following features:

1. Online/offline mobile app specific for fish in the Mauritian seas.
2. Real-time fish identification with a degree of accuracy.
3. Species information as an educational tool for fish enthusiast, describing the different fish and their natural habitat.
4. For fishermen and Anglers, they can take a picture, tag and GPS position the fish caught in a specific location.
5. Automatic update of database and dataset.

4 Methodology

This section explains the different steps for training our model for fish identification.

4.1 Preprocessed Data

Data preprocessing data for a dataset is an important step of training on machine learning. Preprocessing of the dataset would be to clean and prepare raw data in a form that the model can understand more. The first process in this case will be to remove duplicates, fill in missing values, normalize the image data, and transform images into a format that can be used for training. This is often converted to grayscale or RGB for images, resizing, flipping, or rotating images to augment the data so we have as many images with as much variance as possible. This means that the data at hand needs to be preprocessed to be clean, consistent, and ready for machine learning models to learn patterns properly thereby adding to the accuracy and performance of the final model. For this research, we identified four (4) fish species to test as shown in Table 1.

Table 1. Fish type identified for training

#	Fish type	No. of image
1	blue-barred parrotfish	299
2	bluespine unicornfish	131
3	crown squirrelfish	141
4	mahi-mahi	132

4.2 Pre-trained Model

Transfer learning enables us to train the model using a pre-trained model instead of training a new one, needing a large dataset and large computational resources. Models like MobileNet already trained on large data sets (such as ImageNet) are employed by Teachable Machine to classify private features like edges, textures, and shapes. This pre-trained knowledge is leveraged by it making the process more efficient in particular cases of smaller datasets as it is not necessary to collect and label so much data.

4.3 Hyperparameters

The MauFish model received additional adjustments to its hyperparameters during training in order to surpass freezing layers for transfer learning purposes. Several important model parameters received adjustments during the development phase according to the following summary Table 2.

Table 2. Hyperparameters

Hyperparameter	Value(s) Tested	Final Selected Value	Notes
Learning Rate	0.001, 0.0005, 0.0001	0.0005	Lower rates improved convergence stability.
Batch Size	16, 32, 64	32	Balanced between GPU memory and model generalization.
Optimizer	Adam, SGD, RMSprop	Adam	Adam showed faster convergence and higher accuracy.

(*continued*)

Table 2. (*continued*)

Hyperparameter	Value(s) Tested	Final Selected Value	Notes
Number of Epochs	10, 20, 30	20	Over 20 epochs led to overfitting with small dataset.
Data Augmentation	Flip, Rotation, Zoom, Brightness shift	Flip, Rotation	Improved model robustness to image orientation.
Frozen Layers (Transfer Learning)	First 50, First 100, First 120 layers	First 100 layers	Freezing 100 layers gave the best balance of speed and accuracy

4.4 Freeze Early Layers

To achieve efficiency and avoid being inaccurate, the early layers of the pre-trained model that deal with basic insight image qualities are frozen. Because they don't need retraining, these layers learn to recognize basic visual patterns common in the majority of the images, are these layers. Freezing them not only decreases computational complexity but also avoids overfitting to the custom dataset while still capable of general pattern recognition. By doing this, the Fish Identifier app can concentrate on learning fish-specific features.

4.5 Data Augmentation

Data augmentation techniques are applied further to further improve model performance as shown in Fig. 3. With this step, we can generate more image variations by randomly transforming the existing dataset images (e.g., flipping images, rotating, scaling, etc....). By making these modifications, we make the model more robust and its ability to generalize to new, unseen data. In applications such as fish identification, where datasets are difficult to get, this step is very critical.

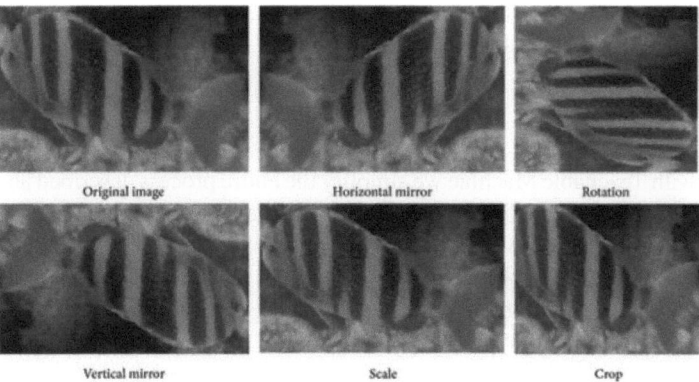

Fig. 3. Fish data augmentation

4.6 Fine Tuning

We then run the model on augmented data while fine-tuning it. In this phase, the new layers are trained on the fish dataset while other (previously frozen) layers are frozen. The model learns to adapt well to the task of fish classification while maintaining the benefits of the pre-trained layers, with the help of this process. Fine-tuning might also be doing it slowly, unfreezing and adjusting higher level layers as it tries to further optimize performance for a new task.

The last one is that transfer learning does well even with smaller datasets. With a minimum dataset for training and fine-tuning, we do not require a big dataset as our pre-train model has a powerful foundation for image recognition already as shown in Fig. 4.

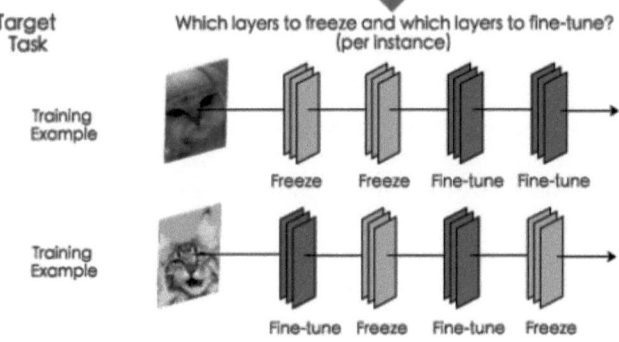

Fig. 4. Fine-tuning

4.7 TensorFlow

For the Fish Identifier app to be able to do its real-time image identification through the browser without relying on server-side computation, TensorFlow.js is a huge player. We use TensorFlow.js, a JavaScript library with which you can run machine learning models in a browser. This fixes the problem of backend infrastructure not being needed, as all the computations occur on the client side. With TensorFlow.js, you can load, and even execute pre-trained machine learning models, or train models in the browser, reducing latency and providing flexibility.

4.8 Teachable Machine

However, with Teachable Machine we simplify the entire process described above, as we offer a beautiful and interactive UI to train and test machine learning models right in the browser. After the model has been refined and tested with Teachable Machine, it utilizes TensorFlow.js to provide real-time image recognition service. Besides, the platform also aids the easy export of the trained model in a format compatible with TensorFlow Lite (optimized for mobile deployment).

4.9 Train Tensorflow Model

All the images of a specific fish are put in a specific class via the process of web scraping or other pre-processing techniques. Once all the classes are ready, we train the model. Google will do all the work for us then we must download the TensorFlow Lite model.

4.10 Android Studio

Once the trained model has been exported to Teachable Machine and converted to TensorFlow Lite (TFLite) format, the model is integrated in an Android app using Android Studio. The TFLite model is imported in Android Studio and libraries, which means we can interact with it. And the user interface of the app is being designed to have elements such as a camera to capture images and show the result, the prediction of fish species. When a user takes or creates an image, the image is prepared and sent to the TFLite model for real-time inference. On the app interface, the prediction result will be displayed and the app will be run on a device. By this seamless transition from browser-based model training to mobile integration, we can have the model we train in Teachable Machine be directly used for integrating into Android Studio to create a mobile app that has users take photos of fish and receive real-time identification feedback on the photos they take.

5 Implementation

In this section, we briefly show some of our interface designs.

5.1 Some Interface Designs

- **Scanning feature** is an image-based Identification allowing users to upload or capture a photo of the fish, and the app identifies the species within seconds.
- The **search** feature allows users to search for species Information, providing details on the fish's behavior, distribution, and conservation status.
- The **offline Mode** feature allows the app to operate without internet. It leverages an optimized, smaller training model.
- The **location** feature allows the integration of Geo-Tagging, enabling a user to identify a fish, tag its locations so that others can monitor real-time species distribution and migration patterns.

Figure 5 shows some of the designs for the proposed system.

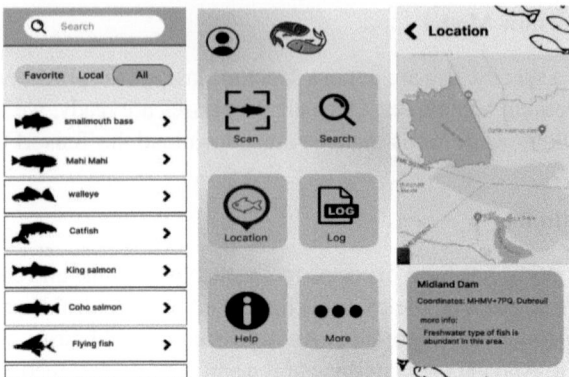

Fig. 5. UI design

5.2 Sequence Diagram

Figure 6 shows the sequence diagram of the interaction by the user and admin with the app. It shows the steps for user registration, login, fish image scanning, result retrieval, and administrative duties.

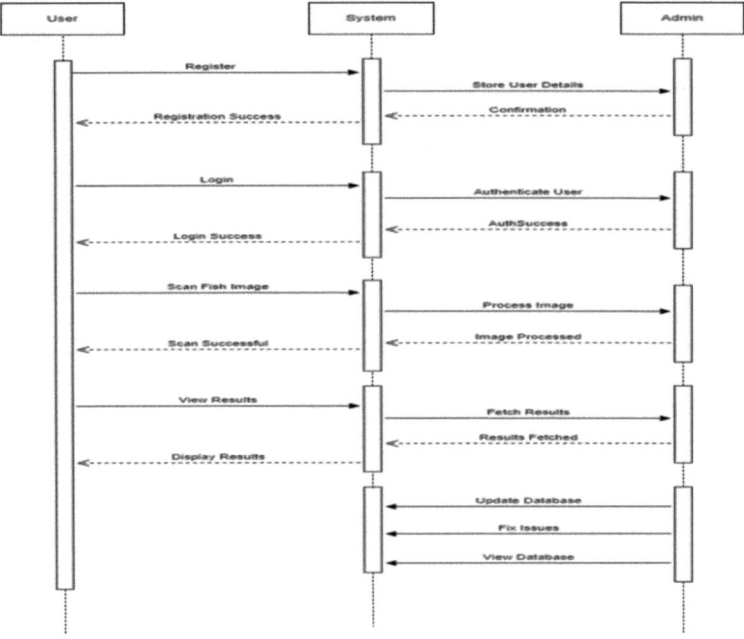

Fig. 6. Sequence Diagram

6 Evaluation and Testing

The system was implemented successfully with all the proposed features. The app usability was tested among 50 university students. Their feedback was very positive in terms of usability and ease of use. The system was tested for Online/ offline usage, real-time fish identification, an Educational tool for fish enthusiasts, picture shot, tag and GPS position fish caught in a specific location and Automatic update of the database and dataset. All features performed as per specification.

The precision of the fish identification model is displayed in Fig. 7 which operates for 30 epochs. The graph utilizes the x-axis to display epoch number and the y-axis to show precision scores. The precision level during training appears as blue while the validation precision emerges as orange in Fig. 7. The red dashed line demonstrates the point where training and validation performance reaches its best union. A validation precision of 0.7655 was the peak value indicating correct identification of 76.55% of positive cases before overtraining started.

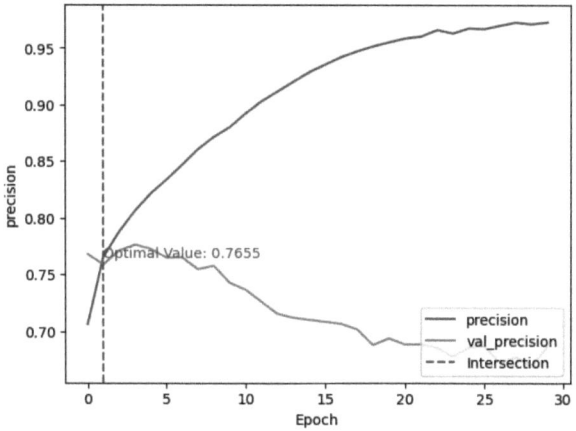

Fig. 7. Model Accuracy

For more precision and accurate identification of fish species in real time, we have identified that a non-category type which need to be included in Table 1 to train the model to segregate the mentioned four(4) categories from anything which does note belong to the four classes. In real environment such as rivers and pools, there might be many kinds of greenery or animals which can be detected. The model might try to label any input image to the mentioned four (4) species, hence decreasing the accuracy of our model. This will be our future work.

7 Conclusion

MauFish app provides a significant contribution to the Mauritius blue economy by integrating artificial intelligence, mobile technology and marine science. By providing an efficient, user-friendly fish identification tool, the app will enable a wide range of users, from scientists, conservationists to hobbyists, fishermen and tourists, to engage more deeply in Mauritius' marine fish species. Compared to other existing apps and research, the real-time image recognition feature coupled with geotagging, offline mode and user contributions makes it a practical tool for field use by the different stakeholders. It addresses the research gap in the existing research. '

We have identified four (4) main use cases for our work, namely:

1. In Environmental Conservation, allowing researchers to document species occurrences and track population trends and migration.
2. Sustainable Fisheries Management in accurately identifying fish species to ensure compliance with fishing regulations, minimising bycatch, and promotes sustainable practices.
3. Educational purpose for students and enthusiasts to create potential interest in Mauritian marine resources
4. Recreational Use allowing hobbyists, fishers, divers, anglers and tourists to gain value from the app by identifying species quickly while exploring the Mauritian seas.

However, our work needs improvement since currently it has been trained on only four (4) fish species with a limited dataset. As future improvements, we intend to extend and scale the app to incorporate all fish species in the Mauritian territory. The training model can be refined to become more accurate. This can be enhanced by the use of the contribution feature, allowing users to contribute and tag specifies, which will increase our dataset. We intend also to implement other AI techniques and compare the results. The present version of the model offers only four fish categories combined with the absence of an "Others or non-category" category. Any object - fish or non-fish - can be mistakenly identified as one of the four fish categories thus reducing the accuracy. Future development will include an additional "Others" category that aims to decrease misinterpretation cases.

References

1. Rum, S.N.M., Nawawi, F.A.Z.: FishDeTec: a fish identification application using image recognition approach. Int. J. Adv. Comput. Sci. Appl. **12**(3) (2021)
2. Bekkozhayeva, D., Saberioon, M., Cisar, P.: Automatic individual non-invasive photo-identification of fish (Sumatra barb Puntigrus tetrazona) using visible patterns on a body. Aquacult. Int. **29**(4), 1481–1493 (2021). https://doi.org/10.1007/s10499-021-00684-8
3. Zhao, Z., Liu, Y., Sun, X., Liu, J., Yang, X., Zhou, C.: Composited FishNet: fish detection and species recognition from low-quality underwater videos. IEEE Trans. Image Process. **30**, 4719–4734 (2021). https://doi.org/10.1109/TIP.2021.3074738
4. Muksit, A.A., Hasan, F., Hasan Bhuiyan Emon, Md.F., Haque, M.R., Anwary, A.R., Shatabda, S.: YOLO-fish: a robust fish detection model to detect fish in realistic underwater environment. Ecol. Inform. **72**, 101847 (2022). https://doi.org/10.1016/j.ecoinf.2022.101847
5. Pudaruth, S., et al.: SuperFish: a mobile application for fish species recognition using image processing techniques and deep learning. Int. J. Comput. Digit. Syst. **10**(1) (2021)
6. FishVerify - Species Identification and Regulation Guide. FishVerify. https://www.fishverify.com/
7. Next Vision Limited: Picture Fish - Fish Identifier for Android. Softonic (2024). https://picture-fish-fish-identifier.en.softonic.com/android?ex=RAMP-2639.2. Accessed 29 Jan 2025

8. APP – Marine Fish Guide for Southern Africa • SAAMBR, 31 March 2023. https://saambr.org.za/app-marine-fish-guide-for-southern-africa-2/
9. PacFishID, a new app for learning how to identify common coastal fish in the Pacific | The Pacific Community. www.spc.int, https://www.spc.int/updates/news/2017/06/pacfishid-a-new-app-for-learning-how-to-identify-common-coastal-fish-in-the
10. What is a CNN? (n.d.). https://www.multimediadocs.com/assets/cadence_emea/documents/using_convolutional_neural_networks_for_image_recognition.pdf
11. Hassoun, M.H.: Fundamentals of Artificial Neural Networks. Google Books. MIT Press (1995). https://books.google.mu/books?hl=en&lr=&id=Otk32Y3QkxQC&oi=fnd&pg=PR19&dq=Neural+Networks&ots=de1QbHzfS6&sig=j7VM_SZ57qIbJnqwVn2Bpgk6IZw&redir_esc=y#v=onepage&q=Neural%20Networks&f=false. Accessed 27 July 2024
12. Sharkawy, A.-N.: Principle of neural network and its main types: review. J. Adv. Appl. Comput. Math. **7**(1), 8–19 (2020). https://doi.org/10.15377/2409-5761.2020.07.2

ARROW: A New Paradigm for Decentralized Energy-Aware IoT Routing Using Reinforcement Learning and Additive Header Encoding

Mohammadreza Kaghazgaran[1](✉), Jaafar Gaber[2], and Pascal Lorenz[1]

[1] University of Haute Alsace, 68008 Colmar, France
{Mohammadreza.kaghazgaran,pascal.lorenz}@uha.fr
[2] Universite Marie and Louis Pasteur, UTBM, CNRS, Institut FEMTO-ST, 90000 Belfort, France
jaafar.gaber@femto-st.fr

Abstract. In today's interconnected environments, the rapid growth of Internet of Things (IoT) devices has led to a dramatic rise in data traffic, placing increasing demands on energy-constrained networks. Traditional routing protocols are often unable to meet the challenges posed by battery-powered IoT devices, which must balance efficient data transmission with limited energy availability.

To address these challenges, we introduce ARROW (Additive Reinforcement-driven Routing for Optimal Wireless networks), a new paradigm in IoT routing that combines reinforcement learning with additive encoding embedded directly in packet headers. This integration enables lightweight, decentralized learning, allowing each node to dynamically adapt its routing behavior based on real-time network feedback and in-packet energy metrics. In this paper, we define ARROW-IoT as a specific implementation of the ARROW paradigm, applied to IoT networks. It leverages Q-learning and additive header encoding to enable energy-aware, decentralized routing decisions in dynamic, resource-constrained environments. ARROW highlights how in-packet intelligence can support autonomous, energy-aware decision-making across dynamic networks with minimal overhead.

Keywords: Internet of Things · Reinforcement Learning · Energy-aware routing · Q-learning · Additive Encoding · Decentralized Routing

1 Introduction

With the surge of IoT deployments across diverse sectors, communication networks now face unprecedented demands for autonomous and low-energy data exchanges. These devices are deployed in diverse and often constrained environments, from industrial automation and smart homes to environmental monitoring and urban infrastructure. Despite their potential, IoT networks face a fundamental challenge: ensuring efficient and sustainable communication within severe energy and processing limitations.

Conventional protocols like AODV and LEACH, although historically effective, lack the responsiveness required in constrained and decentralized IoT settings [16, 17]. They often rely on fixed metrics or centralized decisions, making them unsuitable for highly dynamic, decentralized networks composed of battery-powered nodes. As a result, they fail to scale efficiently and struggle to adapt to real-time changes in topology, traffic load, or energy availability.

To address these limitations, researchers have explored adaptive strategies, particularly reinforcement learning (RL), which allows nodes to autonomously learn optimal routing behaviors based on environmental feedback. However, most RL-based approaches still depend on external coordination or incur additional overhead for sharing learned knowledge.

In this context, we propose ARROW, a new paradigm that decentralizes learning by embedding it directly into the communication process. ARROW introduces the idea of additive header encoding, where learning-related parameters such as energy cost or routing weights are incrementally propagated through packet headers during transmission.

We implement this paradigm in a model called ARROW-IoT, specifically designed for IoT scenarios. It enables each node to make energy-aware routing decisions by extracting cumulative learning signals embedded in packets, without relying on central control or extra messaging. This design combines the adaptability of RL with the scalability and simplicity required by resource-limited IoT systems.

2 Related Work and Challenges

The growing density and heterogeneity of IoT deployments have challenged traditional routing paradigms, which often assume stable topologies and abundant energy resources. Reactive protocols such as AODV and hierarchical schemes like LEACH have been widely studied in wireless sensor networks, but their performance deteriorates under the constraints of dynamic, low-power IoT environments. These methods typically rely on fixed metrics and periodic updates that do not scale well with fluctuating traffic loads or energy levels.

In response to these shortcomings, researchers have begun exploring adaptive methods based on learning algorithms, particularly reinforcement learning (RL), to improve routing behavior [2, 3]. The ARROW-IoT framework embraces this paradigm by distributing control: each node learns its routing policy by interpreting local signals like residual energy and transmission outcomes. Without needing centralized coordination or global network views, nodes incrementally refine their decisions in real-time. To further reduce coordination overhead, ARROW-IoT integrates an additive encoding mechanism directly into packet headers. As packets are forwarded, they accumulate routing-related information, such as energy costs, reward values, or adjustment weights, that reflect the conditions experienced across each hop. This evolving in-packet summary serves as a lightweight substitute for explicit message exchanges, allowing nodes to make decisions based on embedded feedback. The combination of additive encoding and local RL enables each node to learn in real-time and adapt its routing behavior without centralized synchronization, forming a continuous feedback loop aligned with network dynamics.

Despite recent advances, several challenges remain open. Reinforcement learning models must be tailored for ultra-low-power nodes with limited processing capabilities. Furthermore, efficient encoding of learning signals in compact packet headers is essential to avoid increasing communication load [2]. Finally, aligning real-time routing decisions with long-term energy sustainability, reliability, and latency goals requires further investigation, particularly in highly dynamic and heterogeneous IoT environments [1].

To better highlight the distinguishing features of the ARROW-IoT framework, we present a structured comparison with traditional routing approaches. This comparison outlines how our model extends existing paradigms by integrating decentralized learning with inline energy-aware signaling. Table 1 summarizes the key differences in terms of adaptability, routing intelligence, coordination strategy, and multi-objective capabilities.

Table 1. Comparative Features: ARROW-IoT vs. Classical Protocols.

Design Dimension	Conventional Protocols (e.g., AODV, LEACH)	ARROW-IoT (RL + Additive Header Strategy)
Adaptation to Network Changes	Rely on predefined paths; slow to react to topology dynamics	Continuously adapts based on node-level experience and real-time metrics
Energy-Aware Behavior	Energy consumption is not directly embedded in routing logic	Routes are dynamically shaped by cumulative energy costs encoded in packets
Routing Control Mechanism	Centralized updates or static cluster schedules	Fully distributed: routing cues evolve through packet-carried updates
Embedded Intelligence	No learning: metrics are fixed or threshold-based	Reinforcement signals and node weights are updated hop-by-hop via headers
Optimization Objectives	Focus on a single criterion (e.g., hop count or distance)	Jointly optimizes energy use, delivery reliability, and latency in real time

3 The Proposed Model

At the core of the ARROW-IoT framework lies a routing decision mechanism based on Q-learning, adapted to operate in a fully decentralized manner through encoded packet interactions. Each node updates its routing preferences by evaluating the long-term impact of forwarding actions, while simultaneously taking into account real-time energy metrics and locally observed transmission success.

The value function is updated using the following formulation:

$$Q_{t+1}(s,a) = \underbrace{\iint_{\tau=0}^{T} \iint_{d=0}^{D} \alpha \cdot e^{-\lambda(\tau+d)} \cdot C(s,a,\tau,d)\, d\tau\, dd}_{\text{Cumulative Energ Cost}} + \underbrace{\sum_{k=1}^{N} \sum_{h=1}^{H} \beta_k \cdot \gamma^h \cdot R(s_h, a_h)}_{\text{Aggregated Hop-wise Rewards}}$$

The breakdown of components is the model's cumulative energy consumption over time (τ), and spatial distance (d), where λ indicates a decay factor balancing temporal and spatial energy costs. $C(s, a, \tau, d)$ is the energy cost function, dependent on state s, action a, time τ, and distance d. . Also, we consider the aggregate rewards across nodes (k) and hops (h). β_k is h eader-encoded weight for node k and γ is the discount factor for delayed rewards. R (s_h, a_h) denotes the reward at hop h, combining energy savings and packet delivery success.

Each packet header encodes β_k, a node-specific weight updated via additive coding that enables distributed learning with minimal overhead.

$$\beta_k^{(h+1)} = \beta_k^{(h)} + \eta \cdot \left(\frac{\partial Q}{\partial \beta_k}\right)_h$$

$\beta_k^{(h+1)}$ is the updated weight for node k at hop $h + 1$. Replacing the previous weight $\beta_k^{(h)}$ in the packet header. This update encodes refined routing strategies based on new observations (e.g., energy consumption, network congestion). It facilitates decentralized learning by allowing nodes to iteratively improve routing decisions and ensures adaptability to dynamic IoT environments (e.g., node failures, traffic fluctuations). The value $\beta_k^{(h)}$ represents the current weight for node k at hop h and reflects he accumulated knowledge about the network state up to that point. It influences routing decisions (e.g., prioritizing paths with lower energy costs), maintains continuity in the learning process, avoiding abrupt changes in routing policies, and enables nodes to leverage historical data for informed decision-making. The learning rate η controls the step size of the weight update. It determines how aggressively β_k is adjusted in response to the gradient $\frac{\partial Q}{\partial \beta_k}$. A higher η accelerates convergence but risks instability; a lower η ensures stability at the cost of slower adaptation. This parameter balances the trade-off between exploration (trying new paths) and exploitation (reusing known paths) and must be tuned based on network dynamics (e.g., high η for volatile environments).

The gradient $\left(\frac{\partial Q}{\partial \beta_k}\right)_h$ measures the sensitivity of the Q-value to changes in β_k. It is derived from the RL objective function, which balances energy efficiency, latency, and packet delivery success. A positive gradient indicates increasing β_k improves the Q-value (e.g., selecting energy-efficient paths), while a negative gradient suggests that decreasing β_k is beneficial (e.g., avoiding congested nodes). This gradient directs the weight update to maximize long-term rewards (e.g., network lifetime) and ensures alignment with global optimization goals such as minimizing total energy consumption.

The sign of $\frac{\partial Q}{\partial \beta_k}$ determines the update direction:

- If positive gradient ($\frac{\partial Q}{\partial \beta_k} > 0$), increasing β_k improves the Q-value,
- If negative gradient ($\frac{\partial Q}{\partial \beta_k} < 0$), decreasing β_k improves the Q-value.

This ensures that the update moves in the direction that maximizes long-term expected rewards. For example: if node k is congested; reducing β_k helps avoid routing through it.

To modulate exploration pressure during decision-making, ARROW-IoT employs a sigmoid-based temperature control function. The parameter μ evolves as a function of residual energy:

$$\mu = \frac{1}{1 + e^{-\theta \cdot (E_{local} - E_{min})}}$$

Here, θ controls the sensitivity of the adjustment, while E_{local} and E_{min} sent the current and baseline energy levels. This mechanism promotes conservative routing when energy is scarce and encourages broader path testing when resources are abundant.

The feedback function guiding ARROW-IoT's routing policy is constructed as a weighted composite of performance indicators. Specifically, it balances transmission success with minimal energy usage and timely delivery:

$$R(s_h, a_h) = \omega^1 \cdot \left(\frac{1}{(E_{used} + \varepsilon)}\right) + \omega^2 \cdot SuccessRatio(h) - \omega^3 \cdot Delay(h)$$

where ε is a small constant for stability, and the weights $\omega_1, \omega_2, \omega_3$ are periodically adjusted via packet-level feedback to reflect current network trade-offs.

3.1 Structured Algorithm of the ARROW-IoT Framework

The routing routine in ARROW-IoT unfolds over periodic intervals during which each node re-evaluates its local environment. The process begins with energy sensing and neighbor state assessment, followed by next-hop selection guided by the current routing policy. Learning proceeds through in-network updates: each node refines its internal weights based on recent transmission outcomes and encodes the resulting adjustments into outgoing packets. This recursive exchange allows nodes to co-evolve their strategies, progressively optimizing the routing landscape with minimal external coordination.

Algorithm ARROW-IoT

Input: Network topology, node energy levels, neighbor tables
Output: Energy-efficient routing paths with adaptive header updates

1: Initialize routing weights **W**, energy table **E**, and packet counters
2: **for** each time step **t** do
3:    **for** each node **n** do
4:       Sense current energy level **E[n]**
5:       Observe neighbor states and channel quality
6:       Select next-hop node **h** using policy $\pi(W, E)$
7:       Update routing weights **W** using RL feedback
8:       Compute gradient-based header adjustment **ΔH**
9:       Encode **ΔH** and **E[n]** into packet header
10:      Transmit packet to next-hop node **h**
11:      Receive reward **r** based on:
           - Local energy variation **ΔE**
           - Packet delivery success
12:      Update policy π using reward **r**
13:    **end for**
14: **end for**
---

4 Experimental Results and Analysis

To evaluate the performance of the proposed ARROW-IoT model, we selected two widely used baseline protocols for comparison: AODV (Ad hoc On-Demand Distance Vector) and LEACH (Low-Energy Adaptive Clustering Hierarchy):

- AODV is a reactive routing protocol widely used in mobile ad hoc and IoT networks. It starts the route discovery process only when needed, which makes it a strong benchmark for testing how well ARROW-IoT can adapt in fast-changing network environments.
- LEACH is a classical hierarchical protocol specifically designed for energy-constrained wireless sensor networks. It periodically rotates cluster heads to balance energy consumption, which makes it a relevant benchmark for assessing energy efficiency.

The arrangement of elements used in the simulation is outlined in Table 2.

Table 2. Simulation Setup

Number of nodes	100
Simulation area	100 × 100 m²
Initial energy per node	2 Joules
MAC protocol	IEEE 802.15.4
Propagation model	Two-ray ground
Simulation duration	50-time steps

The evaluation focuses on key performance indicators, including adaptability, energy efficiency, network lifetime, energy consumption, and packet delivery ratio (PDR), to assess performance against both reactive and hierarchical routing strategies. These metrics are selected to reflect the energy efficiency, reliability, and sustainability of each routing protocol in dynamic, resource-constrained IoT environments.

The Fig. 1, compares the network lifetime of ARROW-IoT, AODV, and LEACH after 50-time steps. ARROW-IOT shows the slowest energy decline and maintains the highest energy due to its energy-efficient design with learning and heading coding. AODV (orange line) exhausts energy the fastest, caused by frequent route discovery and high direction discovery. LEACH shows a slight energy consumption affected by the rotation of the cluster head. Overall, ARROW-IOT significantly extends the network's life compared to AODV and Leach, emphasizing its suitability for energy constrained IoT environments. This shows the sustainability and efficiency of ARROW-IOT while maintaining the longevity of the network.

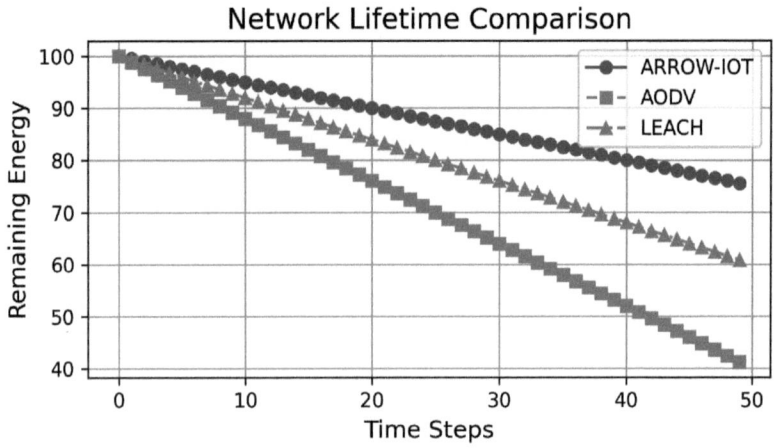

Fig. 1. Network lifetime comparison

Figure 2, presents the packet delivery ratio (PDR) for the three protocols. ARROW-IoT achieves the highest PDR, reflecting its stable and intelligent routing behavior. AODV, being reactive, suffers from packet losses due to frequent rediscoveries. LEACH performs moderately but is impacted by cluster reformation phases. The results show that ARROW-IoT maintains higher delivery success in dynamic IoT environments.

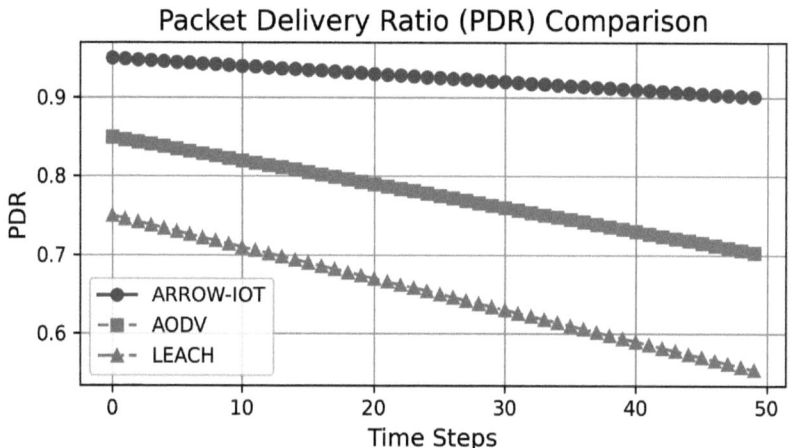

Fig. 2. Packet Delivery Ratio (PDR) Comparison

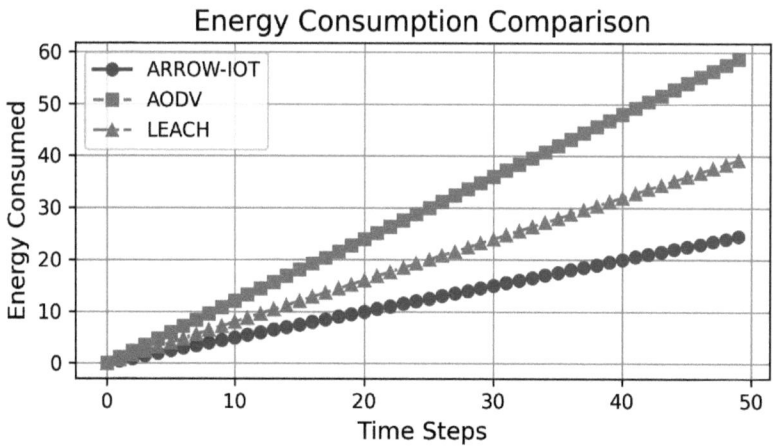

Fig. 3. Energy Consumption Comparison

Figure 3, illustrates the energy consumption trends of the protocols. ARROW-IoT shows the lowest overall energy utilization, increasing gradually thanks to its optimized learning mechanism and header-based adaptation. AODV exhibits rapid energy exhaustion due to repeated route discoveries, while LEACH maintains relatively moderate consumption due to scheduled cluster rotations. ARROW-IoT consumes approximately 49% less energy than AODV and 28% less than LEACH, underlining its energy efficiency and adaptability for IoT networks with limited power resources.

It is worth noting that Fig. 1 and Fig. 3 focus on different aspects of energy performance. Figure 1 illustrates network lifetime, showing how long each protocol sustains its operation before energy is exhausted, with ARROW-IoT outperforming AODV and LEACH. Meanwhile, Fig. 3 compares energy consumption at various points, highlighting ARROW-IoT's efficiency in using less energy compared to AODV and LEACH. Together, these figures demonstrate ARROW-IoT's ability to extend network operation while optimizing energy usage.

4.1 Experimental Insights

The simulation results demonstrate that ARROW-IoT significantly outperforms the reference protocols (AODV and LEACH) across all key performance indicators. The model achieves improved network lifetime by reducing energy depletion rates, thanks to in-packet learning and adaptive routing. It also maintains a higher PDR, indicating more reliable communication under dynamic conditions. Moreover, ARROW-IoT consumes considerably less energy compared to baseline protocols, confirming its effectiveness in energy-constrained environments. These results confirm that the integration of RL with additive header encoding enables lightweight, decentralized, and energy-aware decision-making, well-suited to IoT scenarios.

5 Conclusion

The exponential growth of IoT devices has highlighted the urgent need for energy efficient and adaptive routing protocols to address the challenges of dynamic, resource constrained networks. While traditional routing methods are effective in static environments, they fail to meet the demands of IoT ecosystems, which are characterized by limited energy resources, fluctuating operating patterns, and decentralized architectures. To overcome these challenges, we propose ARROW-IoT—an energy-efficient framework based on the ARROW paradigm—that integrates RL with additive header coding to optimize energy consumption and minimize fluctuations in energy usage.

Key components such as energy-aware learning mechanisms, hybrid reward functions, and gradient-based header adjustments contribute to the model's ability to balance energy savings with reliable data transmission. Simulation results show that ARROW-IoT, built upon the ARROW paradigm, outperforms conventional protocols such as AODV and LEACH in terms of energy efficiency, network lifetime, and packet delivery ratio. Additionally, its modular design facilitates integration with emerging technologies such as federated learning, cloud computing, and blockchain, paving the way for future advancements.

The ARROW paradigm addresses critical gaps in IoT routing, not only extending the operational life of IoT networks but also laying the foundation for sustainable, intelligent communication ecosystems. This paradigm shift enables energy-efficient, scalable, and adaptive routing, making ARROW-IoT a suitable solution for next-generation IoT networks.

6 Limitations and Future Work

While ARROW-IoT offers promising improvements in adaptability and energy efficiency, several limitations remain. First, the current implementation has been evaluated in a moderate-scale, static simulation environment; scalability to large-scale or mobile IoT networks still requires validation. Second, the model's performance relies on the proper tuning of learning rates and header parameters, which may be challenging in highly dynamic or heterogeneous environments.

Future work will focus on three main directions:

- Extending ARROW-IoT to larger and mobile topologies with varying traffic patterns,
- Exploring its integration with federated learning to enable collaborative model updates without global coordination,
- Investigating cross-layer optimization strategies to further align routing decisions with MAC and physical layer constraints.

These directions aim to enhance the robustness, generalization, and interoperability of the ARROW paradigm in next-generation IoT and 6G networks.

References

1. Sharma, S., et al.: The role of 6G technologies in advancing smart city applications: opportunities and challenges. Sustainability, MDPI **16**(16), 7039 (2024). https://doi.org/10.3390/su16167039
2. Motlagh, N.H., Mohammadrezaei, M., Hunt, J., Zakeri, B.: Internet of Things (IoT) and the energy sector. Energies, MDPI **13**(2), 494 (2020). https://doi.org/10.3390/en13020494
3. Zhang, Z., et al.: 6G wireless networks: Vision, requirements, architecture, and key technologies. IEEE Veh. Technol. Mag. IEEE **14**(3), 28–41 (2019)
4. Yang, Z., Hu, D., Guo, Q., Zuo, L., Ji, W.: Visual E2C: AI-driven visual end-edge-cloud architecture for 6G in low-carbon smart cities. IEEE Wirel. Commun. IEEE **30**(3), 204–210 (2023)
5. Liwen, L., Qamar, F., Liaqat, M., Hindia, M.N., Ariffin, K.A.Z.: Towards efficient 6G IoT networks: a perspective on resource optimization strategies, challenges, and future directions. IEEE Access, IEEE **12**, 76606–76633 (2024)
6. Marinakis, V., Doukas, H.: An advanced IoT-based system for intelligent energy management in buildings. Sensors, MDPI **18**(2), 610 (2018)
7. Foruzan, E., Soh, L.K., Asgarpoor, S.: Reinforcement learning approach for optimal distributed energy management in a microgrid. IEEE Trans. Power Syst. IEEE **33**(5), 5749–5758 (2018)
8. Pack Kaelbling, L.P.L., Littman, M.L., Moore, A.W., Reinforcement learning: a survey. J. Artif. Intell. Res. AI Access Foundation **4**, 237–285 (1996)
9. Littman, M.L.: Markov games as a framework for multi-agent reinforcement learning. Mach. Learn. Proc. Morgan Kaufmann **1994**, 157–163 (1994)
10. Chowdhury, M.Z., Shahjalal, M., Ahmed, S., Jang, Y.M.: 6G wireless communication systems: applications, requirements, technologies, challenges, and research directions. IEEE Open J. Commun. Soc. IEEE **1**, 957–975 (2020)
11. Abbas, M.T., et al.: Towards zero-energy: navigating the future with 6G in Cellular Internet of Things. J. Netw. Comput. Appl. Elsevier, 103945 (2024)

12. Liu, G., Jiang, D., 5G: vision and requirements for mobile communication system towards year 2020. Chin. J. Eng. Hindawi, 1–8 (2016)
13. Rashid, H.U., Jeong, S.H.: AI empowered 6G technologies and network layers: recent trends, opportunities, and challenges. Expert Syst. Appl. Elsevier, 125985 (2024)
14. Park, S., et al.: Reinforcement learning-based BEMS architecture for energy usage optimization. Sensors, MDPI **20**(17), 4918 (2020)
15. He, Q., Wang, Y., Wang, X., Wu, W., Li, F., Yang, K.: Routing optimization with deep reinforcement learning in knowledge defined networking. IEEE Trans. Mob. Comput. IEEE **23**(2), 1444–1455 (2024)
16. Patel, N.R., Kumar, S., Singh, S.K.: Energy and collision aware WSN routing protocol for sustainable and intelligent IoT applications. IEEE Sens. J. IEEE **21**(22), 25282–25292 (2021)
17. Daanoune, I., Abdennaceur, B., Ballouk, A.: A comprehensive survey on LEACH-based clustering routing protocols in Wireless Sensor Networks. Ad Hoc Netw. Elsevier **114**, 102409 (2021)

The Improvement of Organizational Value Chains Using Distributed Sensor Networks

C. Atsango and J. P. van Deventer(✉)

Department of Informatics, University of Pretoria, Pretoria, South Africa
`phil.vandeventer@up.ac.za`

Abstract. This paper explores the enhancement of organizational value chains through the implementation of Distributed Sensor Networks (DSNs) within the context of the Internet of Things (IoT). The study begins by establishing the significance of DSNs in facilitating automated data collection and analysis, which are crucial for improving operational efficiency and decision-making processes. A systematic literature review (SLR) was conducted, focusing on the implementation of distributed sensors, networks, devices, and their impact on various value chains. Key findings reveal that advancements in sensor technology, including low-power consumption strategies and predictive modelling capabilities, significantly contribute to optimizing value chains. The research identifies adaptive sampling and energy harvesting as effective methods for prolonging sensor battery life and reducing power consumption, which improves overall system performance. Furthermore, the paper discusses the importance of addressing challenges related to data security and reliability to fully leverage the potential of DSNs. The study concludes by emphasizing the need for future research to explore the integration of IoT technologies with Blockchain to enhance data interoperability and security. The study also highlights the potential for tailored applications of sensor technologies across different value chain segments, ultimately advocating for continuous improvement of sensor hardware and software to foster sustainable practices and maintain cutting-edge technology in an ever-evolving landscape.

Keywords: distributed sensor networks · IoT · devices · value chain · artificial intelligence · machine learning

1 Introduction

Sensor technology continues to rapidly evolve, which positions sensors as the primary data source across different domains, thanks to their high speed, low-power, and high-resolution features [1]. The continuous development of information and communication technologies has made the use of Distributed Sensor Networks (DSNs) more prevalent, meaning they play a crucial role in capturing environmental conditions such as mechanical, thermal, and optical changes, thereby enabling them to provide precise and continuous data [2]. DSNs are essentially spatially distributed autonomous sensors which are used to monitor either physical or environmental conditions to combine their real-time data to a central location. There are wired and wireless sensor networks in which the components of a sensor include sensor nodes, a gateway within a sensor field, and a management node. Sensors operate on multiple distributed platforms and range from active and passive sensors, contact and non-contact sensors, as well as absolute and relative sensors to measure temperature, motion, acoustics, and pressure [3].

Developments in sensor technology have led to the creation of compact, energy-efficient sensors enabling them to control various parameters like air quality, traffic lights, pressure, and temperature, which highlights their versatility and adaptability across different applications [3]. The continuous integration of sensors into Internet of Things (IoT) systems has positioned sensor data as the standard source of information, driving the development of predictive models and enhancing the quality and efficiency of data collection and analysis in supply chains and beyond [4]. The quintessential goal of DSNs is to make decisions or gain knowledge based on the information accumulated from distributed sensors' input [5]. In the current era, DSNs have been implemented in multiple applications and have become imperative in the way organizations collect data, making them relevant devices in the broader area of IoT [6].

Advances in sensor technology have also brought forth challenges, specifically in the processing of large amounts of data in, bandwidth limited, power-constrained, unstable, and dynamic environments [5]. Some sensors are battery powered and have a finite lifespan. Depending on the environment sensors are located, batteries could be difficult to replace or upgrade [7]. Battery-less sensors also have challenges because they operate intermittently. The hindrance caused by this is that at times the timekeeping of the sensor is not as reliable. Low-power real-time clocks in sensors suffer from long start-up times and have low timekeeping granularity, meaning they often tend to not match timing requirements of devices that experience power outages [8]. These challenges may have unintended consequences in systems that sensors have been implemented in, which could affect organizations that have invested in sensors to function sustainably and rely on their data to perform specific operations.

Additionally, there are concerns that arise with the evolution of sensor technology. Politically, issues of data ownership and privacy arise, which necessitates the need for regulations to protect stakeholders from cyberthreats and data breaches [9]. Economically the integration of IoT may lead to increased costs and market disruptions due to rapid digitalization. Socially, the digital divide may worsen inequalities, affecting access to technology. Technologically, the reliance on interconnected systems raises vulnerabilities such as data silos and security challenges. Environmentally, the impact of digital agriculture on ecosystems and animal welfare may be a consideration. Legally, the lack of standardized data privacy legislation poses challenges for compliance. Ethically, the implications of automation on labor and human agency in value chains remain a critical concern.

Despite advancements in sensor technology and networks, gaps remain in the literature regarding their optimization and integration into value chains. The objective of this paper is to therefore consolidate, compare, and contrast existing literature on DSNs, IoT and value chains to investigate approaches in which distributed sensors can be leveraged to improve organizational value chains. This paper aims to build on the accumulated academic research through synthesizing the knowledge surrounding DSNs by conducting a systematic literature review.

2 Background

The IoT has emerged as a disruptive force that can revolutionize value chains with interconnecting devices. Enabled by smart sensors, embedded microelectronics, high speed connectivity, and internet standards, IoT facilitates seamless communication and data exchange across diverse domains. This connectivity generates a large amount of data which is characterized by its volume, velocity, and variety of formats, collectively known as Big Data. The symbiotic relationship between IoT and Big Data underscores the transformative potential of data-driven decision-making in various sectors.

The datafication of business which is fueled by IoT-generated data presents both opportunities and risks, necessitating robust modelling tools to mitigate technical challenges inherent in managing interconnected systems. The influx of structured and unstructured demands novel IT platforms and architectures capable of processing and storing information in real-time. Advanced analytics tools play a pivotal part in extracting actionable insights from this flood of data, making data science a strategic asset in the IoT era.

In an IoT environment, sensors play the crucial role of collecting data and transmitting it wirelessly using various protocols. Sensor nodes deliver data streams via Wi-Fi and Message Queuing Telemetry Transport (MQTT) protocol, which is a lightweight messaging protocol designed for small sensors and mobile devices in low-bandwidth, high-latency, or unreliable networks [10]. Different protocols are utilized for networking, such as Radio Frequency Identification (RFID), a technology widely used in supply chains for tracking physical objects without line of sight, as for example when used alongside Ultra-Fast Heating (UFH) Gen 2 technology processes [11]. Wired internet protocols like Transmission Control Protocol/Internet Protocol (TCP/IP), and wireless options such as Wi-Fi and Bluetooth are chosen based on factors such as power consumption, range, security, and network topologies [8]. These protocols are significant in enabling seamless connectivity, data transmission and interaction within IoT ecosystems which enables efficient monitoring, control, and automation of various processes in value chains as well as a broad range of different applications [11]. There is an emphasis in selecting the right protocol for efficient sensor communication in IoT applications similar to IoT environments.

Standardization emerges as a critical factor in the success of IoT deployment which ensures interoperability across heterogeneous systems. Fundamental standardization activities lay the groundwork for seamless integration and compatibility, facilitating the widespread adoption of IoT technologies. Real-time processing techniques and analytics tools are indispensable components in harnessing the potential of IoT-generated data, driving innovation and efficiency across various domains.

Different components functioning together or separately, add value to the overall IoT solution which benefits the end user [12]. In this context, a value chain refers to the interconnected activities and processes within a network that adds value to a product or service, which enables companies to gain a competitive advantage [12]. The integration of IoT technologies such as wireless sensor networks and machine-to-machine systems enhances information exchange, decision-making, and cooperation within a value chain, which leads to improved efficiency and transparency [13]. This creates opportunities for companies to leverage IoT for revenue optimization through improved tracking, tracing, and management of products, contributing to overall value chain revenue growth [14]. The continual optimization of a value chain is crucial due to its ever-present role in enhancing corporate success through cost reduction, increased responsiveness, and elevated service levels. This optimization provides flexibility, especially in situations where quick adjustments in value chains are essential for continuity and success.

3 Research Method: Systematic Literature Review

The research method used to meet the objective of this paper is a Systematic Literature Review (SLR). This research method provides a comprehensive framework to identify, select and evaluate the findings of the studies, ensuring a thorough examination of the literature on DSNs, the IoT, and value chains. The SLR aims to synthesize findings from various studies to uncover patterns, themes, and inconsistencies, which will enhance the understanding of how distributed sensors can improve organizational value chains. The Preferred Reporting Items for Systematic reviews and Meta-Analyses (PRISMA) flowchart is utilized to guide the review process and facilitate a structured analysis of the literature and helps identify key trends and gaps for future research [15]. In the following section the process followed as per Fig. 1, will be considered.

3.1 Data Sources and Search Terms

Databases that were searched for peer-reviewed papers include IEEE Xplore, ACM Digital Library, EBSCO and Scopus. Database searches for articles from these identified databases were performed using keywords contained in the title, topic and abstract of papers, such as (distributed sensor networks) AND (production methods) AND ((devices) OR (Internet of Things)) AND (value chain).

3.2 Selection Criteria

The literature search was broad in an effort to include all available research on DSNs in relation to value chains. The focus was narrowed down to articles published in English, articles between the years 2014 – 2024, articles with Open Access, as well as peer-reviewed articles.

Inclusion Criteria. All studies were filtered based on the inclusion of: (1) studies focusing on DSNs, (2) studies focusing on the IoT and devices, (3) studies focusing on value chains, (4) studies that examined and/or mentioned the role of IoT in value chains/supply chains, (5) conference papers and peer-reviewed journal articles, and (6), open access publications.

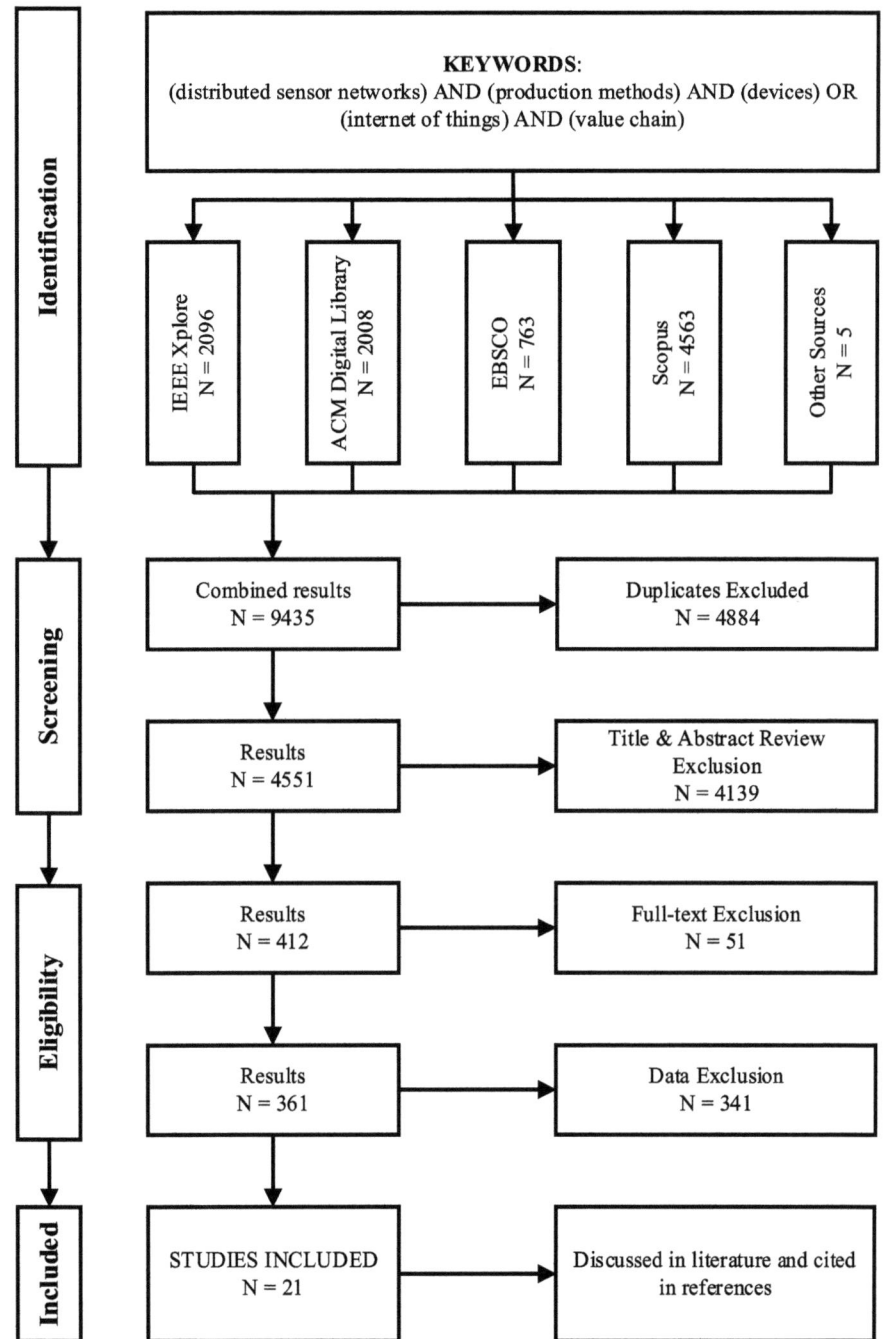

Fig. 1. Complete PRISMA flowchart

Exclusion Criteria. All studies were filtered based on the exclusion of: (1) studies published in languages other than English, (2) studies not published in peer-reviewed journals, (3) studies without open access availability, (4) studies conducted more than a decade ago.

PRISMA Flowchart. A total of 9435 studies were retrieved across four databases, of which 5 were from other sources. Once the duplicates were removed, a total of 4551 studies remained. Within these studies, 4139 were excluded based on their Title and Abstracts. Studies were primarily excluded due to filters (year, language, document type) and correlation studies or re-reviews. The remaining 412 studies were reviewed in their entirety, of which 361 of them contained usable data that could be extracted via tables, figures, and text statistics. Of these, 21 studies were sampled (based on citation index) and selected for a meta-analysis and review.

Data Extraction. The data extracted focused on gathering articles pertaining to distributed sensors, networks, and devices particularly in the context of the IoT and their impact on various organizational value chains. This process involved selecting relevant studies that align with the research objective, ensuring that the extracted data is pertinent and comprehensive. The data collected serves as a foundation for analyzing how DSNs can enhance organizational efficiency and effectiveness. By highlighting these specific areas, the SLR aims to provide valuable insights into the integration of technology within organizational frameworks, ultimately contributing to the understanding of value chain improvements.

Data Analysis. The data analysis method employed in this SLR on DSNs adhered to the guidelines outlined by the Preferred Reporting Items Systematic Reviews and Analyses (PRISMA) flowchart. The PRISMA flowchart provided a structured framework for each stage of the review process, including study identification, screening, eligibility assessment, and inclusion in the final analysis. This systematic approach facilitates a comprehensive analysis of the existing literature on DSNs, the IoT, and value chains which enables the identification of key trends, gaps, and areas for future research.

4 Findings

To enhance sensor battery life and reduce power consumption, various strategies can be implemented. One approach is subsampling, where sensors transmit only a subset of measurements reducing the amount of data that needs to be processed and transmitted to conserve energy [7]. A derivation of subsampling is adaptive sampling, which is a family of algorithms commonly used in low-power sensors to manage energy consumption efficiently by sampling frequently in unpredictable environments and collecting fewer values in predictable settings, consequently optimizing energy usage based on the observed data [7]. By adapting the sampling strategy based on the environment and observed data, sensors can achieve lower error rates under energy constraints, which makes adaptive sampling a viable option in low-power devices in various applications such as environmental monitoring and healthcare [7].

Another approach is a prototype called "Sirius", a self-localization system that uses a single receiver for low-power and resource-constrained IoT sensors [16].

Sirius dynamically switches the beam pattern of the antenna to embed a direction specific signature to the received signal, meaning the vector of amplitudes contain the unique signature which then map to the Angle-of-Arrival (AoA) represented by (0) [16]. Traditional methods that rely on antenna arrays and tight synchronization are not sustainable for low-power IoT nodes because of resource constraints, which makes the Sirius approach a significant advancement in self-localization for IoT sensors [16]. The system's innovative technique allows for AoA estimation without compromising the regular communication channel, which ensures seamless integration with existing IoT systems. By reducing power consumption by means of systems such as for example Sirius, there would inherently be minor gains in terms of the system's carbon footprint.

Sirus appears to be a viable system that can be implemented in a manufacturing environment. Radio Frequency (RF) signals can be detected and harvested at specific locations on an assembly line to enhance operational efficiency [4].

The RF map's suggested design focused on optimizing manufacturing operations by utilizing RF signals for energy harvesting and monitoring purposes along the conveyor belt [4]. This sort of system would however require the development and integration of an Android application that is tailored to the manufacturing system's requirements, including conveyors, pallets, wireless sensors, and web-service-enabled controllers. The application interfaces with the manufacturing information system which would track pallet locations on the conveyor path in real-time ensuring efficient asset management and control [4]. By leveraging an RF map, users can visualize the exact location of pallets on the conveyor path which will enable better decision-making, improved operational efficiency, reduced maintenance costs in manufacturing processes and reduced power consumption [4].

DSNs need to be able to reorganize themselves when nodes fail or lose contact for various reasons such as energy depletion, adversarial actions by bad actors, adverse reactions such as signal degradation, or natural causes [17]. As sensor nodes may join, leave, or change roles within a network, the topology constantly evolves which necessitates re-organization to maintain connectivity and functionality. It is important to establish keys between small groups versus the entire sensor network.

Since DSNs operate in dynamic environments where routes between nodes are not initially known and can change due to factors like energy levels and communication noise, the keying scheme used need to provide the necessary level of confidentiality and authentication for the entire network to function effectively [17]. Adaptability to changing conditions within the network allows for seamless communication and secure data transmission even in the events of node failures and network reconfigurations. Additionally, re-organization supports fault tolerance by allowing the network to seamlessly degrade performance when nodes fail which ensures overall network robustness and reliability, therefore the ability of DSNs to autonomously reorganize is fundamental for their operational efficiency and resilience in dynamic environments.

In the interest of enhancing DSNs, Machine Learning (ML) can achieve this by improving anomaly detection through sophisticated algorithms to detect unusual patterns in sensor data. ML algorithms can optimize network performance by enabling efficient data aggregation and processing within the network itself to reduce the need for centralized processing [18]. Leveraging ML enables DSNs to benefit from faster decision-making processes, allowing real-time adjustments based on the data collected from distributed sensors. These algorithms are also capable of assisting with traffic classification and prediction within sensor networks, enabling more accurate forecasting of network behavior and resource allocation [18].

DSNs offer various costs and benefits across different factors; Politically, they can enhance data security. Economically they can lead to cost-effective distributed manufacturing approaches [10]. Socially, DSNs may bring up ethical dilemmas related to data ownership and consent, but also ensure policies for fair use of information [19]. Technologically, DSNs improve operational efficiency and advanced data processing capabilities, including real-time analytics and predictive modelling which enables proactive responses to potential issues. Environmentally, DSNs enhance monitoring with real-time data on parameter such as air quality and pollution levels, leading to better decision-making for sustainable resource management [19]. Legal considerations of DSNs include liability issues related to the accuracy of data collected by the sensors, which makes it important to determine responsibility in cases of errors and malfunctions. Legal frameworks with regards to Intellectual Property Rights are also needed because issues such as the ownership of data generated from DSNs could be ambiguous, therefore it is important to ensure fair distribution of benefits and protection of innovations [19].

5 Discussion

The data-driven nature of adaptive sampling and subsampling possesses privacy challenges. The data collection rates can leak information about captured measurements thereby presenting an inherent risk in maintaining privacy for sensors using energy efficient communication methods. Adaptive Group Encoding (AGE) has been introduced to address privacy concerns and to protect adaptive samplers by encoding measurement batches as fixed-length messages, which reduces information leakage while preserving the low error rates of adaptive sampling [7].

By grouping similar measurements together and encoding them collectively, AGE can conceal individual data points which minimizes the risk of privacy breaches during data transmission [7]. DSNs that utilize AGE can enhance their privacy protection measures without compromising the efficiency and accuracy of their adaptive sampling processes, allowing DSNs to also dynamically adjust the encoding strategy based on the sensitivity of the data being transmitted, providing a more flexible and customizable approach to privacy protection in adaptive sampling [7]. The benefits of RF energy harvesting allow for the continuous powering of sensors and devices without the need for frequent battery replacements, which leads to improved operational efficiency in manufacturing processes and a reduction of battery related pollution [4]. Cost reduction is also a benefit because the maintenance required for checking and replacing batteries is minimized. Overall RF energy harvesting enhances productivity through a continuous and reliable power supply, ensuring manufacturing assets and sensors remain operational [4].

Low-power sensors offer significant advantages in monitoring and healthcare applications through subsampling and adaptive sampling [7, 20]. Sensor energy preservation has emerged as a crucial factor for DSN sustainability because collection and communication tasks consume most of the energy, with wireless communication being particularly energy-intensive [8]. Advancements in energy harvesting technology have enabled battery-less sensors to operate perpetually, reducing the need for costly and maintenance-intensive battery powered devices [1]. Generally, the benefits of low-power sensors lie in their ability to enable continuous monitoring in various applications.

A clear advantage of low-powered sensors and sensors that harvest energy from the environment is that it has a cumulative effect on power consumption. Thus, low-powered sensors and power harvesting sensors optimizes how power is used, saves energy and, as such, has a positive environmental impact by reducing waste. Additionally, low-powered sensors can be used in for example agriculture where the improved turnaround time as per the agricultural value chain can prevent food wastage.

The political environment can influence the deployment and operation of sensor networks, especially in terms of data privacy, security protocols, and cross-border data flow regulations. Political decisions can also impact the development of global value chains and industry standards related to sensor technologies, including the integration of digitalization and the IoT into governmental strategies and initiatives [17]. Technological advancements in Artificial Intelligence (AI) and Data Analytics shape the future of DSN features and functionalities, which could positively impact their use cases and interfaces. The functionality of DSNs would need to take sustainability practices and energy consumption in their data centers under consideration to ensure that they align with environmental standards thereby improving sustainability [19].

DSNs enhance value chains by enabling automated data collection and analysis. Hardware improvements of sensor technology include predictive modelling capabilities such as Time-Temperature Indicators (TTIs) and data loggers [1]. Software enhancements include developed applications for the integration of predictive models with sensors to ensure integrity of IoT data, leading to increased efficiency, throughput, and reduced overhead in production environments. The continuous improvement of sensor hardware and software enables DSNs to further optimize value chains by providing real-time insights and facilitating seamless communication across networks. In a broader scope, DSNs can be scalable, adaptable, and efficient which is paramount for companies to maintain seamless communication and security [17].

Yet again, the environmental benefit is a reduction of wastage by for example reducing power consumption through enhancing the efficiency of an organizational value chain.

DSNs have a wide range of applications across various fields, with the most common being in healthcare, agriculture and in industrial settings [20]. The biggest clusters within these themes are AI, wireless sensor networks and protocols, with a total of 410 links between the clusters. In the medical field, sensor networks are used for monitoring patient physiological data, tracking doctors and patients within hospitals, and managing drug administration. The sensors mainly support applications such as fall detection, vital sign monitoring, as well as tele-monitoring which enhances patient care and reduces costs enhancing organizational sustainability.

In agriculture, sensor networks are increasingly used for tasks such as greenhouse monitoring, irrigation automation, and managing water systems. DSNs assist in approving yield, reducing pesticide usage and enhancing turnaround time, therefore again, reducing wastage or precious resources. The sensors help farmers monitor environmental conditions, control irrigation systems, and optimize resource use which leads to more efficient farming practices [21]. In industrial settings, sensor networks facilitate condition-based maintenance of machinery which allows for cost savings and improved operational efficiency. Sensors can be deployed in previously inaccessible areas which means their monitoring capabilities are enhanced in various industries. The recurring themes in these applications include "enhanced monitoring capabilities", "improved efficiency" and "cost reduction" which makes DSNs a promising approach for various sensing tasks across multiple domains.

What can be noted however is that addressing security concerns are lacking in literature. Research states that security might be a concern [8], but this is never clearly addressed. A possible solution could be the application of a general ledgering system such as for example the application of Blockchain. Blockchain can for example assist in tracking datapoints and DSN data transactions by creating unique identifiers per sensor and sensor datapoint. This would in essence prevent network interception and data tampering driven by malicious parties and bad actors. This is however speculation as there is limited research on Blockchain applied to DSNs.

6 Conclusion and Future Research

The implementation of DSNs into organizational value chains presents a transformative opportunity for enhancing operational efficiency and decision-making processes. The findings in this review underscore the critical role that DSNs play in enabling real-time data collection and analysis, which is integral for optimizing various aspects of value chains. By leveraging the advancements in sensor technology including predictive modelling and low-power consumption strategies, organizations may be able to achieve greater responsiveness and adaptability in their operations.

Additionally, the research highlights the importance of addressing existing challenges such as data security, and the reliability of sensor performance to fully harness the potential of DSNs. Ultimately the continuous improvement of both hardware and software components of DSNs will not only facilitate seamless communication across networks, but also contribute to more sustainable practices within organizations by for example reducing costs, limiting waste and enhancing turnover time going to market. As industries progressively adopt these technologies, the hope is that the insights gained from this study may serve as a guiding principle for future innovations so that organizations may harness cutting-edge sensor technology in an ever-evolving landscape.

Future research on DSNs should focus on exploring the integration of IoT technologies with Blockchain because one of the main challenges with emerging technology and devices is data security [1, 12]. This would improve data interoperability and address challenges like high operational costs and concerns associated in IoT applications. Additionally, studies could investigate the application of various IoT, and sensor technologies tailored to specific value chain segments. Future research should also emphasize the development of comprehensive modelling tools and analytics platforms to be able to process the vast amounts of data generated by sensor networks, to ensure real-time decision-making capabilities and successful implementation across various industries.

References

1. Tamplin, M.L.: Integrating predictive models and sensors to manage food stability in supply chains. Food Microbiol. **75**, 90–94 (2018)
2. Koot, M., Mes, M.R., Iacob, M.E.: A systematic literature review of supply chain decision-making supported by the Internet of Things and Big Data Analytics. Comput. Ind. Eng. **154**, 107076 (2021)
3. Jesse, N.: Internet of Things and Big Data: the disruption of the value chain and the rise of new software ecosystems. AI & Soc. **33**(2), 229–239 (2018)
4. Tahir, M.A., Ramis Ferrer, B., Martinez Lastra, J.L.: An approach for managing manufacturing assets through radio frequency energy harvesting. Sensors **19**(3), 438 (2019)
5. Qi, H., Iyengar, S.S., Chakrabarty, K.: Distributed sensor networks—a review of recent research. J. Franklin Inst. **338**(6), 655–668 (2001)
6. Alaerjan, A.: Towards sustainable distributed sensor networks: an approach for addressing power limitation issues in WSNs. Sensors **23**(2), 975 (2023)
7. Kannan, T., Hoffmann, H.: Protecting adaptive sampling from information leakage on low-power sensors. In: Proceedings of the 27th ACM International Conference on Architectural Support for Programming Languages and Operating Systems, pp. 240–254 (2022)
8. de Winkel, J., Delle Donne, C., Yildirim, K.S., Pawełczak, P., Hester, J.: Reliable timekeeping for intermittent computing. In: Proceedings of the Twenty-Fifth International Conference on Architectural Support for Programming Languages and Operating Systems, pp. 53–67 (2020)
9. Klerkx, L., Jakku, E., Labarthe, P.: A review of social science on digital agriculture, smart farming and agriculture 4.0: new contributions and a future research agenda. NJAS-Wageningen J. Life Sci. **90**, 100315 (2019)
10. Lemme, G., Nölscher, K.A., Bei, E., Hermeling, C., Ihlenfeldt, S.: Secure data storage and service automation for cyber physical production systems through distributed ledger technologies. J. Mach. Eng. **21** (2021)
11. Rejeb, A., Keogh, J.G., Treiblmaier, H.: Leveraging the IoT and blockchain technology in supply chain management. Future Internet **11**(7), 161 (2019)
12. Egwuonwu, A., Mordi, C., Egwuonwu, A., Uadiale, O.: The influence of blockchains and IoT on global value chain. Strateg. Chang. **31**(1), 45–55 (2022)
13. Butollo, F., Gereffi, G., Yang, C., Krzywdzinski, M.: Digital transformation and value chains: introduction. Global Netw. **22**(4), 585–594 (2022)
14. Shousong, C., Xiaoguang, W., Yuanjun, Z.: Revenue model of supply chain by IoT technology. IEEE Access **7**, 4091–4100 (2018)
15. Rother, E.T.: Systematic literature review X narrative review. Acta paulista de enfermagem **20**, v–vi (2007)
16. Garg, N., Roy, N.: Sirius: a self-localization system for resource-constrained IoT sensors. In: Proceedings of the 21st Annual International Conference on Mobile Systems, Applications and Services, pp. 289–302 (2023)
17. Carman, D.W., Kruus, P.S., Matt, B.J.: Constraints and approaches for distributed sensor network security (final). DARPA project report, (cryptographic technologies group, trusted information system, NAI labs), **1**(1), 1–39 (2000)

18. Swamy, T., Rucker, A., Shahbaz, M., Gaur, I., Olukotun, K.: Taurus: a data plane architecture for per-packet ML. In: Proceedings of the 27th ACM International Conference on Architectural Support for Programming Languages and Operating Systems, pp. 1099–1114 (2022)
19. Mayer, M., Baeumner, A.J.: A megatrend challenging analytical chemistry: biosensor and chemosensor concepts ready for the IoT. Chem. Rev. **119**(13), 7996–8027 (2019)
20. Núñez-Carmona, E., Abbatangelo, M., Sberveglieri, V.: Internet of food (Iof), tailor-made metal oxide gas sensors to support tea supply chain. Sensors **21**(13), 4266 (2021)
21. de Abreu, C.L., van Deventer, J.P.: The application of Artificial Intelligence (AI) and Internet of Things (IoT) in agriculture: a systematic literature review. In: Jembere, E., Gerber, A.J., Viriri, S., Pillay, A. (eds.) SACAIR 2021. CCIS, vol. 1551, pp. 32–46. Springer, Cham (2022). https://doi.org/10.1007/978-3-030-95070-5_3

Comparative Analysis of Predictive Models for Analysing Demographics and Academic Features to Predict Student Performance Using Machine Learning Techniques

Harshvardhan Tiwari(✉) and Neel Pandey

School of Tech, New Zealand Skills and Education Group, Auckland, New Zealand
`harsh@nzse.ac.nz, neel@nzseg.com`

Abstract. This study presents a comprehensive analysis of various regression models to predict student performance, focusing on the impact of preprocessing, feature selection, and model evaluation. The research leverages a dataset comprising key academic, demographic, and social factors affecting student outcomes. Initial preprocessing involved converting categorical variables into numerical formats using Label Encoding and One-Hot Encoding, ensuring the dataset was suitable for machine learning algorithms. Feature selection techniques and correlation analysis, were employed to identify the most significant predictors of student performance, optimizing model efficiency. Six regression models were evaluated: Linear Regression, Support Vector Machine (SVM), K-Nearest Neighbors (KNN), Decision Tree, Random Forest, and Gradient Boosting. Each model was trained on the selected features, and performance was assessed using standard regression metrics-Mean Absolute Error (MAE), Mean Squared Error (MSE), Root Mean Squared Error (RMSE), and R^2 Score. The results revealed that Linear Regression achieved the highest R^2 score and the lowest error metrics, outperforming the other models. While SVM and Gradient Boosting also demonstrated strong predictive capabilities, Decision Tree models showed signs of overfitting, and Random Forest, though effective, did not surpass the top models.

Keywords: Regression Models · Feature Selection · Student Performance · Preprocessing · Model Evaluation · Machine Learning

1 Introduction

Massive databases have resulted from the rapid growth of information technology and digital platforms in education. Educational institutions hold extensive data on student demographics, academic achievement, health, family history, and social relationships. This study uses data on a wide range of factors affecting higher education student achievement and retention. It covers demographic data like address, gender, age, and school and health data like student health. Along with extracurricular activities and ambitions for higher education, which are evaluated by final grades, academic indicators-absences, commute time to school, weekly study time, past failures, and other academic support indicators-school support (schoolsup) and family support (famsup)-are also included in the dataset. Families' size, parental education status, parent's cohabitation levels, and job categories are also included. Finally, it measures internet access, romantic relationships, family relationship quality, idle time, social events, weekend and workday alcohol usage. This vast collection provides a solid foundation for studying higher education student retention and performance in multiple ways.

This study provides a complete analytical approach that uses the dataset's plethora of data to predict student success and retention using demographic, academic, health-related, family, and social characteristics.

Machine learning is a useful analytical tool for teachers and scholars to analyse vast educational databases. Machine learning helps schools uncover trends and patterns in student behaviour and performance. These technologies identify at-risk students, learner models, and disengagement, which are critical to academic performance. Machine learning algorithms identify student performance variables in this study. This work seeks to use the dataset to help teachers and institutions help at-risk students, enhance learning environments, and increase academic achievement.

The paper is organised as follows: Sect. 2 presents the literature review, Sect. 3 presents the dataset, data preprocessing, and machine learning approaches employed in order to predict student performance. Section 4 goes over the evaluation procedure including model assessment and performance measures. It also explores the outcomes with an eye towards important findings. Section 5 ends with a conclusions and some future improvements.

2 Literature Review

Teachers and programs increasingly leverage student involvement, however users may fail to explain or justify their knowledge, limiting its efficacy in understanding and modifying learning. Beyond involvement as behaviour, empirical research on student engagement is sparse. Physical campuses and face-to-face delivery underpin most engagement, but this understates student participation. The study in [1] critiques how research should be rethought in light of changing learning settings and how to investigate involvement in two blended learning Initial Teacher Education programs. The results support past research on student involvement's multiple levels and interpretations and more complex and multidimensional models. The study supports the reevaluation of student involvement in modern digital contexts and verifies students' complicated participation perspectives.

The article in [2] discusses the need for a new perspective on higher education student achievement and retention. It proposes that the educational interface symbolically represents the individual psychosocial area where institutional and student factors mix and how these interactions effect participation. Four psychological constructs: self-efficacy, emotions, belonging, and well-being- moderate the relationships between student and institutional factors and student engagement and achievement.

The paper contributes to engagement theory by emphasising that student or institutional factors rarely affect student involvement alone and that their combination is vital.

The interface's four major components mediate engagement and success, not guarantee either. The report also highlights non-traditional student experiences and suggests procedures that may explain cohort results. Low self-efficacy, loss of belonging, negative emotions, poor well-being, and stress may cause these issues. The new framework acknowledges non-traditional students' challenges and underlines how institutional measures engaging these mediators could benefit all students, especially non-traditional ones. Government, institutions, and students are responsible for student perceptions of education. The approach emphasises fostering positive student-institution interactions to improve learning.

In [3] researchers explore socio-demographic and study environment factors affecting Open Polytechnic student persistence using 2006–2009 enrolment data. Performance was influenced by ethnicity, course program, and course block, with Pacific Islands and Māori students at increased risk. With ~60% accuracy, classification algorithms demonstrate that enrolment data alone cannot accurately predict. Support systems might benefit from early at-risk student identification. Academic achievement and advanced machine-learning should be used in future studies to improve accuracy.

The study in [4] predicts student performance using a machine learning model based on academic accomplishment. The model predicts first-year success or failure based on a student's performance in their last year of school and first semester of university. The program can accurately predict whether a student will pass or fail with 87% accuracy, suggesting its usage in education to improve results.

The research in [5] examines college academic achievement prediction using machine learning to predict dropout and retention. It analyses 6690 records with 21 variables using CRISP-DM. At 87.75% AUC, the XGBoost model accurately predicted success in 8 of 10 cases, whereas a decision tree model did 7 out of 10. Data preparation and model simplification enhance student retention strategies and decision-making by creating predictions that are efficient and interpretable.

The study in [6] examines student educational success determinants from student, parent, and school perspectives. Using machine learning (Lasso, Random Forest, AdaBoost, and Support Vector Regression), it finds that parental demand is the best predictor for girls, followed by school effort. Parents and educators must work together to improve academic performance. In order to reduce educational inequalities and improve student performance, the study suggests strengthening school efforts and motivational approaches.

Authors in [7] used ML to predict higher education student performance. The study examines academic outcome prediction utilising K-means clustering, SVM, Decision Tree, Naïve Bayes, and KNN classifiers. The SVM model has the highest accuracy (96%), followed by Decision Tree (93.4%) and Naïve Bayes (83.3%) following parameter tweaking. The research stresses data mining tools' importance for forecast accuracy and customised therapies. Future studies will focus on larger datasets and model interpretability, highlighting progress through longitudinal analysis and stakeholder feedback.

This study in [8] addresses student performance concerns, especially after the 2020 coronavirus epidemic lowered educational results. It stresses the importance of projecting student performance for timely interventions. The suggested machine learning model outperforms conventional models in accuracy, recall, and F1 score at 84%, 95%, and 82%. The study highlights student success factors and shows how machine learning can discover latent trends in student data. Adding features and data points improves the model, making it a better tool for learning. Future studies will expand the model to include more complex characteristics and combine interventions to improve student performance.

Another study in [9] predicts student performance using personal data, academic tests, VLE activities, psychological factors, surroundings, and attendance. KNN, C4.5, and SVM were used, together with Big Data technology to manage massive volumes of data and speed up execution. SVM prediction success was 87.32% after attribute selection. Performance was determined by academic assessments, economic status, parent education, child interest, and virtual classroom access.

In [10], researchers predicted student academic success using artificial neural networks (ANN) and feature selection. 161 students completed a 61-question survey about academics, health, and social events. With academic factors most relevant, FS techniques—Info Gain, Correlation, SVM, PCA—identified the top 30 influential questions. The algorithm predicted student grades with 87% accuracy, outperforming previous models and analysing student achievement factors.

In the [11], proposed study helps teachers anticipate student growth using data mining, addressing non-technical user challenges. Methodical framework for major choices, rules, and best practices. Predicting academic achievement using historical performance, demography, e-learning, and psychological factors is key. The paper covers Educational Data Mining (EDM) for non-experts, with potential uses in various sectors, particularly undergraduate education. It suggests adding data to improve forecasts and discover new student success variables.

Data science and machine learning have transformed education by predicting student achievement. These approaches identify at-risk students and improve instruction, which is crucial for university accreditation. ANN, SVM, Naïve Bayes, Linear Regression, and Decision Trees are often used machine learning approaches for predicting student results. These models' accuracy depends on choosing relevant traits, improving prediction accuracy, and letting teachers personalise interventions to improve student achievement [12].

3 Methodology

This study aims to predict student academic achievement by utilising demographic, social, academic, and health-related variables, with the final grade (G3) serving as the dependent variable in a regression models. The dataset comprises essential predictors including parental education, study duration, previous failures, and health-related behaviours. Data preprocessing encompassed addressing missing values, transforming categorical variables through one-hot and label encoding, and implementing Z-score normalisation on numerical features to enhance model performance. Outliers were detected by Z-score analysis but preserved to maintain critical data trends. Correlation analysis was performed to identify the most pertinent factors, including G1, G2, study time, and parental education. The dataset was divided into 80% for training and 20% for testing to assess model generalisation. A variety of machine learning techniques were examined, encompassing tree-based models such as Decision Tree, Random Forest, and Gradient Boosting, as well as non-tree-based methods like Linear Regression, Support Vector Machines (SVM), and K-Nearest Neighbours (KNN). This methodology establishes a thorough prediction framework for student performance, facilitating data-driven interventions to improve educational results.

3.1 Dataset

Student performance dataset is accessed from UCI at https://archive.ics.uci.edu/dataset/320/student+performance. Student demographics, social background, academic behaviours, and health are described in the dataset to predict academic success, specifically grades (G1, G2, G3). This dataset is useful for understanding student performance determinants and constructing a model to predict student performance. Key features of the dataset include demographic information such as sex, age, family size, and parental relationship status, providing insight into the student's background. Educational factors such as study time, school support, and prior failures indicate a student's academic engagement and preparedness. Health and well-being factors including health, alcohol usage, and family relationships are also included that might affect a student's academic performance. Parental influence factors such as education, job, and cohabitation status can impact student motivation and resources are included in the dataset.

The continuous numerical variable G3, the final grade, is the outcome variable. Therefore, the task is presented as a regression problem to predict student performance as a final grade based on independent factors.

The student's final academic performance is measured by G3 in this study. We want to construct models which predict student achievement at the final assessment factor using G3 directly as the target, making it a more accurate indicator of academic success. This approach allows for a deeper investigation of factors affecting final grades and clarifies the links between features and academic achievement. Additional dataset information is provided in Table 1.

Table 1. Dataset Description

Variable	Description
school	The name of the student's school (categorical: GP or MS)
sex	The gender of the student (categorical: M = male, F = female)
age	The age of the student (numeric)
address	The type of home address of the student (categorical: U = urban, R = rural)
famsize	The family size (categorical: LE3 = less than or equal to 3, GT3 = greater than 3)
Pstatus	The parent's cohabitation status (categorical: T = living together, A = apart)
Medu	The mother's education level (numeric: 0–4 scale)
Fedu	The father's education level (numeric: 0–4 scale)

(continued)

Table 1. (*continued*)

Variable	Description
Mjob	The mother's job (categorical: teacher, health, services, at_home, other)
Fjob	The father's job (categorical: teacher, health, services, at_home, other)
reason	The reason for choosing the school (categorical: course, home, reputation)
guardian	The student's guardian (categorical: mother, father, other)
traveltime	Time taken to travel from home to school (numeric: 1 =< 15 min, 2 = 15–30 min, 3 = 30 min–1 h, 4 => 1 h)
studytime	Weekly study time in hours (numeric)
failures	Number of past class failures (numeric)
schoolsup	Whether the student receives extra educational support (categorical: yes/no)
famsup	Whether the student receives family educational support (categorical: yes/no)
paid	Whether the student takes paid classes (categorical: yes/no)
activities	Whether the student participates in extra-curricular activities (categorical: yes/no)
nursery	Whether the student attended nursery school (categorical: yes/no)
higher	Whether the student wants to pursue higher education (categorical: yes/no)
internet	Whether the student has internet access at home (categorical: yes/no)
romantic	Whether the student is in a romantic relationship (categorical: yes/no)
famrel	Quality of family relationships (numeric: 1–5 scale)
freetime	Free time after school (numeric: 1–5 scale)
goout	Going out with friends (numeric: 1–5 scale)
Dalc	Workday alcohol consumption (numeric: 1–5 scale)
Walc	Weekend alcohol consumption (numeric: 1–5 scale)
health	Current health status (numeric: 1–5 scale)
absences	Number of school absences (numeric)
G1	First period grade (numeric: 0–20 scale)
G2	Second period grade (numeric: 0–20 scale)
G3	Final grade (numeric: 0–20 scale)

3.2 Dataset Preprocessing

Before developing a predictive model, data must be cleaned, formatted, and ready for analysis. The demographic, academic, and social elements of the student performance dataset must be carefully prepared before model training. Data preparation for this dataset involves the following steps:

Handling Missing Data: First, we analysed the and fixed the missing or null values in the dataset. Missing data might influence model predictions or prevent model training.

The dataset initially had no missing values, removing the need for imputation or other treatment.

Data Type Conversion: The dataset had category and numerical variables, requiring correct data type assignments for model inputs. Dataset variables such as school, sex, address, and family size are encoded into numeric variables. Multi-category variables like school and Mjob were encoded one-hot to create binary columns for each category. Binary categorical variables like higher and internet are converted into 1 and 0 using label encoding. Age, studytime, and failures were verified as numerical data. To reflect their four levels of mother's and father's education, Medu and Fedu were transformed from objects to numbers. These preprocessing processes guaranteed consistency and eased machine learning workflow integration.

Outcome Variable: G3 is the result variable in this modelling technique to predict student achievement. This method preserves the grading system and lets the model estimate final performance based on other features.

Feature Scaling: Machine learning algorithms sensitive to data range, such as linear regression, support vector machines, and k-nearest neighbours, require feature scaling to ensure that all features contribute equally to model training. To increase model performance and consistency, we used feature scaling to normalise numerical variables in this study. The dataset features: age, famrel, freetime, Dalc, and absences vary in scale, which can cause some aspects to dominate the learning process in model training and lead to inferior performance. Standardisation (or Z-score normalisation) was used to centre numerical values around zero with a unit variance. Each feature is transformed by subtracting its mean and dividing by its standard deviation.

This approach was used to scale the columns Medu (mother's education) and Fedu (father's education), which were categorical variables with ordinal values (1–4). This ensures that all numerical features, including ordinal columns, are evenly scaled for machine learning models. Standardising these columns removes scale's effect on the model, enabling algorithm convergence and improving model predictive power.

Handling Outliers: The dataset's outliers were discovered using the Z-score approach, which analyses data points' standard deviations from the feature mean. A Z-score larger than 3 or less than -3 indicates an outlier since it deviates significantly from the mean. This approach found outliers in "age," "studytime," and "failures."

We confirmed that these outliers were valid data points after rigorous review. A student with extremely high studytime may be an outlier, but it may indicate extraordinary education devotion. High failure rates may indicate particular academic issues for some students. We kept these outliers because they gave useful insights into extraordinary cases and had no data entry problems.

Outliers were recognised in 242 records across all 40 features in the (649, 40) dataset. These outliers are actual extreme cases that may reveal significant patterns or behaviours, therefore removing them would lose 37% of the dataset. We used tree-based prediction models for predictive systems instead of deleting outliers, which would greatly reduce the data. Random Forest and Gradient Boosting split data recursively based on feature values, making them less influenced by outliers.

We maintained dataset integrity and minimised outlier effects on model performance by preserving outliers and employing tree-based models. This strategy lets us collect potentially meaningful patterns from extreme occurrences, making the model more accurate and dependable without sacrificing much data.

3.3 Feature Selection Based on Correlation with the Target Variable (G3)

Correlation analysis was used to determine the best features for predicting G3 (final grade). The prediction models prioritized features with significant positive correlations to G3, while those with lower or negative correlations were less important. G2 (0.9185) and G1 (0.8264) were essential model features due to their substantial positive connection. Feature higher education (0.3322), expressing students' goal for higher education, and studytime (0.2498), showing weekly study time, also showed moderate positive associations with G3 and were retained for the model. Medu (mother's education) and Fedu (father's education) had moderate positive associations with G3 (0.2402 and 0.2118, respectively), suggesting parental education affects student performance. However, failures (-0.3933) and school (-0.2843) had moderate negative relationships with G3, showing that past academic failures and school attended negatively affect ultimate grade achievement. Despite the negative correlation, failures were chosen because of their impact on academic progress. Walc (-0.1766) and Dalc (-0.2047), which represent alcohol intake, and age (-0.1065) and freetime (-0.1227) were eliminated from the feature set due to their lower correlations. Choosing features with the highest correlations to G3 guarantees that the model includes the most important factors, optimising forecast accuracy and efficiency. Top-correlated features with G3 (final grade) were selected for feature selection. Based on association analysis, the following factors were selected: G2 (prior grade), G1, higher (if the student aspires to higher education), Medu (mother's education), studytime (weekly study time), Fedu (father's education), and Mjob. These variables were chosen for their significant and relevant connections with G3, which highlights student academic performance. This guarantees that only the most relevant elements with the highest target correlation are used to forecast students' final grades, improving the model's efficiency and performance (Fig. 1).

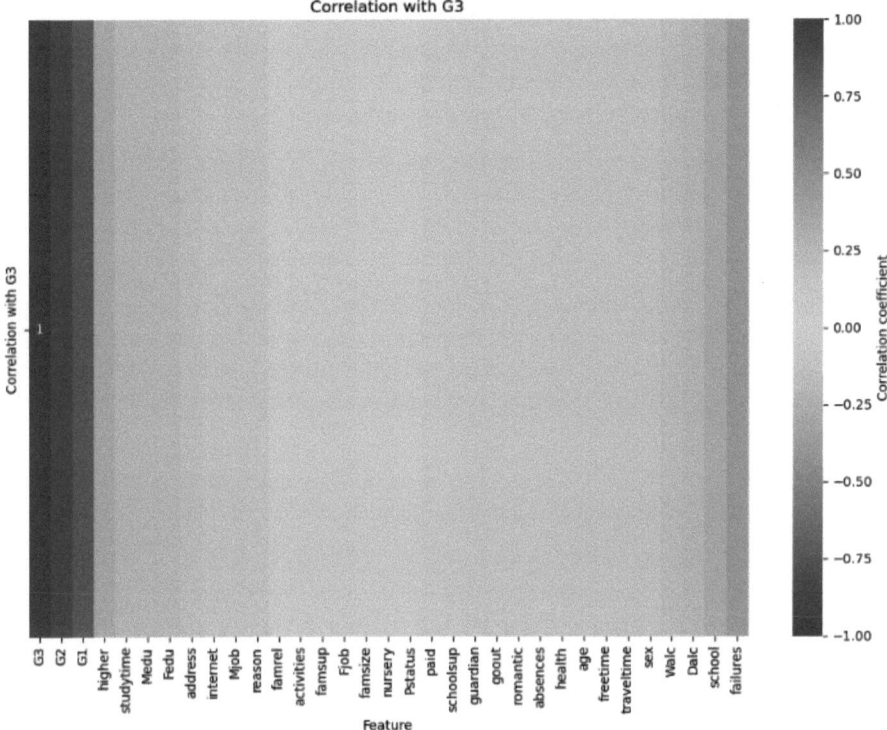

Fig. 1. Correlation between predictors and G3

3.4 Splitting the Data

The dataset was split into training and testing sets to test the model and ensure generalisation. The model learns feature-target variable associations from the 80% training set. Test data, 20% of the data, is preserved for model evaluation. This split evaluates the model's predicted accuracy on unseen data for impartiality. The split provides a fair trade-off between training and testing. This ratio provides enough data for models to learn and reliably test performance as compared to other ratios. Holding back some data for testing ensures that the model's performance is not unduly optimistic and that it can generalise to new, unseen real-world cases. A fixed random seed ensured reproducibility across runs.

3.5 Predictive Models

Multiple machine learning techniques predicted student performance using various features. These algorithms can be tree-based or non-tree-based. Each group includes strengths and characteristics that suit distinct issues. The following models were tested for predictive power and performance:

Algorithms Based on Trees: Ensemble tree-based techniques train models using several decision trees to increase accuracy and reduce overfitting. These models are interpretable and work well with complex, high-dimensional datasets.

Decision Tree: The Decision Tree algorithm divides data by feature values and creates branches that predict. This model is easy to understand and apply for classification and regression. Decision Trees can overfit when their tree structure is excessively deep and complicated, rendering them vulnerable to data noise.

Random Forest: This ensemble technique uses numerous decision trees trained on a random subset of data and features. The predictions from all trees are pooled to reduce overfitting and boost robustness. Due to its ensemble nature, Random Forest performs well in regression and classification and overfits less than Decision Trees.

Gradient Boosting: Another ensemble method that iteratively adds weak learners (typically decision trees) to address historical model mistakes. By addressing previous errors, each subsequent tree improves the model. Gradient Boosting is accurate and powerful for regression problems, but it can be computationally demanding and overfit if not optimised.

Non-tree-based Algorithms: These algorithms use mathematical functions and assumptions to model data and uncover linear or complicated correlations between features and the target variable.

Linear Regression: By fitting a linear equation to the data, linear regression describes the connection between the dependent variable and one or more independent variables. This simple, interpretable model works effectively when characteristics and goal variables are linearly related. In other cases, it struggles with complex or nonlinear interactions, losing effectiveness.

SVM: SVM is a powerful classifier that finds the hyperplane that best divides data into classes in a higher-dimensional space. It works well with linear and nonlinear data, especially high-dimensional data. While computationally expensive for large datasets, SVM performs well when decision boundaries are complex.

K-Nearest Neighbours (KNN): This instance-based learning technique predicts data points based on their proximity. KNN finds and averages nearest neighbours for regression on a test sample. KNN is simple and doesn't require training, although it tends to predict slowly in large datasets. It works well with non-linear data and difficult-to-define decision boundaries.

By separating algorithms into tree-based and non-tree-based techniques, we may take advantage of their capabilities. Decision Trees, Random Forests, and Gradient Boosting are ensemble-based algorithms that handle complex, high-dimensional data well and resist overfitting. However, non-tree-based algorithms like Linear Regression, SVM, and KNN perform well with simpler data with linear or proximity-based feature relationships. Both sorts of algorithms can be evaluated to compare their prediction capability and task fit.

3.6 Evaluation

It's important to evaluate machine learning algorithms using measures that represent the model's accuracy, efficiency, and ability to generalise to new data. Regression tasks that predict continuous outcomes like student grades utilise numerous metrics to evaluate model predictive power. This study evaluated its algorithms using the following criteria:

Mean Absolute Error (MAE): This simple statistic evaluates the average absolute discrepancies between predicted and actual values. It helps determine how far predictions are from actual results by providing an interpretable number of the model's prediction error in the target variable's units. MAE is less sensitive to outliers than other error metrics but may not detect large error severity.

Mean Squared Error (MSE): MSE estimates the average squared difference between anticipated and actual values. MSE penalises greater errors more than MAE, making it more outlier-sensitive. If not regulated, this feature can cause overfitting but is important for minimising greater errors. Model performance improves with lower MSE.

Root Mean Squared Error (RMSE): Another popular regression evaluation metric is Root Mean Squared Error (RMSE), which is the square root of the Mean Squared Error. It penalises significant errors like MSE but is in the same units as the target variable, like MAE. RMSE is sensitive to outliers and measures model accuracy, especially when big prediction errors must be minimised.

R-Squared (R^2): The coefficient of determination, or R-squared, measures the amount of variance in the target variable explained by the independent variables in the model. An R^2 value near 1 implies the model well explains target variable variance, while a value near 0 indicates limited variability capture. For regression models, larger R^2 values indicate better performance.

Combining these evaluation criteria allows us to evaluate the strengths and limitations of the machine learning algorithms, guaranteeing that the selected model is correct, generalises well to new data, and is efficient.

4 Results and Discussion

Machine learning models used to predict student academic achievement (with G3 as the target variable) vary in accuracy and predictive ability. The models' performance and capacity to generalise to new data are evaluated using MAE, MSE, RMSE, and R^2 Score measures. These evaluation criteria are used to analyse the models' results (Table 2 and Fig. 2):

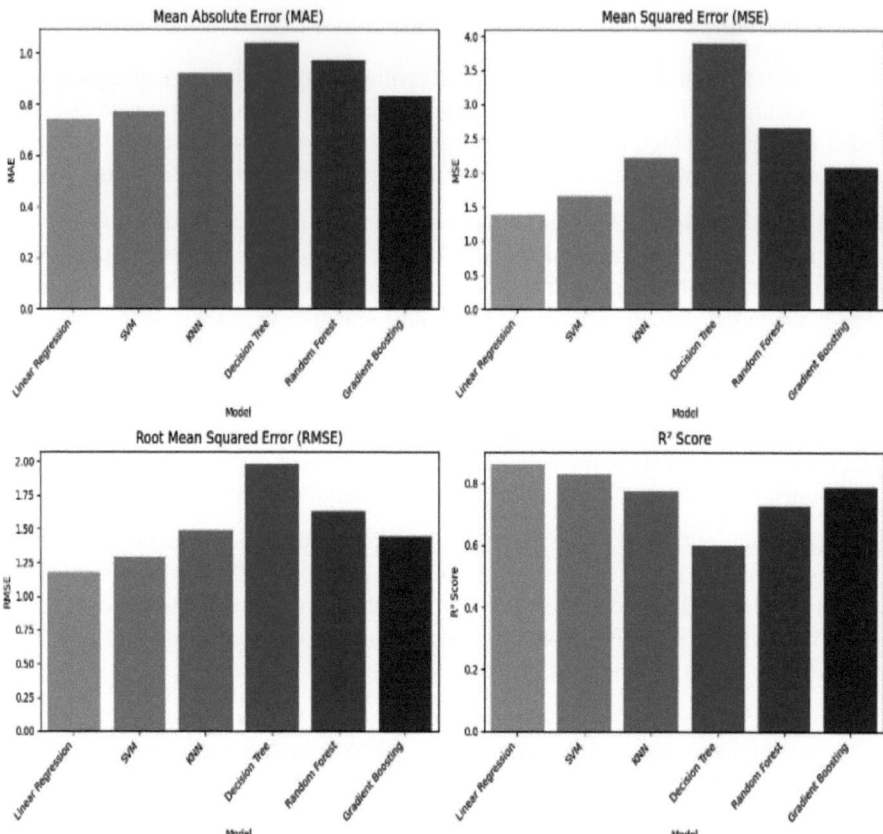

Fig. 2. Comparison of MAE, MSE, RMSE, and R^2 for different predictive models

Linear regression performs well, with a R^2 score of 0.858, explaining 85.8% of variation in the target variable (G3). Low MAE (0.740) and MSE (1.387) values indicate that the model's predictions are generally accurate. The model's 1.178 RMSE suggests a low average error. Linear Regression is one of the best models for predicting student grades.

The SVM model, however less effective than Linear Regression, nevertheless performs well with a R^2 score of 0.829. The model explains 82.9% of target variable variance. The MAE of 0.770 and RMSE of 1.291 are greater than Linear Regression, suggesting the model may predict less accurately. It predicts student achievement with competitive accuracy, making it a good contender (Fig. 3).

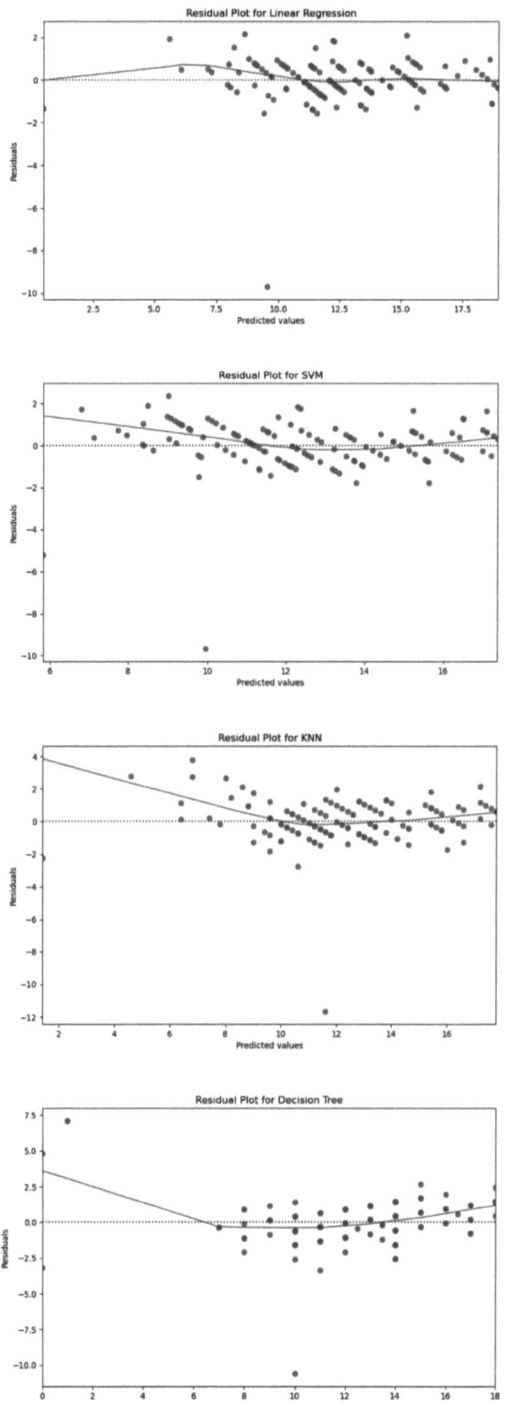

Fig. 3. Comparison of Residual Plots for different predictive models

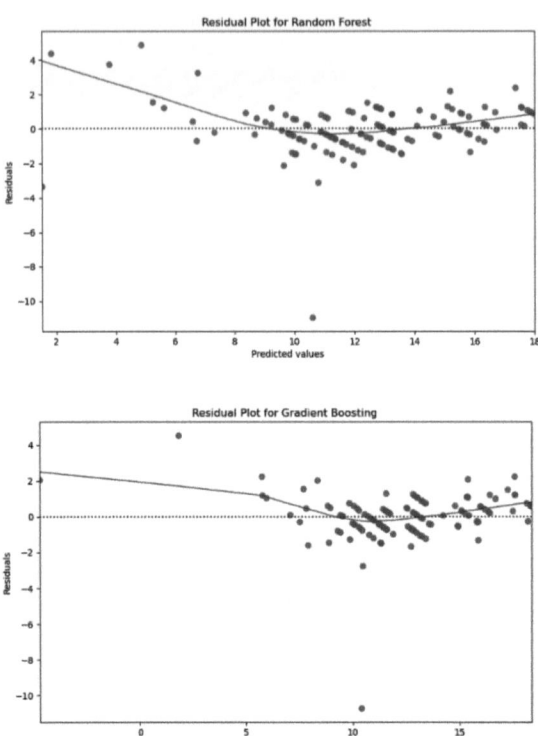

Fig. 3. (*continued*)

With the highest MAE (0.920) and RMSE (1.490), KNN performs worse. The MSE of 2.221 implies KNN predicts student grades less accurately than the other models. The R^2 value of 0.772 implies that the model explains only 77.2% of variance, which is lower than other techniques. This may be related to the KNN model's sensitivity to distance metrics and the curse of dimensionality, especially with many features.

The Decision Tree model has a higher MAE (1.042) and MSE (3.902), indicating poor student performance prediction. The R^2 score of 0.600 indicates a low explanation for the target variable, with just 60% explained by the model. A greater RMSE (1.975) supports the conclusion that the model is less accurate than others. Decision Trees overfit, especially deep ones, which may explain the decreased performance in this scenario.

Random Forest outperforms Decision Tree with lower MAE (0.972) and MSE (2.657). The R^2 value of 0.728 shows that the model explains 72.8% of the target variable's variance. A lower RMSE of 1.630 than KNN and Decision Tree indicates lower error. Random Forest, an ensemble of decision trees, is less likely to overfit and makes more accurate predictions, making it a competitive model.

Table 2. Comparison of performance metrics

Model	R^2 Score	MAE	MSE	RMSE
LR	0.858	0.74	1.387	1.178
SVM	0.829	0.77	1.667	1.291
KNN	0.772	0.92	2.221	1.49
DT	0.6	1.042	3.902	1.975
RF	0.728	0.972	2.657	1.63
GB	0.787	0.833	2.078	1.442

Gradient Boosting performs well with an MAE of 0.833 and MSE of 2.078. With a R^2 value of 0.787, the model explains 78.7% of target variable variance, outperforming Random Forest while being inferior to Linear Regression. Gradient Boosting predicts student performance with modest accuracy, as shown by its RMSE of 1.442. Gradient Boosting's ensemble technique adds weak learners to increase predicting performance.

Residual plots are essential for assessing regression model accuracy and suitability. A Linear Regression model with a R^2 score of 0.858 is expected to show a residual plot with a random dispersion about zero, showing low bias in capturing data trends. The SVM model, with a R^2 score of 0.829, may exhibit a similar pattern, but requires more tuning to incorporate all data nuances. However, the KNN model, with the lowest R^2 score of 0.772, may show a more structured residual plot, indicating potential overfitting or hyperparameter sensitivity issues, leading to higher residuals. The Decision Tree model, with a R^2 value of 0.600, may have considerable overfitting, resulting in clustered residuals and poor generalisation. Random Forest and Gradient Boosting models explain 72.8% of variation and produce more equally distributed residuals, however small patterns or outliers may still be observed. The residual plots reveal that Linear Regression and SVM are the most dependable models, Decision Tree needs improvement, KNN, Random Forest, and Gradient Boosting are in between, each with varied predicted accuracy and generalisability.

5 Conclusion

Several steps were taken to establish a reliable student performance prediction technique in this study. Data preprocessing began with Label Encoding and One-Hot Encoding to convert category variables to numerical values. This phase formatted all variables for machine learning models. To protect dataset integrity, missing values were resolved. Next, feature selection identified the best indicators for student performance. Correlation analysis selected a subset of attributes with the greatest target impact. This concentrated the approach, removing irrelevant variables and boosting model efficiency. This study uses Linear Regression, SVM, KNN, Decision Tree, Random Forest, and Gradient Boosting. Popular and regression-friendly models were chosen. The models were trained on preprocessed data and evaluated using common metrics such as MAE, MSE, RMSE, and R^2 Score.

This study used different regression models to predict student performance with mixed results. With a R^2 score of 0.858, the Linear Regression model performed best overall, effectively explaining variance in the target variable. It had the lowest MAE and RMSE of the models, indicating the most accurate forecasts. The Support Vector Machine (SVM) model had a good R^2 score of 0.829, but had greater MAE and RMSE than Linear Regression, indicating poorer accuracy. The K-Nearest Neighbours (KNN) model performed poorly, with a R^2 score of 0.772 and higher MAE and RMSE values, indicating ineffective data pattern capture. The Decision Tree model performed poorly, ranking lowest with a R^2 score of 0.600 and higher MAE and RMSE values, suggesting overfitting. Despite being more resilient than Decision Tree, the Random Forest model fared poorly compared to Linear Regression and SVM, with a R^2 score of 0.728 and moderate prediction errors. Finally, Gradient Boosting model showed strong prediction ability with a R^2 value of 0.787, but still lagging behind Linear Regression. Linear Regression was the best model for this dataset because to its accuracy and efficiency, while SVM and Gradient Boosting also showed potential. These findings highlight the relevance of model selection, feature engineering, and preprocessing in educational data analysis predicted accuracy.

References

1. Tai, J.H.-M., Bellingham, R., Lang, J., Dawson, P.: Student perspectives of engagement in learning in contemporary and digital contexts. High. Educ. Res. Dev. **38**, 1075–1089 (2019). https://doi.org/10.1080/07294360.2019.1598338
2. Kahu, E.R., Nelson, K.: Student engagement in the educational interface: understanding the mechanisms of student success. High. Educ. Res. Dev. **37**, 58–71 (2017). https://doi.org/10.1080/07294360.2017.1344197
3. Kovacic, Z.: Predicting student success by mining enrolment data. Res. High. Educ. J. (2012)
4. Al Mayahi, K., Al-Bahri, M.: Machine learning based predicting student academic success. In: 2020 12th International Congress on Ultra Modern Telecommunications and Control Systems and Workshops (ICUMT), p. 264 (2020)
5. Guanin-Fajardo, J.H., Guaña-Moya, J., Casillas, J.: Predicting academic success of college students using machine learning techniques. Data **9**, 60 (2024). https://doi.org/10.3390/data9040060
6. Jin, X.: Predicting academic success: machine learning analysis of student, parental, and school efforts. Asia Pac. Educ. Rev. (2023). https://doi.org/10.1007/s12564-023-09915-4
7. Ahmed, E.: Student performance prediction using machine learning algorithms (2024)
8. Umamaheswari, P., Vanitha, M., Devi, P.V., Theporal, J.G., Basha, B.R.: Student success prediction using a novel machine learning approach based on modified SVM. Multidisc. Sci. J. **6**, 2024ss0110 (2023). https://doi.org/10.31893/multiscience.2024ss0103
9. Ouatik, F., Erritali, M., Ouatik, F., Jourhmane, M.: Predicting student success using big data and machine learning algorithms. Int. J. Emerg. Technol. Learn. (iJET) **17**, 236–251 (2022). https://doi.org/10.3991/ijet.v17i12.30259
10. Hamoud, A.K., Humadi, A.M.: Student's success prediction model based on artificial neural networks (ANN) and a combination of feature selection methods. J. Southwest Jiaotong Univ. **54**, (2019). https://doi.org/10.35741/issn.0258-2724.54.3.25

11. Alyahyan, E., Düştegör, D.: Predicting academic success in higher education: literature review and best practices. Int. J. Educ. Technol. High. Educ. **17** (2020). https://doi.org/10.1186/s41239-020-0177-7
12. Yadav, N.R., Deshmukh, S.S.: Prediction of student performance using machine learning techniques: a review. Adv. Comput. Sci. Res. 735–741 (2023). https://doi.org/10.2991/978-94-6463-136-4_63

TRACK-02: Pattern Recognition

Integration of Security Elements into the Honeybee Work Sharing Framework

Sarvesh Chand(✉), Krishneel Sharma, Mansour H. Assaf, and Bibhya Sharma

School of Information Technology, Engineering Mathematics, and Physics, University of the South Pacific, Suva, Fiji
{s11146171,s11133165}@student.usp.ac.fj, {mansour.assaf, bibhya.sharma}@usp.ac.fj

Abstract. The increased computation load of the modern era presents an opportunity for Mobile edge computing models like the Honeybee models, as they offer a significant potential in optimizing computational load balancing. Being as it is the data security is an essential part of any computing system. This paper aims to provide the security enhancement to the Honeybee model by integrating user authentication, data encryption for data in transit and at rest and provide a secure channel for communication. The prototype system to simulate work-sharing capabilities of the Honeybee model has been developed, where users submit and solve simple mathematical tasks, which will be used to evaluate can compare the performance before and after integrating the security features. This performance comparison will demonstrate what computational overhead will be introduced with the security integration while significantly improving data integrity and user privacy. The results of the integration will offer an insight into the fine balance between security and performance in the mobile edge computing cloud environment.

Keywords: Mobile Edge Computing · Honeybee Model · Data Security · Computational Load Balancing

1 Introduction

Mobile edge computing has become a viable solution to the increased offloading of heavy computational tasks from the cloud environment to nearby resource rich devices. This approach reduces the strains on a central cloud server, offering improved efficiency of distributed system. The Honeybee Model introduced by [1], is a promising framework that uses the decentralized approach to its advantage for load balancing and work sharing across mobile devices. With its novel work stealing algorithm, the frame is able to dynamically distribute computation tasks across various mobile computing devices based on factors that optimized resources utilization among all worker devices.

The authors of the Honeybee framework did manage to improve the effectiveness of work-sharing application but did state that the model they had developed lacked security measures that would need to be looked at if the model were to be a viable option for today's data intensive world. With this research, we aim to integrate security measures such as user authentication, data encryption both at rest and in transit, and establish secure communication protocols. To showcase the functionalities and measure the performance, a simple mobile app has been developed as a prototype that will be used to measure and assess the performance before and after security integrations to the mobile app. As part of the functionalities of the application in relation to the work sharing framework, registered users will be able to submit simple mathematical equations to the systems, which would represent work being shared. The application would then receive work to complete it. This would be the testbed that will be used to evaluate the performance under a secure and a non-secure environment. The before and after comparison will be used to demonstrate how effective security measures can be integrated without significant reducing performance in the mobile edge computing environment.

2 Literature Review

The fast-growing landscape of the computational capabilities required by modern computing devices has found its place in Mobile Edge Computing (MEC) which is today one of the rapidly progressing technologies [2, 3]. Due to decentralization and efficient practices the processed data at the network edges is more and more, MEC has managed to compute and offload very many tasks [2, 4]. Looking at European Telecommunications Standards Institute (ETSI) [5] mention, there are three main types of MEC architectures: centralized, decentralized and hybrid models. Each of these models has some advantages which include expansion, adaptability, and resource allocation efficiency. Architectures meant for the deployment of the MEC systems, as discussed for instance, by Satyanarayanan et al. [6] and Drolia et al. [7], are in the forefront for effective deployment of the MEC systems. Such frameworks employ an approach of sharing workload that is decentralized therefore allowing effective allocation of work to be done through different mobile devices. Using dynamic resource allocation allows for better utilization of resources for the tasks hence improving the effectiveness and efficiency of the MEC implementations. Such frameworks mitigate issues like the scalability and flexibility limits that are typically experienced in traditional on-demand cloud systems.

The remarkable aspects of Mobile Edge Computing (MEC) come with their own unique challenges that must be surmounted to protect the data and services offered from threats to their confidentiality, integrity, and availability [8–10]. Among them, are the issues of data leakage, hacking or other forms of unauthorized access, and even DDoS as seen in research done in [8, 9]. The very decentralization that endowed MEC its advantages also make the system easily susceptible to threats compared to a conventional system. [8–10]. A broad overview of the security concerns regarding MEC was examined by Garg et al. [10] who even recommended how such concerns can be alleviated, for example, by putting in place comprehensive security structures. Furthermore, Yu [11] equally posits that like a security architecture for the transmission channels and databases, it is also essential to put in place a security architecture for service provision and user information within MEC. In view of its heterogeneous operational structure core to its design, user centric MEC presents vast challenging issues that need improved measures to bolster security against emerging threats. Jin et al. [9] state the importance for the development of mobile computing and mobile communication specific security framework which would focus on the issues of security, and include data encryption, secure log-in and access control. All of these components of security are very much necessary to ensure the credibility and dependability of the MEC systems, more so considering the sensitive content such MECs are likely to handle. Recent studies note an increasing sophistication of cyber attacks on MEC environments which indicate that proactive and adaptive security measures are now required [19]. It also investigates the specific weaknesses induced by the introduction of AI and machine learning into MEC systems [20]. While federated learn may offer privacy benefits, it could also present new specific security challenges in the MEC context [21]. Moreover, such dynamic and distributed nature of MEC entails novel intrusion detection and prevention systems specifically for the edge environment [22].

In addition, authentication is one of the areas that can improve security in a particularly important way, especially in the case of the MEC environment [12, 13]. Yang et al. [12] identify various approaches to authentication, arguing that any approach chosen must be weighted based on security, efficiency, and user experience. Yang et al. [13] present a review of various authentication techniques in terms of their pros and cons. The authors advocate for the deployment of multifactor authentication solutions and the application of blockchain technology to provide additional security with minimal performance hit. In addition, the assumption advanced by Garg et al. [10] is that there exist robust authentication protocols coupled with effective access control which itself does not facilitate resource compromise. Data encryption is yet another element that makes a system secure, for instance, while ensuring that data is encrypted both when stationary and when moving about the system. Yu [11] provides an overview of the different forms of data encryption including single key encryption forms, public key encryption forms and combined key encryption forms. After assessing the approaches in terms of the strength of security, costs in computing power and resources, and the difficulties of putting the techniques into practice, the research asserts that the choice of encryption methods should be in line with the application of MEC. Another aspect of security is the use of secure communication channels by MEC applications when communicating and exchanging data with other devices. A review of various communication protocols such as Transport Layer Security (TLS) and Internet Protocol Security (IPsec), as well as up-and-coming innovations such as blockchain, was conducted by Bassole et al. [14]. The article pointed out the importance of choosing the right protocol for the use of the MEC applications owing to its ability to mitigate threats such as the man-in-the-middle threat, wiretapping, and the alteration of messages while at the same time reducing the processing power needed. Recent investigations conducted were about the study of biometric authentication methods in supplementing the existing security in the MEC environments [23]. The rise of increasing applications of blockchain-based decentralized identity management systems to provide secure access control towards distributed MEC deployments has gained considerable attention [24]. Lightweight cryptographic algorithms so far under study aim at efficient data encryption for resource-constrained MEC devices [25]. The integration of secure enclaves as well as trusted execution environments (TEEs) is also being conducted with the aims of providing protection for sensitive data and computations on the edge [26]. Post-quantum cryptography has also begun to attract research attention to the future proof of such MEC systems from threats coming from developing quantum computing [27].

Providing security components in the MEC architecture comes at a cost of processing resources, which can affect the system performance. [8, 10, 14]. In the work done by Fazeldehkordi and Grønli [8], it is pointed out that any measures such as encryption, authentication, access control, and so on, should be thoroughly examined prior to being introduced into the final MEC application. The analysis may also include measuring the performance impact of the different security elements in the MEC application. Garg et al. [10] analysis the implications of several security approaches in terms of latency and throughput, power and processing overheads, and also how these approaches affect and enrich the overall application performance. The paper notes that performance degradation of the MEC application should be considered when designing security protocols. Bassole et al. [14] look at it from a different perspective by proposing how such performance impacts could be reduced by use of security that include, low complex lightweight encryption techniques, fast and efficient authentication schemes, and smart access control. Achievements in practical implementations and analysis provide more explanations on the application of security measures such as encryption, authentication, access control, and their impact on the performance of MEC applications. In recent studies, trade-offs security-performance in various MEC appli-cations have been investigated to propose an optimized security architecture that aims at overhead minimization [28]. Machine learning techniques are now employed to dynamically adapt security levels according to the current threat scenario and resource availability [29]. Another research area is the use of hardware acceleration for speeding up cryptographic operations-it aims at improving the performance of security-intensive MEC applications [30]. Additionally, various security protocols are under extensive scrutiny to characterize their impact on the Quality of Service (QoS) of MEC-based services [31]. Energy-efficient mechanisms that incorporate security are also a major object of study, particularly for extending mobile device battery life within the MEC environment [32].

3 Methodology

The objective of this research is to improve the existing security aspects of the Honeybee Framework for Mobile Edge Computing (MEC) in a manner that is well coordinated. The emphasis, by contrast, is on considering the effect of adding more security on aspects like CPU usage, memory usage, power usage, among others, all while ensuring the application performs well. The methodology is broken down, into different major steps which are: designing the system, developing the security features, implementing the system, assessing the impact on performance and lastly assessment of the security features on both the server side and the client side.

3.1 System Design

The first step is the system design where additional security features will be added to the system. This is important to cover user authentication, data encryption (at rest and in transit) and secure channels. The Honeybee framework modular design enables the security components to be added into an already existing workload sharing without interfering with its operation. This modular design offers easy system upgrades for security enhanced features can take place in the future without compromising the overall functioning of the system [1], as shown in Fig. 1.

Key Architectural Components:

- User Interface (UI)
- User Login Screen
- Data Encryption Modules
- Secure Communication Services
- Workload Management Module

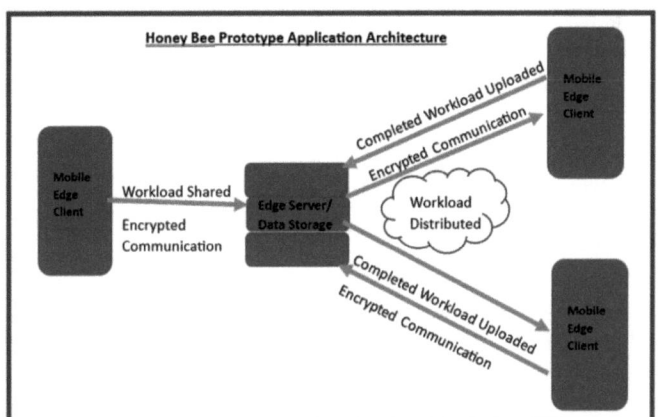

Fig. 1. Honey Bee Prototype.

3.2 Security Features Development

Security feature development in this context includes the design of both the frontend and backend security measures. The purpose is to consider the level of impact these security features have on the system resource consumption specifically how CPU resources, memory, and power are utilized.

Backend Security Integrations

1. **Controlling the Environment**- It was practiced defining variables, for instance SECRET_KEY and ALGORITHM, in the environment so that these sensitive details would not be hard coded wherever required.

2. **The Passwords are In Encrypted Form**- Passlib together with bcrypt hashing algorithm was used to encrypt user passwords prior to them being kept, thus meaning no plain user passwords are kept at any time.

3. **JWT Authentication JSON Web Tokens (JWT)** was used for authentication of users in a secure manner and without maintaining any pertinent user information on the system.

4. **Method of OAuth2 Password Flow** - The fastapi.security .OAuth2PasswordBearer class was used to implement the password grant flow of OAuth2 so that user security is poor.

5. **Customizing CORS** Fastapi.middleware.cors.CORSMiddleware was utilized in implementing Custom CORS (Cross-Origin Resource Sharing) to allow requests from only a specific set of domains.

6. **Protection of API Routes and Role-Based Access Using Permi** - New User Access to API routes was protected by means of authentication and authorization to protect sensitive pages from non-permitted users.

7. **Exception Handling**- Redundant error messages were effectively applied through HTTP Exception so that error messaging systems do not give any information concerning the system which can be vital to its security.

8. **Secure Database Interactions SQL Alchemy Object Relational Mapper (ORM)** - facilitated secure communication with the database while preventing SQL injection attacks.

9. **Data Protection Information** security was enhanced in that data at rest was secured via AES-256 encryption technique while data in transit was protected from threats using RSA encryption technique.

10. **Timed JWT Expires** times were also assigned for use of JWT tokens to prevent long periods of usage limits which would minimize adverse effects in case of misuse of the tokens.

Frontend Security Integrations

1. **Use of Flutter** libraries for Storing Information flutter_secure_storage set feature was used to secure authentication tokens in the mobile device.

2. **Active Directory Integrated Token-based** Authentication To allow secure access to users I worked on Non-interactive JWT based authentication to maintain the user's session.

3. **Network Security** - Procedure for encrypting the sensitive data transmission to backend using encodes and pointycastle libraries.

4. **Certification Authority** - The application contained integrated the server's public encryption key for secure transfer of encrypted data.

5. **Managing request and response HTTP** - headers The appropriate headers such as Content-Type and Authorization were adjusted to provide secure communication with the APIs.

6. **Managing Exceptions** - and that user can view the errors a dom error management which entails giving feedback to user without compromising security was employed.

7. **Management of states within the application** - Secure management of application authentication states was done using provider package.

8. **Addressing Problems with Data** - Extra validation by the client was done to ensure that the data sent to the backend, which is referred to as server-side validation, is not changed.

9. **API Secure the Integrated** - All communication with the API was required to take place over HTTPS so that data would be sent securely.

10. **Improvement of Record Keeping Techniques** - Unnecessary chronicling out of classified information was restrained or obscured to avoid the leakage of private information.

11. **Middleware and Additional Security Layers Enhanced security** - by incorporating RSA encryption with other methods such as rate limiting and input sanitization.

3.3 System Development

During the development phase, the security features discussed above were integrated into both the frontend and backend of the Honeybee Framework, with a focus on assessing the impact on CPU usage, memory consumption, and power utilization.

Backend Development:

• The backend was developed with **FastAPI**, which offers **JWT authentication** and secure tokens by using the **OAuth2 password flow**.
• To interface with the database, the **SQLAlchemy ORM** was used, while **AES 256** encryption was used to encrypt the data at rest.
• Data in transit was secured by the usage of **TLS 1.3** and **IPsec** between mobile devices and edge servers.

Frontend Development:

• The mobile application was constructed using **Flutter** based on accessibility to various platforms.
• Management of state securely was achieved via the use of the provider package.
• Transmission of sensitive information to the server was protected with confidential **RSA encryption**.
• Store sensitive mobile tokens in **secure storage** offered by the Flutter framework.

3.4 Overhead Performance Assessment

It was significant to evaluate benefits relating to security features since attention was given to primary metrics: how much CPU was utilized, how much memory was disproportionately consumed, as well as how much power was drained. The focus was rather on measuring performance degradation caused by imposed security measures.

Experimental Protocol:

1. **Baseline Measurement**: Prior to the integration of the security elements, a set of performance metrics was recorded to establish the base against which variations will be compared.

2. **Post-Integration Measurement**: Metrics were assessed and measured for a second time after the methods or processes were secured, holding all other variables constant.

3. **Comparison and Analysis**: The pre-and post-integration phase data was examined to assess the effect of the security features.

Metrics Evaluated:

1. **CPU Usage**: Processor workload was examined in order to determine the computational burden imposed by the additional security features.
2. **Memory Consumption**: The memory parameters of the application were tracked in a bid to assess the effectiveness of solutions put in place for security.
3. **Power Utilization**: Power levels were recorded to analyze how amelioration of security upgrades would hamper the battery life which is always a consideration for mobile devices.
4. **Latency**: Latency, or the state of request processing before and after the integration of security features, was measured.

3.5 Evaluation of Frontend and Backend Security Integrations

A thorough assessment of the security features added to the front end as well as the back end was performed to provide assurance on their success. Their effect on the CPU and memory and power consumption was noted.

1. Frontend Evaluation: There were performance tests for secure storage, token management, data protection, and state management.
2. Backend Evaluation: The influence of processing times and resourcing on password protection, token use and active databases was assessed.

4 Experimental Results and Analysis

The purpose of enhancing the Honeybee Work Sharing Framework with security components was to ensure that the data was protected, and the users were kept private without adversely affecting the system's operation in the Mobile Edge Computing (MEC) architecture. This study evaluated the effects of user authentication, data encryption, and secure communication mechanisms and protocols on the back-end server and the mobile front-end applications in terms of CPU usage, memory usage, power usage, and latency.

4.1 Impact on Backend Performance

Figures 2 and 3 present the Fast API Backend Results, before and after security integration.

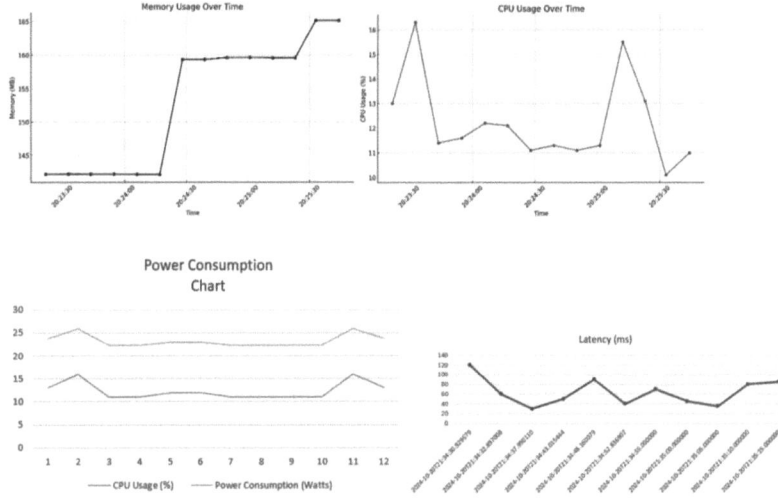

Fig. 2. Before security integration.

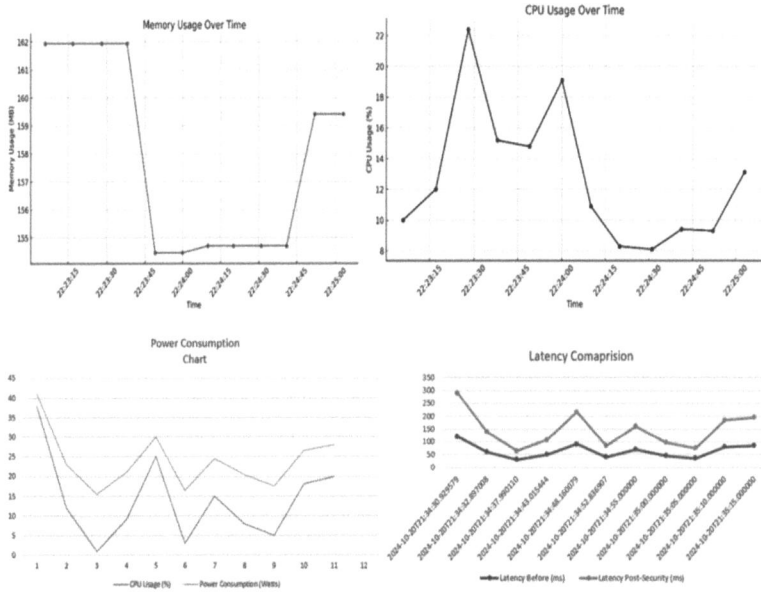

Fig. 3. After security integration.

Once the security enhancements were added to the FastAPI backend server, there was a visible difference in the following operational metrics of the system:

• Memory Usage: The noticeable decrease in memory usage came right after the security enhancement. Where average memory went from about 162 MB to 157 MB, representing

a 3.09% reduction. This signals more efficient memory usage, possibly due to better memory management in secure operations.
• CPU Usage: There was a spike due to heavy usage. The average CPU usage went from about 13% to 17%, at random times exceeding 20%) after the integration. This constitutes a ~ 30.77% increase attributed to process activities such as encryption, JWT validation, and hashing computations.
• Power Consumption: An increase was recorded that could be easily noticed. Average power consumption went from 23 Watts to about 30 Watts, which represents an increase of about ~ 30.43%. This increase aligns with CPU usage and considerable computation activity that follows by security protocols.
• Latency: There was notable increase recorded through all measured intervals. Latency before the security implementation averaged about 135 ms, while after the security integration it rose to 215 ms (~59.26% increase). These overheads are expected mainly due to the cost of the TLS handshakes, encryption/decryption, and token validations.

This clearly indicates that while security integrations such as BCRYPT password hashing, JWT creation/validation, AES-256 and RSA encryption/decryption, and secure transport layers (TLS 1.3 and IPsec) added computational overhead, still the backend performed satisfactorily in terms of speed. In fact, the changes present a perfect scenario illustrating the "Law of Diminishing Returns"; there is a point at which security enhancements begin to come at greater trade-offs in performance and cost, but this is nonetheless justified by their increased resilience and thorough protection of data.

Figure 4 shows the impact on frontend performance.

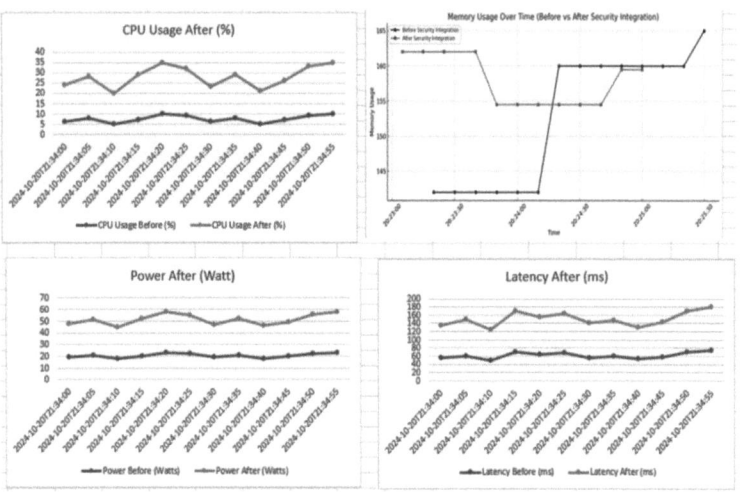

Fig. 4. Significant resource consumption.

Following the implementation of security measures in the mobile app built with Flutter, the frontend of the mobile application laid more stress on the resources:
• CPU Usage: Increased three times than the baseline measurement.

- Memory Usage: Decreased by where average memory went from about 162 MB to 157 MB, representing a 3.09% reduction.
- Power Consumption: Power consumption went up by 10.42 Watts (baseline value not mentioned).
- Latency: There was an increase of 10.42 ms Latency.

The marked rise in CPU utilization is linked to the use of different libraries of encryption, safe storage systems for authentication tokens, plus the better state management that is expected for security reasons. The CPU usage has more than doubled mainly due to the processes involving encryption and decryption as well as the protocols for secure communication which most mobile devices find extremely taxing.

4.2 Interpretation of Findings

Backend Efficiency vs. Frontend Constraints

The contrary effect that such a strategy has on the performance indicators of backend and frontend reveals the difficulty of implementing security measures in devices with limited resources, such as mobile phones. The backend server, for example, was able to accommodate the additional processing burden without an appreciable effect on performance; however, in the frontend application the performance impact was more noticeable.

Despite the growth, however, the values of resource consumption on the front end still are within the threshold limits of modern-day mobile devices. The growth in memory usage to 16,400 bytes is negligible considering the memory limits of today's mobile devices. The rise in latency of 10.42 ms is not expected to impact user experience adversely especially for applications where real time interactivity is not a requirement.

Limitations.

In analyzing the findings, a few constraints need to be kept in mind:

1. **Workload simplification**: The prototype application used a simple enacting over input and output mathematical operations, which can be far from the true nature of real-world MEC framework applications which go a step further in computation and data usage.
2. **Limited settings**: The assessments were performed in limited settings and thus it lacked some of the real-world factors such as network delays or changes in hardware configurations and user concurrency.
3. **Narrow Security Range**: The security measures in place accounted for only some of the possible security concerns. No evaluation of multi factor, threat detection or extensive user privilege preventative action was conducted.
4. **Influence on battery life**: The research failed to consider the effect of security applications on the battery life of mobile devices over extended periods which is important for the acceptance of such applications.

Implications for MEC Environments.

The results denote that it is possible to include security mechanisms in MEC designs, but the hardware limitations of the client devices ought to be addressed. For infrastructure systems, the overhead is insignificant; however, with mobile software, the security devices are the ones that need to be developed in such a way that their use does not interfere with the users' normal work.

The problems associated with mobile device performance can be mitigated by the following means:

- **Utilization of crypto lite** - Usage of cryptosystems otherwise designed for not so computing demanding external usage for devices that have limited resources.
- **Accelerated processing** - Make use of the mobile device with its inbuilt features that allow for faster encryption and decryption processing.
- **Code optimization** - Restructure the code in a way that reduces wastefulness of resources, properly managing memory and ensuring that certain calculations if done are not repeated for the better part of the code.
- **Adaptive Security Mechanisms** - Enforce beyond security that are flexible in ensuring that low resource consuming security levels are enforced when the device performance or battery capacity is low.

5 Conclusion

Adding security features into the Honeybee Work Sharing Framework proved that improving the data integrity and the users' privacy in an MEC environment can be done with some acceptable increase of performance costs. The management of the back-end system was able to incorporate the security related processes efficiently with no much effect on the resources and latency. On the contrary, the frontend mobile application suffered more from the increase in the CPU usage, memory usage and power consumption.

These results reinforce the need to consider the effective cost of security strategies on devices with limited resources. Even though it is notable that there is such a huge resource requirement imposed on the front end, it is still manageable with today's handheld devices. In turn, this resource requirement is excused by the major merits that come with allowing higher levels of security.

Key Points

- **Feasibility**: It is possible and imperative to include security measures in MEC frameworks to protect confidential information and keep the user's data private.
- **Performance Balance**: It is necessary to find a balancing point because too much emphasis on security affects performance particularly in client devices where resources are limited.
- **Optimization**: Security features should be designed in such a way that they do not bring a big drop in performance and lightweight cryptography, hardware acceleration are some of the techniques that can be used.
- **User Experience**: Considering the fact that security measures are put in place, and they are costly in resources, it's important to make certain that user satisfaction is not compromised, so as to promote adoption.

Future Work

To further improve the security position of MEC frameworks, prospective research will include exploring high-level security strategies like blockchain authentication, machine learning anomaly detection systems, and quantum secure encryption algorithm. What's more is that expanding the prototype to support more edge devices and different applications scenarios will give a better understanding on the scalability and effectiveness of the combination security features.

Taking into considerations the challenges identified and results from this research, there is possibility that Honeybee Work Sharing Framework can be modified so that it fits the current MEC applications without changes in the performance and security aspects which aids in the provision of mobile distributed computing across devices.

References

1. Yu, Y.: [Retracted] Encryption Technology for Computer Network Data Security Protection. Secur. Commun. Netw. **2022**(1), 1789222 (2022)
2. Ahmed, A., Ahmed, E.: A Survey on Mobile Edge Computing (2016). https://doi.org/10.1109/ISCO.2016.7727082
3. Hassan, N., Yau, K.-L., Wu, C.: Edge Computing in 5G: a review. IEEE Access **PP**, 1 (2019). https://doi.org/10.1109/ACCESS.2019.2938534
4. Mao, Y., You, C., Zhang, J., Huang, K., Letaief, K.: A Survey on mobile edge computing: the communication perspective. IEEE Commun. Surv. Tutor. **PP**, 1 (2017) .https://doi.org/10.1109/COMST.2017.2745201
5. ETSI. Multi-access Edge Computing (MEC); Framework and Reference Architecture. GS MEC 003, V3.1.1, Mar 2022, www.etsi.org/deliver/etsi_gs/MEC/001_099/003/03.01.01_60/gs_mec003v030101p.pdf. Additional information can be found at the ETSI website
6. Satyanarayanan, M., Bahl, P., Caceres, R., Davies, N.: The case for VM-based cloudlets in mobile computing. IEEE Pervasive Comput. **8**(4), 14–23 (2009)
7. Drolia, U., et al.: The case for mobile edge-clouds. In: Proceeding IEEE 10th International Conference on Ubiquitous Intelligence & Computing and 10th International Conference on Autonomic & Trusted Computing, pp. 209–215. IEEE (2013). https://doi.org/10.1109/UIC-ATC.2013.94
8. Fazeldehkordi, E., Grønli, T.-M.: A survey of security architectures for edge computing-based IoT. IoT **3**, 332–365 (2022). https://doi.org/10.3390/iot3030019
9. Jin, X., Katsis, C., Sang, F., Sun, J., Kundu, A., Kompella, R.: Edge Security: Challenges and Issues. (2022). https://doi.org/10.48550/arXiv.2206.07164
10. Garg, S., Kaur, K., Kaddoum, G., Garigipati, P., Aujla, G.S.: Security in IoT-driven mobile edge computing: new paradigms, challenges, and opportunities. IEEE Netw. **35**(5), 298–305 (2021). https://doi.org/10.1109/MNET.211.2000526
11. Yu, Y.: Encryption technology for computer network data security protection. Secur. Commun. Netw. **2022**, 1–9 (2022). https://doi.org/10.1155/2022/1789222
12. Yang, C., Peng, J., Xu, Y., Wei, Q., Zhou, L., Tang, Y.: Edge computing-based VANETs' anonymous message authentication. Symmetry **14**, 2662 (2022). https://doi.org/10.3390/sym14122662
13. "Secure and Anonymous Authentication Scheme for Mobile Edge Computing Environments | IEEE Journals & Magazine | IEEE Xplore. Accessed 21 Oct 2024. [Online]. Available: https://ieeexplore.ieee.org/document/10230274
14. Bassolé, D., Kaboré, K., Traoré, Y., Sie, O., Ben Sta, H.: Design and implementation of secure communication protocols for Internet of Things systems, pp. 112–117 (2019). https://doi.org/10.1109/ISC246665.2019.9071738

15. Dastjerdi, A V., Buyya, R., Ghosh, S. K.: Fog computing: principles, architectures, and applications. J. Cloud Comput. Adv. Syst. Platforms **5**(1), 1 (2016). https://doi.org/10.1186/s40 888-016-0045-5
16. Vhora, F., Gandhi, J.: A comprehensive survey on mobile edge computing: challenges, tools, applications, p. 55 (2020). https://doi.org/10.1109/ICCMC48092.2020.ICCMC-0009
17. Haibeh, L.A., Yagoub, M.C.E., Jarray, A.: A survey on mobile edge computing infrastructure: design, resource management, and optimization approaches. IEEE Access **10**, 27591–27610 (2022). https://doi.org/10.1109/ACCESS.2022.3152787
18. Vivekanandan, M., Sastry, V., Reddy, U. S.: Biometric based user authentication protocol for mobile cloud environment, p. 6 (2019). https://doi.org/10.1109/ISBA.2019.8778529
19. Ahmed, Md.R., Islam, A.K.M.M., Shatabda, S., Islam, S.: Blockchain-based identity management system and self-sovereign identity ecosystem: a comprehensive survey. IEEE Access **10**, 113436–113481 (2022). https://doi.org/10.1109/ACCESS.2022.3216643
20. Mahenge, M.P.J., Li, C., Sanga, C.A.: Energy-efficient task offloading strategy in mobile edge computing for resource-intensive mobile applications. Digital Commun. Netw. **8**(6), 1048–1058 (2022). https://doi.org/10.1016/j.dcan.2022.04.001
21. "Federated Learning: A Survey on Enabling Technologies, Protocols, and Applications | IEEE Journals & Magazine | IEEE Xplore. Accessed 07 Apr 2025. [Online]. https://ieeexplore.ieee.org/document/9153560
22. Almogren, A.S.: Intrusion detection in edge-of-things computing. J. Parall. Distrib. Comput. **137**, 259–265 (2020). https://doi.org/10.1016/j.jpdc.2019.12.008
23. Al Shebli, H. M. Z., Beheshti, B. D.: Light weight cryptography for resource constrained IoT devices. In: Proceedings of the Future Technologies Conference (FTC) 2018, vol. 880. Arai, K., Bhatia, R., Kapoor, S., (eds.) in Advances in Intelligent Systems and Computing, vol. 880. , Cham: Springer International Publishing, pp. 196–204 (2019). https://doi.org/10.1007/978-3-030-02686-8_16
24. "Network Function Virtualization - an overview | ScienceDirect Topics." Accessed: Apr. 07, 2025. [Online]. Available: https://www.sciencedirect.com/topics/computer-science/network-function-virtualization
25. Hussien, A., Maolood, A., Gbashi, E.: A systematic review: post quantum cryptography to secure data transmission. Iraqi J. Sci. 3975–3992 (2024). https://doi.org/10.24996/ijs.2024.65.7.35
26. Bibi, A., Majeed, M., Ali, S., Abbasi, I., Samad, A., Baseer, S.: Secured optimized resource allocation in mobile edge computing. Mobile Inf. Syst. **2022**. 1–14 (2022). https://doi.org/10.1155/2022/9952993
27. Liao, R.-F., et al.: Security enhancement for mobile edge computing through physical layer authentication. IEEE Access **7**, 116390–116401 (2019). https://doi.org/10.1109/ACCESS.2019.2934122
28. Meuser, T., et al.: Revisiting edge AI: opportunities and challenges. IEEE Internet Comput. **28**(4), 49–59 (2024). https://doi.org/10.1109/MIC.2024.3383758
29. Hu, B., et al.: Secure and efficient mobile DNN using trusted execution environments. In: Proceedings of the 2023 ACM Asia Conference on Computer and Communications Security, in ASIA CCS '23. New York, NY, USA: Association for Computing Machinery, pp. 274–285 (2023). https://doi.org/10.1145/3579856.3582820
30. Verdecchia, R., Lago, P., de Vries, C.: The future of sustainable digital infrastructures: a landscape of solutions, adoption factors, impediments, open problems, and scenarios. Sustain. Comput. Info. Syst. (SUSCOM) **35**(100767), 1–20 (2022). https://doi.org/10.1016/j.suscom.2022.100767

31. "The Security and Privacy of Mobile Edge Computing: An Artificial Intelligence Perspective." Accessed 07 Apr 2025. Available: https://arxiv.org/html/2401.01589v1
32. "Towards Blockchain-IoT Based Shared Mobility: Car-sharing and Leasing as a Case Study - CBS Research Portal. Accessed 07 Apr 2025. [Online]. Available: https://research.cbs.dk/en/publications/towards-blockchain-iot-based-shared-mobility-car-sharing-and-leas

Origins, Models, Current Status, and Challenges in Textual Emotion Recognition

Abid Hussain Wani[1(✉)] and Faezeh Mesrinejad[2]

[1] Department of Computer Science, University of Kashmir, South Campus, Anantnag, India
abid.wani@uok.edu.in
[2] Department of Information Science, Faculty of Management, University of Tehran, Tehran, Iran
fmesrinejad@ut.ac.ir

Abstract. Emotion Recognition in Text has received profound attention in recent years especially with the proliferation of the social media platforms and advancements in human-computer interaction. In the past decade, the research in this area has been propelled by the new developments in deep learning and multimodal integration. This article discusses affect detection in text and reviews recent work conducted in the field of automatic detection and classification of emotions in text. We also discuss how the opinion mining, sentiment analysis and emotion classification differ from each other. We delve into various theories and models of emotion recognition in text. Different approaches for recognizing emotions in text are discussed outlining their strengths and weaknesses. We discuss different contemporary approaches for emotion detection and outline the major challenges in the field.

Keywords: Emotion recognition · emotion theories · computational linguistics · deep learning

1 Opinion Mining, Sentiment Analysis and Emotion Classification

The domain of affect detection and analysis has received significant attention due to rapid increase in affect-rich textual data composed of reviews, recommendations, blogs, tweets etc. on the web, particularly social networking sites [1]. Automatic Emotion Recognition has vast applications in sentiment analysis, human-computer interactions, mental health monitoring, social media analysis and a number of other applications. Though a lot of progress has been made in this direction, researchers still confront a number of obstacles in this field. In this article, we will explore the origins, different models, current status, and the major challenges in the field of Textual Emotion Recognition. This section outlines the broader concepts of Opinion Mining, Sentiment Analysis and Emotion Classification. Section 2 covers different emotion models used by various researchers. Section 3 discusses different approaches to automatic emotion recognition in text. In Sect. 4, we outline the current status of progress made in automatic emotion detection and major challenges faced and finally Sect. 5 concludes this article.

Three terms which are predominant in the affect computing literature include opinion mining, sentiment analysis and emotion classification. In common usage, Opinions refer to what a person is thinking about something. According to Pang and Lee [2], an opinion encompasses a conclusive thought about something which is still open to dispute; which implies that different people can have very different opinions on a topic, based on different observation and evidence and is subject to change. Young [3] describes opinions as "rationalizations, explanations, and justifications". Fishbein and Ajzen [4] define opinion as the perception held by a subject towards an object that has certain features or is related to some other object.

Sentiments represent a feeling about something and can be positive, negative or neutral [5]. Although Sentiments and opinions are often used interchangeably due to the fact that much of the work on opinions has mostly taken into consideration the subjective part, often referred by some authors as sentiment [6]. A subtle distinction between them is that opinions are personal interpretations of observation or information and not always constrained by social norms, but sentiments are typically socially generated, formed, and maintained, which is why they are sometimes referred to as "settled opinions reflective of one's feeling[2]. Moreover, opinions are predominantly according to subjective or objective probabilities of observations and information about an event, person, situation or topic, whereas sentiments are mostly elicited by feelings. Thus, opinions represent personal interpretations of observation and information without the expressions necessarily being emotionally charged. The terms emotion and sentiment fundamentally differ in the way they are targeted towards an object and the time frame for which they are perceived. Not all emotions are directed at a specific object but generally the sentiments are generated and focused on an object [7]. On the same count, sentiments are more individualistic, stable and retained longer amount of time whereas emotions are often characterized by brief episodes of behavioural feelings [8] A number of authors in Computational Linguistics, constrain the definition of "sentiment analysis" to the specific application of classifying text (reviews, feedback, comments) according to its polarity (either positive or negative). Table 1 provides the definitions and the primary structural parts of Opinion Mining, Sentiment Analysis and Emotion Classification.

Table 1. Opinion Mining, Sentiment Analysis and Emotion Classification

Base term		Primary Structure
Term	Definition	Structural Components
Opinion	Opinion encompasses a conclusion which is not final but open to debate and subject to change	• Topic • Opinion holder • Claim
Sentiment	Sentiment suggests an enduring and settled disposition developed over time	• Sentiment Holder • Disposition • Object
Emotion	Emotion is a state of feeling usually accompanied by brief behavioural and autonomic changes directed towards a specific object	• Experiencer • Emotion experience • Target

2 Emotion Modelling

Recognition of emotions from text necessitates the adoption of an emotion model for their computational treatment The primary factor to be taken into account is how accurately models depict emotions. For emotion recognition, psychologists have suggested three major modelling approaches: (1) the categorical emotion modelling, (2) the dimensional modelling, and (3) the cognitive appraisal modelling [9]. A brief description of each of these is shown as follows:

2.1 Categorical Emotion Modelling

Emotions are represented using categorical modelling as distinct expressive classes that are domain-specific. According to D'Mello et al. [10] each emotion in categorical model is distinguished by a distinct set of characteristics and attributes that convey triggering conditions and/or responses/reactions. Ekman's six basic emotions—ANGER, DISGUST, FEAR, HAPPY, SAD, and SURPRISE—have been the subject of the majority of emotion recognition research to date [11]. Many academics contend, however, that affective computing should not be limited to the six fundamental emotions and that, depending on the field and the intended use, a different set of emotions should be considered. BOREDOM, CONFUSION, DELIGHT, FLOW, and FRUSTRATION are the five categories proposed by D'Mello et al. [13] to describe affect states in an intelligent tutoring system that facilitates learning by having a discussion in natural language with students. They contend that while students usually feel bored or confused, they hardly ever feel sad, afraid, or disgusted. As a result, numerous writers have suggested that domain-specific emotion categories are necessary. However, because there are so few labels, it has a number of drawbacks. For instance, the emotional categories are made up of distinct components, and it is common to see a wide range of feelings within each of these distinct categories. Because several emotions are lumped together under one category, there may be instances where classifications are insufficient to cover all feelings. Additionally, linguistic, contextual, cultural, or psychological variables might cause the same affective states to be expressed through various emotional categories, which can result in a low level of agreement between emotional categories. These results suggest that, despite the fact that the collection of emotion categories is specified, a representative set of them might not accurately describe different affective states. Furthermore, in certain situations, inadequate and thus incorrect conceptualization may lead to ineffective or suboptimal affect detection. Additionally, it may result in a forced-choice identification issue. Instead of identifying an emotion label on their own, the respondents are likely to discriminate among the categories that are offered, which may compel them to select an incorrect and irrelevant category. A more significant issue that is connected to the first one is that respondents may not always be able to choose the right category as it is not included in the set of predefined labels. As a result, when it comes to trying to pinpoint the exact emotional states that people perceive, a categorical model has the limits of figuring out intended emotion. When NEUTRAL emotion is included, for example, participants are unable to choose between the six basic emotions (ANGER, DISGUST, FEAR, HAPPY, SAD, and SURPRISE) even though they feel neutral and would like to. However, because of its ease of use, familiarity, and simplicity, the category model—which includes numerous variations—has become the most popular.

The Parrot's model [12] is another well-known categorical emotion model. It includes a tree structure of emotions with three levels and a set of six fundamental emotions: love, joy, surprise, anger, sadness, and fear. The granularity of the first level of this classification model is improved by these six emotions, and each level after that makes abstract emotions more tangible and fine-grained. The Parrot's model identifies more than 100 emotions, which are arranged in a list with a tree structure. The Parrot's model is thought to be the most sophisticated model for classifying emotions.

2.2 Dimensional Emotion Modelling

A dimensional model uses dimensions to depict feelings or affect states. According to this paradigm, emotional states are connected by a shared collection of metrics and are typically represented in a multidimensional space, usually two or three dimensions, where each emotion has a specific location. To date, several dimensional models have been put forth and examined [13, 14]. A well-known dimensional model that depicts emotions as arousal and valence combinations is Russell's model shown in Fig. 1. While the arousal dimension distinguishes between different stimulus intensities, such as aroused and calm (activated and deactivated) states, the valence dimension depicts positive and negative (pleasurable and unpleasant) feelings on opposite extremes of the spectrum. The conceptual similarity between two emotion categories increases with their proximity in the circumplex. Numerical data representing an emotion is generated the with regard to locations in the two-dimensional bipolar space (comprising of valence and arousal) in a set of coordinates, where the y-axis indicates the degree of arousal and the x-axis measures the valence, from negative to positive emotions. Some studies have made extensive use of the Russell's model [15, 16]. According to these findings, a fine-grained classification of sentiment and emotion can be obtained using the dimensional technique.

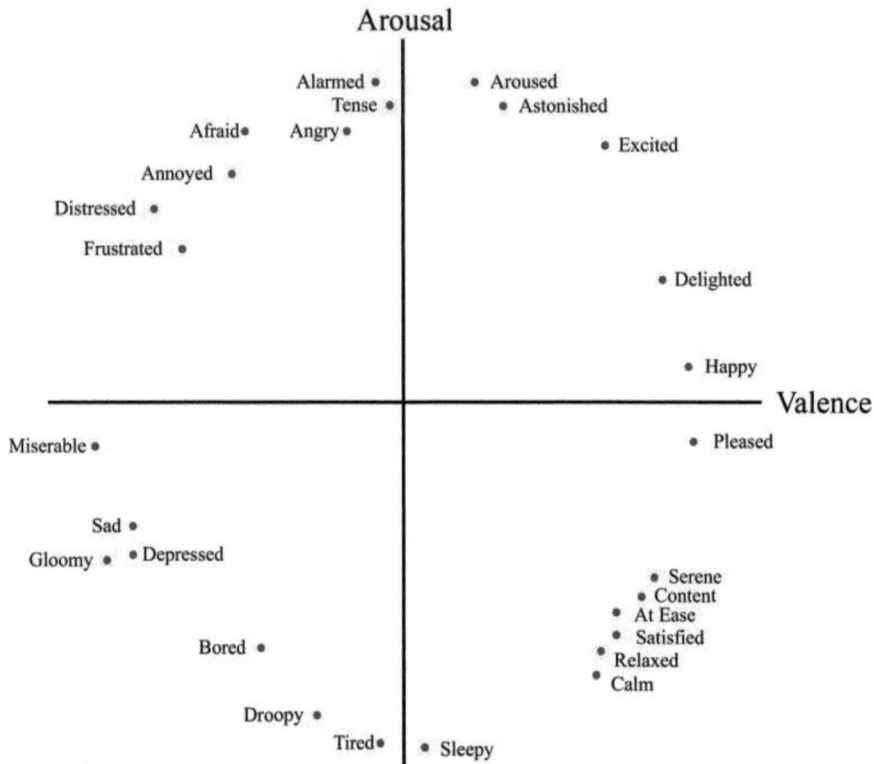

Fig. 1. Russell's circumplex model [17]

There are certain benefits of using emotion dimensions to model and depict emotional states. The fact that dimensional models are not associated with any specific emotional state such as sadness or surprise, is one of their main advantages. Rating is often used to identify two or three dimensions of emotional meaning. Emotion dimensions are able to represent delicate emotion notions that differ just a little from large emotion categories because of their gradual and continuous nature. As a result, dimensional emotion models can represent a wide variety of emotions, including highly specialized ones.

Specifically, the task of measuring the fully described emotional states is a good fit for a dimensional description. Additionally, the dimensional model takes a completely different approach than the categorical model in that it links emotional states in a dimensional space. The degree of similarity and dissimilarity of emotion categories can be measured automatically by a dimensional model; while the opposite categories on the space are obviously distinct from one another, the adjacent categories are rather similar. In conclusion, a dimensional emotion model is a means to compute the similarity across emotion states and is a suitable representation that captures the majority of the possible emotions.

2.3 Cognitive Appraisal Modelling

According to cognitive appraisal theory, an individual's emotional reaction to a circumstance, event, or object is determined or influenced by his or her evaluation (or appraisal) of it. The foundation of the cognitive appraisal emotion model is the idea that emotion has a deep and fundamental cognitive foundation [18]. Three key questions are addressed by cognitive appraisal theory: what are the fundamental traits and qualities inherent in the events being assessed or appraised; what emotions, if any, are felt as a result of this appraisal process; and what are the behavioural reactions to the emotions that are felt? In dimensional modelling, appraisals are the interpretations of distinctive components of events that combine to produce particular emotions, whereas the dimensions represent intrinsic aspects of emotions themselves. For example, players on a team who cheated to win can feel depressed instead of happy because winning a sporting event isn't always interpreted positively. Compared to the dimensional approach, the cognitive appraisals approach offers a more extensive, nuanced, and thorough approach to emotions. According to the cognitive appraisal approach, every emotion has a unique collection of assessment patterns.

A "core relational theme" underlying each distinct type of emotion, even though different people may have different opinions about a given incident or [19]. By describing the framework of cognition of 22 affect states, Ortony et al. established the foundation for the categorical perspective's inability to provide a collection using language structures to identify various textual emotions. Instead of emphasizing the vocabulary of emotion, their model focuses on evoking factors that could differentiate between different types of emotions. We call this approach the OCC model as depicted in Fig. 2. Three scenarios are predicated on these responses or triggering factors. a) objectives of pertinent events, b) responsible agent behaviour, or c) opinions about appealing or unappealing items. Three main branches make up the OCC model's hierarchical classification of emotions: feelings about the effects of events (like joy and pity), agent acts (like pride and rebuke), and characteristics of objects (like hatred and love). Furthermore, some branches come together to form a category called compound emotions, which includes feelings about the results of events brought on by agents' activities (such as thankfulness and rage).

The OCC model is consequently thought to be a suitable model for use in artificial agents since the concepts of events, actions, and objects are also used in agent models.

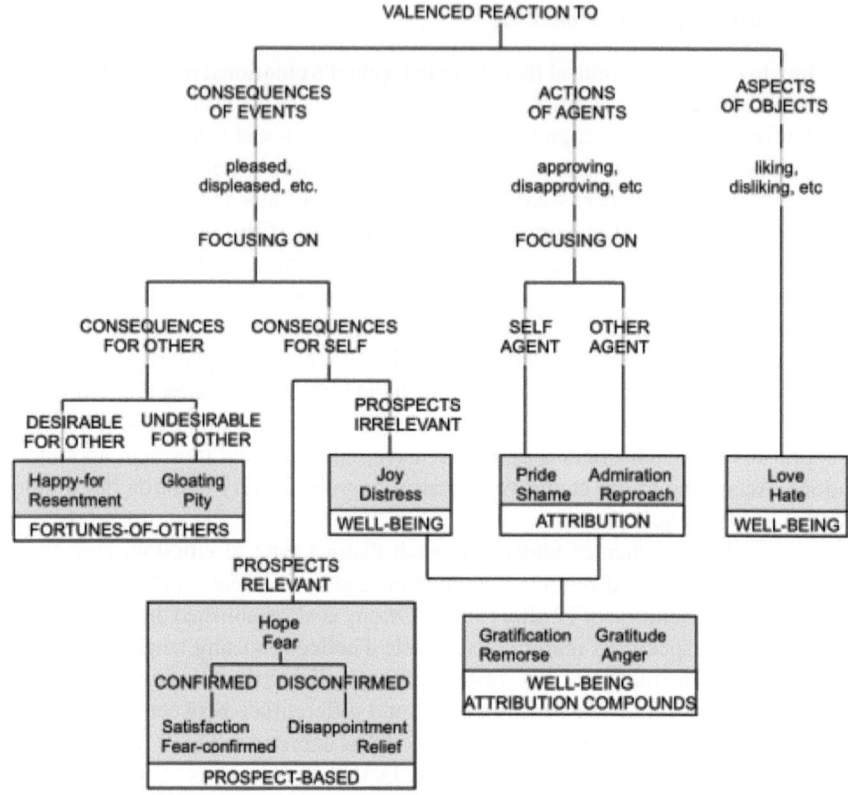

Fig. 2. OCC Model of Emotion [20]

3 Approaches to Emotion Detection in Text

The importance of emotions in human-computer interactions, where machines attempt to behave and act like humans so as to create humane and realistic exchanges with human users, has been steadily established over a period of time. Five prominent approaches to emotion recognition in text are: 1) keyword implied 2) lexicon-formed, 3) manually created rules, 4) knowledge-grounded, and 5) machine and deep learning-based. Evaluating the classification framework's performance is a crucial component of discussing various methods for detecting emotions in textual data. An emotion detection framework's performance is typically assessed by contrasting its predictions with corpora that contain the "correct" emotion labels, or gold standard data. Four standard measures are typically used to assess an emotion classification framework's performance:

1. Accuracy: Proportion of accurate emotion predictions
2. Precision: Proportion of the anticipated number of cases for an emotion that turn out to be accurate
3. Recall: Proportion of positive instances of an emotion that were accurately identified
4. F-score: Harmonic mean between recall and precision

3.1 Pure Keyword-Based Approach

An intuitive means to detect emotions in text is through simply spotting the keywords i.e., the affective or emotion-bearing words in text. This approach is referred to as Keyword Spotting or Keyword-based emotion detection. The fundamental premise of this strategy is keyword independence, and in its pure form it disregards the potential use of various keyword kinds (which was have opposite affect sense) concurrently to convey complex feelings. Nevertheless, this approach serves as the preliminary activity in many other emotion detection approaches. Traditionally this approach encompasses construction and development of a set of related words pertinent to all emotion labels. Once the set of words related to each emotion label is formed, we can systematically check for any affect expressed in a sentence. Keyword-based techniques involve two basic tasks: preprocessing texts to extract affective keywords and creating an emotional keyword dictionary. Most emotion detection parsers are pre-built software packages. Dictionary gathers keywords and relations among them and exhibits itself as a thesaurus. The major advantage of keyword spotting method is that it is quite straightforward and easy to develop and use however, because of its total dependence on presence of keywords for affect sense prediction it suffers from certain shortcomings. The first being ambiguity in keyword definitions; keywords can have many imprecise meanings. A number of words that represent specific emotion categories may have different meanings depending on how they are used and in what context. Furthermore, even the simplest combination of emotion-bearing keywords can transmit many emotional states in extreme circumstances such as satirical or disdainful statements. Secondly, it suffers from an inherent flaw of being incapable of identifying emotions in a sentence which is devoid of affect-bearing words. Many a times utterances with no emotion words are wrongly classified as neutral when infact they may convey a plausible affect decipher. Lastly since no regard is given to linguistic information, syntax structures and semantics (perspectives and stances are disregarded), less accurate emotion detection performance is achieved.

3.2 Lexicon-Based Approach

Lexicon-based approaches employ a lexicon to identify affect in textual utterances, as the name implies. A lexicon is a list of terms specific to a given language. A particular kind of lexicon that includes a list of words or lexemes associated with emotion is called an emotion lexicon. It is well recognized that lexicon-based techniques are simpler to apply than alternative strategies. This method of emotion detection is predicated on the idea that individual words are efficiently represented at the word level and have affinity for a specific emotion class.

The foundation of the lexicon-based approach consists of emotion lexicons. The quality and coverage of the chosen emotion lexicon have a significant impact on the performance of Lexicon-based systems [21]. Typically, in lexicon-based approach, we first extract emotion bearing words from text and then match them to an inventory of lexical terms. As is the norm with most text processing tasks, text is first tokenized then stemmed to return lexical and textual morphological variations of a term to their most basic structure before extraction of emotion bearing words. A number of scoring methods are available which can used to classify a given segment of text into a particular emotion category. Grefenstette, Qu, Shanahan, & Evans [22] using a corpus of newspaper articles calculated the affect score for an object by taking division of positive emotion word-count and negative word-count. Similarly, a corpus of tweets was used to calculate a representative affect score that takes into account the total count of positive and negative words. Subasic & Huettner [23] developed a more sophisticated lexicon by taking into account the fuzzy semantics of the words. An attempt to account for contextual information in the lexicon was made by incorporating metaphorical and modifying words (such as "very," "too," and "not") to the vocabulary. To find the word metaphors and modifiers, they employed the sentence's grammatical structure in the collection of texts. The results achieved showed a precision of 70% on random text, which is impressive.

Although lexicon-based approaches are often unable to handle more complicated linguistic makeup of text and perform badly when emotion words are rare or absent, they have undergone significant evolution over time. By using it on texts from many domains, those who advocate this approach to emotion recognition have conducted studies to prove its resilience. Based on studies, the average accuracy achieved with these enhanced procedures falls between 70% and 80%.

3.3 Manually Constructed Rules

In the manually built method to emotion detection, rules are employed to determine whether or not a textual utterance contains emotion. Usually, rules are formulated manually from a standard corpus: grammatical structures corresponding to each emotion type are identified based on a conceptual language framework, and these structures are then manually transformed into a set of rules that serve as the foundation for an identification engine. Usually, the rules are unique to the realm of the dataset utilized for rule formulation, and they typically deal with both lexical and semantic features.

Emotion detection using manually constructed rules approach came to its existence once the idea of rule-based expert systems flourished. A number of manually constructed rule-based methods construct sophisticated rule base to address the language's intricacy. To complement lexical rule base a number of approaches has been suggested. Similarly, Donath, Karahalios, & Viégas [24], developed a set of rules to identify statements in all uppercase letters, excessive punctuation, and foul language. In gauging the emotion affinity of a sentence, the importance of semantic information is paramount. The general structure of a semantic rule is < subject > < action > < object >. Initially, the OCC model, was put up as a basis for rule-driven frameworks, however, it lacked the linguistic details required to recognize emotions in text. A number of linguistic resources like ConceptNet, semantic parser, scored POS lists etc. were applied in order to associate the OCC concepts with the language indicators. Since there is an abundance of parsers nowadays, applying syntactic rules will not be too difficult, however, the linguistic implementation of semantic rules is quite involved and challenging. Determining all of the linguistic formulations of a notion becomes more challenging when the notion is more abstract.

3.4 Ontology-Based Approach

The construction of a machine-readable systematic description of affects is the foundation of the ontology-based method for recognizing emotions and classification. Ontology refers to "explicit description of cognition for a specific domain". Since the main goal of the researchers in this domain is to establish a comprehensive and universal collection of identifiers [25] that may assist with minimizing the ambiguity in determining the meaning of affect articulated in textual utterance, the introduction of ontology-based techniques for emotion recognition and classification has made a remarkable progress. While Balahur et al. showed how to create emotion ontologies using real-world, common-sense knowledge [26] suggested a basic affect ontology framed on Parrott's hierarchy. Using an ontology representation, appraisal theories characterized circumstances as "action chains" and the emotions that go along with them. An ontological framework called EmotiNet, was developed to identify subconsciously conveyed emotions. Whereas this ontology's foundation was created by hand, the concepts it contained were semi-automatically fed in by utilizing a variety of pre-existing knowledge sources. Although this framework provides a wider variety of information, it is also extremely complex. EmotiNet's accuracy for text emotion recognition is comparable to that of supervised learning techniques. The ontology-based approach suffers from the somewhat similar set of limitations as that of manually constructed rules, for the obvious reason that both operate at semantic level. The input text is first processed by semantic parser in order to align textual language components with an emotion ontology's associated concepts, which implies that the correctness of these approaches is significantly determined by how well the semantic parsers work. To build a comprehensive, consistent and complete ontology extensive efforts are needed which ultimately will provide standardization in the knowledge of emotions. Nevertheless, one serious shortcoming of ontology-based approach is that an ontology could not translate adequately to domains other than the one on which it is based upon as ontologies are inherently domain-specific.

3.5 Machine Learning and Deep Learning-Based Approach

The Learning-based approach employs trained classifier for emotion detection. Learning-based methods are primarily of two types: supervised and unsupervised. We utilize training data which is labelled with designated emotion classes in supervised learning. Unsupervised learning finds the emotional category of input text which is devoid of any labelled training examples (textual utterances).

Different researchers have used various units for the purpose of emotion analysis in text. The most dominant unit being a sentence. Also, classification has also been binary or multi-class. One example of binary classification is the designation of a statement as either emotional or non-emotional. Studies have either labelled textual expressions that contain multiple emotions as "mixed emotions" or allowed for the attachment of multiple labels to each sentence (also known as the multi-label classification problem) [27].

A major drawback of supervised emotion detection techniques is the requirement of a sufficiently large corpus of labelled training examples for classifier to work. Moreover, the classifiers trained on data from one domain generally do not scale well for other domains hence the need for annotating/emotion labelling the text for target domains. This task of emotions labelling is often very tedious and quite subjective. When emotion annotated corpus is available, typically supervised methods are preferred because of higher classification accuracy achievable with them. However, unsupervised learning methods emerge as a better alternative in absence of such a labelled training corpus. Unsupervised methods are also preferable in situations where the input text is devoid of clear emotion-conveying words. Unsupervised learning algorithm based on PMI-IR (Pointwise Mutual Information (PMI) and Information Retrieval) for classifying a review as recommended or not recommended by employing the similarity measure of pairs of words or phrases has been undertaken. One of the early attempts for unsupervised fine-grained emotion detection and classification was made by Strapparava & Mihalcea [28]. In their work, they employed SemEval 2007 task dataset and focused on using latent semantic analysis (LSA) to extract the semantic information to drive the classification algorithm. D'Mello et al.[29] employed latent semantic analysis for the recognition of affect states in students' conversation with the Autotutor. Agrawal & An [30] took this effort to next level by employing semantic information together with contextual information to effect the emotion classification. Agrawal & An evaluated their Pointwise Mutual Information (PMI)-based method on International Survey on Emotion Antecedents and Reactions (ISEAR) dataset, Alm's dataset and Aman's dataset and found the results were comparable to LSA-based methods. Linguistic aspects and sentiment dictionaries that yield polarities for words are employed in an unsupervised algorithm that automatically created a dictionary for each particular context. They employed Cornell Movie Review, Obama-McCain Debate and SemEval-2015 datasets to evaluate their proposed framework and the results obtained by them favourably compare with other affect detection approaches. Alejandro[31]pre-trained models like Bidirectional Encoder Representations from Transformers (BERT) show remarkable robustness to dataset quality disparities when compared with the models that are trained from scratch. Surolia et al. [32] used deep learning models like convolutional neural network (CNN), long short-term memory (LSTM), bidirectional long short-term memory (Bi-LSTM), and bidirectional encoder representations from transformers (BERT) on a dataset comprising of muti-label tweets, and reported better performance of Bi-LSTM over others.

4 Challenges and Future Directions

Although much progress has been achieved in the field of automatic emotion recognition from text, yet there remain a number of hurdles in this task. Dealing with textual utterances composed of sarcasm, irony, and implicit emotions is a challenge. Much of the issues still faced by researchers in emotion stem from the ambiguity and differential subjectivity of the textual utterances. Contextual complexities, shortage of good-quality datasets, incomplete emotional information in text and fuzzy emotional boundaries pose significant hurdles in recognition of emotions [33]. Focus on developing rich datasets and making them readily available to the research community would help in advancing the research on automatic emotion detection. For resource-scarce languages like Kashmiri, Gojri etc. this is particularly much needed intervention. The use of GAN-based techniques such as Text-GAN, SeqGAN has shown promising results to deal with oversampling and undersampling issues [34] providing an opportunity to deal with emotion detection in resource-scarce languages. As is true for any system, one of most desirable features in textual emotion detection is its robustness. It is noteworthy to note that in developing robust emotion detection system for text that Graph Convolution Network (GCN), which encompasses multi-layer neural network generates embedding vectors for nodes as per the characteristics of the surrounding regions. This property of GCN can use a range of state-of-the-art text embedding and classification algorithms to generate reliable text classification findings and create predictive document annotators [35]. The use of explainable AI (XAI) taking into account the basis and trigger as proposed in [36] can be studied for recognition of different types of emotions especially for deep learning-based emotion analysis models which are rather difficult to understand. Table 2 outlines the major challenges faced by researchers in emotion detection from text and Table 3 lists the future directions in the field.

Table 2. Major Challenges in automatic emotion detection from text

Challenge	Description
Ambiguity of Language	Words or phrases can have multiple meanings, making emotion detection difficult
Context Dependency	Emotions can change depending on the surrounding text or conversation history
Sarcasm and Irony	Detection of sarcasm and irony remains a major obstacle in accurate classification
Domain Dependence	Models often fail to generalize well across different domains or topics
Multilingualism	Handling multiple languages with equal accuracy is still a big challenge
Data Scarcity	High-quality annotated datasets for emotions are limited and expensive to obtain
Label Subjectivity	Emotion annotations are subjective, leading to inconsistencies in labeling
Emotion Intensity Detection	Capturing the intensity or degree of emotion is harder than just classifying emotion categories
Model Interpretability	Current models often lack transparency in how they make predictions
Ethical Concerns	Handling sensitive or emotional data raises concerns around privacy and misuse
Ambiguity of Language	Words or phrases can have multiple meanings, making emotion detection difficult

Table 3. Future Directions for emotion detection in text

Future Directions	Description
Context-Aware Models	Develop models that understand and utilize broader context (e.g., conversation history)
Multimodal Integration	Combine text with audio and visual data to improve emotion detection accuracy
Cross-Lingual Emotion Detection	Enable emotion detection across languages using shared multilingual representations
Transfer Learning and Pretraining	Use pre-trained language models and adapt them to emotion detection tasks
Emotion Intensity Regression	Shift from classification to regression models to capture nuanced emotional intensity
Real-time Emotion Detection	Create lightweight models capable of detecting emotions in real-time applications
Ethical and Fair AI	Ensure models are free from bias and respect ethical considerations
Low-resource Language Support	Develop emotion detection tools for underrepresented languages
Interactive Emotion Systems	Enable systems to interact and respond based on detected user emotions
Explainable AI (XAI)	Make model decisions interpretable to end-users and researchers
Context-Aware Models	Develop models that understand and utilize broader context (e.g., conversation history)
Multimodal Integration	Combine text with audio and visual data to improve emotion detection accuracy
Cross-Lingual Emotion Detection	Enable emotion detection across languages using shared multilingual representations

5 Conclusion

A distinction between the concepts of Opinion Mining, Sentiment Analysis and Emotion Classification is brought forth. Different theories of emotions and emotion modelling are discussed. A number of approaches both traditional and state-of the-art for emotion identification are systematically reviewed in this study. It specifically looks into strengths and weaknesses of each of these approaches and brings forth a study on different machine and deep learning methods, accessible datasets, application domains, and assessment measures. The review's findings indicate that ML and DL-based emotion detection is receiving more attention than traditional ones. In order to improve the creation of systems possessing emotional intelligence and having a 'human-touch', the study also emphasized difficulties, gaps, and potential avenues for further study in computational treatment of emotions.

References

1. Clavel, C., Callejas, Z.: Sentiment analysis: from opinion mining to human-agent interaction. IEEE Trans. Affect. Comput. **7**, 74–93 (2016). https://doi.org/10.1109/TAFFC.2015.2444846
2. Pang, B., Lee, L.: Opinion mining and sentiment analysis. Found. Trends R Info. Retriev. **2**, 1–2 (2008). https://doi.org/10.1561/1500000001
3. Young, K.: Social Psychology: An analysis of Social Behavior. Alfred. A. Knopf, New York (1930)
4. Fishbein, M., Ajzen, I.: Attitudes and opinions. Ann. Rev. Psychol. **23**, 487–544 (1972). https://doi.org/10.1146/annurev.ps.23.020172.002415
5. Pak, A., Paroubek, P.: Twitter as a corpus for sentiment analysis and opinion mining. LREc. **10** (2010)
6. Kim, S.-M., Hovy, E.: Determining the sentiment of opinions. In: Proceedings of the 20th international conference on Computational Linguistics - COLING '04, pp. 1367-es. Association for Computational Linguistics, Morristown, NJ, USA (2004). https://doi.org/10.3115/1220355.1220555
7. Russell, J.A., Barrett, L.F.: Core affect, prototypical emotional episodes, and other things called emotion: dissecting the elephant. J. Pers. Soc. Psychol. **76**, 805–819 (1999)
8. Ben-Ze'ev, A.: The subtlety of emotions. MIT Press (2000)
9. Watson, L., Spence, M.T.: Causes and consequences of emotions on consumer behaviour. Eur. J. Mark. **41**, 487–511 (2007). https://doi.org/10.1108/03090560710737570
10. D'Mello, S.K., Craig, S.D., Witherspoon, A., McDaniel, B., Graesser, A.: Automatic detection of learner's affect from conversational cues. User Model User-adapt Interact. **18**, 45–80 (2008). https://doi.org/10.1007/s11257-007-9037-6
11. Ekman, P.: An argument for basic emotions. Cogn. Emot. (1992). https://doi.org/10.1080/02699939208411068
12. Parrott, W.G.: Emotions in Social Psychology: Essential Readings - Google Books. Psychology Press (2001)
13. Mehrabian, A.: Pleasure-arousal-dominance: a general framework for describing and measuring individual differences in temperament. Curr. Psychol. **14**, 261–292 (1996). https://doi.org/10.1007/BF02686918
14. Plutchik, R.: A psychoevolutionary theory of emotions. Soc. Sci. Inf. **21**, 529–553 (1982). https://doi.org/10.1177/053901882021004003
15. Perikos, I., Hatzilygeroudis, I.: Recognizing emotions in text using ensemble of classifiers. Eng. Appl. Artif. Intell. **51**, 191–201 (2016). https://doi.org/10.1016/J.ENGAPPAI.2016.01.012
16. Wang, J., Yu, L.-C., Lai, K.R., Zhang, X.: Dimensional Sentiment Analysis Using a Regional CNN-LSTM Model (2016)
17. Russell, J.A.: A circumplex model of affect. J. Pers. Soc. Psychol. **39**, 1161–1178 (1980). https://doi.org/10.1037/h0077714
18. Ortony, A., Clore, G.L., Collins, A.: The Cognitive Structure of Emotions. Cambridge University Press (1989). https://doi.org/10.2307/2074241
19. Lazarus, R.: Emotion and adaptation. Oxford University Press (1991)
20. Picard, R.W.: Affective computing. MIT Press (1997)
21. Neviarouskaya, A., Prendinger, H., Ishizuka, M.: Affect analysis model: novel rule-based approach to affect sensing from text. Nat. Lang. Eng. **17**, 95–135 (2011). https://doi.org/10.1017/S1351324910000239
22. Grefenstette, G., Qu, Y., Shanahan, J.G., Evans, D.A.: Coupling niche browsers and affect analysis for an opinion mining application. In: RIAO '04 Coupling approaches, coupling media and coupling languages for information retrieval, pp. 186–194. LE CENTRE

DE HAUTES ETUDES INTERNATIONALES D'INFORMATIQUE DOCUMENTAIRE, Vaucluse, France (2004)
23. Subasic, P., Huettner, A.: Affect analysis of text using fuzzy semantic typing. IEEE Trans. Fuzzy Syst. **9**, 483–496 (2001). https://doi.org/10.1109/91.940962
24. Donath, J, Karahalios, K., Viégas, F.: Visualizing conversation J. Comput. Mediat. Commun. **4** (2006). https://doi.org/10.1111/j.1083-6101.1999.tb00107.x
25. Balahur, A., Hermida, J.M., Montoyo, A.: Detecting implicit expressions of emotion in text: a comparative analysis. Decis. Support. Syst. **53**, 742–753 (2012). https://doi.org/10.1016/j.dss.2012.05.024
26. Shivhare, S.N., Khethawat, S.: Emotion detection from text. http://arxiv.org/abs/1205.4944, (2012)
27. Aman, S., Szpakowicz, S.: Identifying expressions of emotion in text. In: Text, Speech and Dialogue, pp. 196–205 (2007). https://doi.org/10.1007/978-3-540-74628-7_27
28. Strapparava, C., Mihalcea, R.: Learning to identify emotions in text. In: Proceedings of the 2008 ACM Symposium on Applied Computing - SAC '08, p. 1556 (2008). https://doi.org/10.1145/1363686.1364052
29. Mello, S.K.D., Craig, S.D., Witherspoon, A., Mcdaniel, B.: Automatic detection of learner' s affect from conversational cues. User Model User-adapt Interact. **1**, 45–80 (2008). https://doi.org/10.1007/s11257-007-9037-6
30. Agrawal, A., An, A.: Unsupervised emotion detection from text using semantic and syntactic relations. In: 2012 IEEE/WIC/ACM International Conferences on Web Intelligence and Intelligent Agent Technology, pp. 346–353. IEEE (2012). https://doi.org/10.1109/WI-IAT.2012.170
31. de León Languré, A., Zareei, M.: Improving text emotion detection through comprehensive dataset quality analysis. IEEE Access. **12**, 166512–166536 (2024). https://doi.org/10.1109/ACCESS.2024.3491856
32. Surolia, A., Mehta, S., Kumaraguru, P.: Deep learning and transfer learning to understand emotions: a PoliEMO dataset and multi-label classification in Indian elections. Int J Data Sci Anal. (2025). https://doi.org/10.1007/s41060-025-00738-7
33. Kusal, S., Patil, S., Choudrie, J., Kotecha, K., Vora, D.: Transfer learning for emotion detection in conversational text: a hybrid deep learning approach with pre-trained embeddings. Int. J. Inf. Technol. (2024). https://doi.org/10.1007/s41870-024-02027-1
34. Werner de Vargas, V., Schneider Aranda, J.A., dos Santos Costa, R., da Silva Pereira, P.R., Victória Barbosa, J.L.: Imbalanced data preprocessing techniques for machine learning: a systematic mapping study. Knowl. Inf. Syst. **65**, 31–57 (2023). https://doi.org/10.1007/s10115-022-01772-8
35. Firdaus, M., Singh, G.V., Ekbal, A., Bhattacharyya, P.: Affect-GCN: a multimodal graph convolutional network for multi-emotion with intensity recognition and sentiment analysis in dialogues. Multimed Tools Appl. **82**, 43251–43272 (2023). https://doi.org/10.1007/s11042-023-14885-1
36. Li, Y., Chan, J., Peko, G., Sundaram, D.: An explanation framework and method for AI-based text emotion analysis and visualisation. Decis. Support. Syst. **178**, 114121 (2024). https://doi.org/10.1016/j.dss.2023.114121

Deep Learning Approaches for Iris Damage Prediction Using CNN and Image Processing

S. Sangeetha[1(✉)] and R. Sujatha[2]

[1] Department of Computer Science, PSG College of Arts & Science (Autonomous) (Affiliated to Bharathiar University), Coimbatore 641014, Tamil Nadu, India
sangeemphil@gmail.com

[2] Department of Information Technology, PSG College of Arts & Science (Autonomous) (Affiliated to Bharathiar University), Coimbatore 641014, Tamil Nadu, India
sujatha@psgcas.ac.in

Abstract. Iris damage prediction plays an important role in ophthalmology, assisting in the identification and prevention of eye impairments. This paper examines a deep learning–based approach using Convolutional Neural Networks (CNN) and advanced image processing techniques to improve the accuracy of iris damage classification. The image is qualified for improved iris data recording, exploiting attribute extraction and enhancement approaches to attain accuracy in identifying irregularities. Essential elements of this study depend on the work of Casia et al. Provide notably to iris feature extraction using machine learning; our system combines data enrichment, reduced noise and difference enhancement strategies to enhance the strength of the image. Investigation findings illustrate a significant increase in prediction accuracy contrasted with conventional methods, emphasizing the effectiveness of CNN in medical imaging applications. The results of this study have implications for automated ophthalmic features, facilitating live iris health assessment and preventive measures.

Keywords: Convolutional Neural Network (CNN) · image processing · deep learning · ophthalmology · feature extraction · medical imaging

1 Introduction

In eyesight, governing pupil entry into the eye and aiding in clear image formation are vital roles of the human iris. However, various diseases, trauma, and external factors can lead to iris damage, possibly impacting the sharpness of vision and overall eye health. Identifying such damage at an initial stage is important for averting issues and facilitates prompt medical treatment. The iris is a collection of intricate muscular and vascular structures that regulate pupil enlargement and compression. Any interruption in these structures because of disorders like aniridia, irido corneal endothelial syndrome or pigment dispersion syndrome may result in disability. Conventional diagnostic techniques depend on ophthalmic inspection and imaging methods such as slit-lamp biomicroscopy and anterior segment optical coherence tomography (AS-OCT). However, sight recognition of iris anomalies is frequently gradual, subjective and error-prone.

Modern innovation in deep-learning, specifically Convolutional Neural Networks (CNN), has modified medical imaging interpretation by facilitating automated and precise classification of ocular diseases. Leveraging past achievements in retinal and fundus image analysis, this paper presented a CNN-based method for predicting iris damage using advanced image processing methods. The absorption of attribute extraction, noise reduction, and emphasizing disparities underscore the model's ability to detect implicit pattern abnormalities in iris images accurately.

Through manipulating CNN models trained on close-up iris datasets, this study aims to offer an effective, computerized analysis tool that supports ophthalmologists in identifying iris damage at an initial stage. The suggested system assures strong, live detection, decreasing dependence on practical explanation and facilitating improved ophthalmic disease management.

Review of Related Literature Saleh (2023) examined the impact of eye diseases on iris segmentation and recollection performance using a deep model based on transfer learning. This research brings a novel iris segmentation model that includes radiance correction and a modified circular Hough transform, followed by a post-processing step to minimize false positives. A verified data set is built to analyze segmentation accuracy. Various deep learning models, including GoogleNet, Inception_ResNet, XceptionNet, EfficientNet and ResNet50, are used for iris recognition through transfer learning. The CASIA V3 interval dataset was used to essentially condition the model, which was previously fine-tuned using the diseased eye dataset from Warsaw Bio Base V1 and V2. Experimental results show that the identification effect has the best accuracy, 98.5% and 97.26%, respectively, and was achieved using the ResNet50 model with two layers of transfer learning. Research results show that eye diseases mostly affect segmentation instead of recognition, and structural changes such as blood eyes and iris pigmentation partially affect recognition. A comparative study confirms the dominance of the proposed method over existing methods on the same dataset.

Liu et al. (2021) introduced an efficient iris recognition algorithm applying a novel compressed 2-channel deep Convolutional neural network (2-ch CNN) to achieve high accuracy with minimal training samples. The proposed method combines a multi-branch CNN with three online enhancement schemes. The Radial attention layer enhances iris classification performance. To optimize efficiency, the model performs branch and channel pruning by analyzing weight distributions, reducing computational complexity while maintaining accuracy. In addition, a fast fine-tuning process is applied further to refine the pruned Convolutional Neural Network (CNN) and improve the recognition ability. The study also explores the encoding capabilities of 2-channel Convolutional Neural Networks, making them applicable to large-scale iris databases. Gradient-based analysis confirms the algorithm's strength in image contamination. Experimental evaluation on three public iris databases shows its superior performance, validating the approach for instant biometric authentication. This research contributes to the advancement of lightweight and effective iris recognition models.

Lee et al. (2021) explored a significant iris scanning method leveraging a Generative Adversarial Network (GAN)-based image regeneration way to enhance the quality of iris images in difficult circumstances. The study handled problems like optical and motion blur, side views and mirror-like reflections, which diminish recognition performance when images are captured in unrestricted regions. The explored technique includes deep-learning-based sharpening methods to improve iris clarity, specifically in optical images obtained from Android phone cameras. Furthermore, the recognition performance was further enhanced by combining identification scores from periocular areas using a Support Vector Machine (SVM) classifier. The approach was evaluated using the booming iris challenge evolution part 2 training database and MICHE database, illustrating improved performance contrasted with state-of-the-art techniques. The research emphasizes the efficiency of GAN-based reconstruction in enhancing iris images and underscores biometric identification precisely in obstructive situations.

Jayadev and Bellary (2021) conducted a mixed method for classifying and detecting iris injury levels in alcoholics using a transformed Deep Learning Network (MDLNN). The research aimed to improve precision and decrease processing time compared to established approaches. Various pattern removal techniques, including Log Gabor (LG), histogram of Oriented Gradients (HOG), GLAC, LGXP and Canny Edge Detection (CED), were working on the iris images of alcoholics. Bacterial Foraging Optimization (BFO) was applied for feature selection, followed by MDLNN classification, which was divided into three steps: more, medium, or less drunk. Adaptive Histogram Equalization (AHE) was working to improve distinctness, while Hybrid Gaussian Bandpass Filter and discrete Wavelet Transform (HGBFDWT) enhanced the highlight details. The division process was experienced using Otsu Thresholding and Morphological Operations (OTMO). The level of iris injury was measured by calculating the Euclidean distance among the original and divided iris images. Experimental outputs illustrated a high level of precise over-functioning techniques, validating the efficiency of the suggested method in evaluating alcohol- influence iris damage.

Alkuzaay and Alshemmary (2020) explored an iris recognition pattern, IRISNet, utilizing deep Convolutional neural network (CNN) for automated pattern extraction and classification unnecessary for field expertise. The structure improves high resolution, separates the iris using cartesian-to-polar coordinate transformation, and retains CNN layers for pattern identification, succeeded by a softmax layer for classification. Backpropagation and Adam optimization methods were applied for effective learning and weight updates. The pattern was tried on the IITD 6 iris database, achieving an identification rate of 97.32% for source images and 96.43% for standardized images. Compared to conventional distinguished systems such as SVM, KNN, DT, and NB, IRISNet showed higher performance.

Furthermore, the system exposed quick identification time, taking less than one second per individual. The study emphasizes the strength of CNNs in biometric identification, highlighting their efficiency in image analysis patterns. The outputs contribute to advancements in robust identification verification systems.

Understanding the Iris and Its Significance The iris is a circular, coloured structure in the human eye that regulates the volume of photoreception by alternating the scale of the pupil. It is made up of muscle cells that bond and flesh out to luminance. The colour and composition of the iris are uncommon to everybody; it is an important feature for biometric identification. Besides biological function, the iris has accumulated importance in biological study, protection systems and artificial intelligence-based biometric verification. Any impairment or anomalies in the iris can impair sight and imply medical conditions like glaucoma, diabetic retinopathy or eye trauma.

Significance of Iris Detection and Damage Analysis Identifying iris damage is important for examination, biometric identification and forensic studies. In medical management, the initial identification of iris anomalies helps in ophthalmology and protects eyesight. In protection systems, biometric identification by iris is applied in biometric verification, as iris features endure constantly throughout one's life. Analyzing injured irises is important for identifying injuries, infections, or genetic diseases that could impair eyesight. In forensics, iris analysis aids in inquiry and identifying individuals. By incorporating CNN and image analyses, iris damage prediction has been optimized, enhancing the accuracy of medical ramifications.

2 Iris Detection Using Image Processing

1. **Image Acquisition and preprocessing**

Iris damage detection involves obtaining sharp visuals and iris images using biometric sensors or special cameras designed for accurate image acquisition, and these are the initial stages of detection. These images must be of adequate clearness to allow for precise feature extraction and analysis. Hence, unrefined images frequently contain sounds; differences in illumination and changing pre-treatment methods are adapted to improve image quality. Greyscale conversion acts to diminish processing overhead; however, improvement and sound reduction enhance resolution by excluding extraneous data. This process ensures that the data record used for analysis is stable, clear, and appropriate for feature derivation, facilitating the CNN model to differentiate between healthy and damaged irises effectively.

2. **Segmentation of iris region**

To ensure precise detection of iris damage, division methods are used to separate the iris area from the pupil and sclera. This action is important because irrelevant information can anxiously impact results. Developed division methods like Hough Transform and active contour models are often used for accurate placement. These methods aid in contouring the edge of the pupil and separating it from the bounding region, assuring that only the appropriate iris area is determined by impairment analysis. Precise division improves the efficiency of later image analysis methods by concentrating on relevant iris features, enhancing overall accuracy.

3. **Feature Extraction for Anomaly Detection**

Feature extraction techniques will be applied when the iris region is accurately and successfully segmented. This technique is used to identify characteristics of the iris that indicate possible damage. It extracts features such as texture patterns, edge structure and colour variations, which are essential for differentiating between healthy and damaged iris. For this feature extraction, various image processing methods are used, such as Gabor filters, Wavelet Transform and Local Binary Patterns (LBP). These methods highlight the important textural differences and structural details within the iris and make it easier for the CNN model to learn and detect lesions, deformations and pigmentation inconsistencies. This step plays a significant role in enhancing the model's classification ability, ensuring that it can effectively identify minor anomalies that indicate iris damage (Fig. 1).

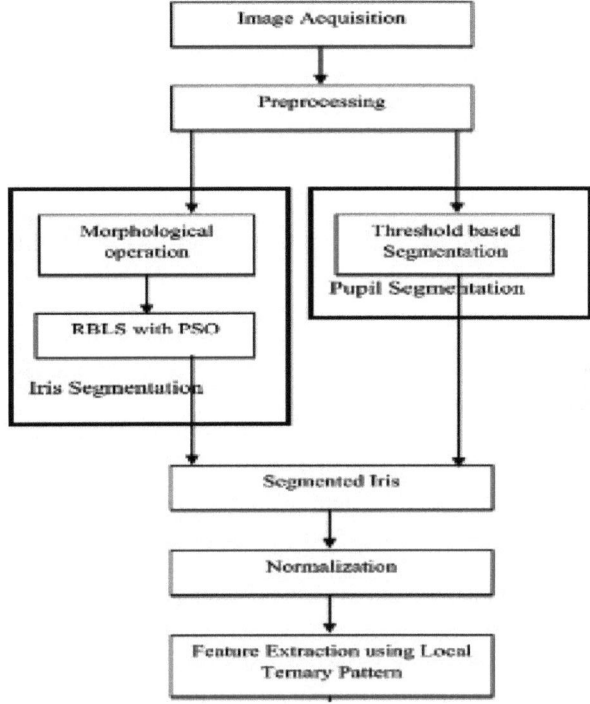

Fig. 1. Block diagram of the proposed iris recognition system (IA → PP → {MO + RBLS–PSO / TBS-PS} → SI → NORM → FE-LTP

Implementation System Requirements for Detection Process in Iris Damage Prediction

1. Hardware Requirements

Processor: Intel Core i7 or higher/AMD Ryzen 7 or higher
RAM: Minimum 16 GB (Recommended: 32 GB for datasets)
GPU: NVIDIA GTX 1080 or higher (Recommended: RTX 3060 0r higher for deep learning acceleration)
Storage: SSD with at least 512 GB of free space (Recommended: 1TB SSD for handling large image datasets)
Camera/Sensor: High-resolution biometric iris scanner or HD Camera

2. Software Requirements:

Operating System: Windows 10/11, Linux (Ubuntu 20.04+), or macOS

Programming Language: Python 3.7 or later
Deep Learning Frameworks: TensorFlow 2.x, PyTorch
Image Processing libraries: OpenCV, PIL, Scikit-image
Database (Optional for Storage): MySQL, PostgreSQL, or MongoDB
Development Environment: Jupiter Notebook, PyCharm, or VS Code

3. **Additional Dependencies**

Numpy, Panda, Matplotlib, Seaborn (for data handling and visualization)
Flask/Django (for GUI-based deployment if required)
CUDA Toolkit (for GPU acceleration in deep learning models)

3 Proposed Solution for Iris Damage Prediction Using CNN and Image Processing

Proposed Approach A CNN-based model will be developed that combines advanced image processing techniques to strengthen image analysis and pre-processing. This model improves the accuracy and efficiency of iris damage detection. This new approach involves the process of collecting datasets, pre-processing data collection and analyzing various iris datasets. It ensures a strong and effective model for iris damage prediction. The new CNN model will detect different abnormalities and structural changes in the iris with high precision by combining deep learning, image enhancement techniques and feature extraction.

The proposed methodology will start with the collection of high-quality iris images from biometric datasets. After collecting datasets, pre-processing techniques such as black-and-white conversion, noise reduction, edge sharpening, and partitioning were used to improve the clarity and image quality. Edge detection and texture analysis will be applied to highlight significant features before feeding the images into the CNN model. A multiple dataset of iris images will be trained by using the CNN model. Also CNN model learns to address various types of iris damage, lesions, minor deformations and major irregularities. The new CNN model will automate the feature extraction by composing multiple layers followed by pooling layers to decrease the size of the image while maintaining the necessary details. For non-linear patterns and classification processes, the CNN model utilizes activation functions such as ReLU and Softmax. Further, this model will undergo methods such as wide hyper-parameter tuning, data segmentation and optimization to develop its generalization and capability. It is examined against performance measures like accuracy, precision, recall and F1-score to validate its efficiency.

Additionally, this approach includes various techniques such as comparative analysis, support vector machines (SVM), and forest classifiers. These techniques will display the superiority of CNN accuracy in detection, speed and reliability. The final CNN model will be ready and tested on original iris images to confirm its robustness and adaptability to different conditions. The combination of real-time iris prediction and real-time reporting features will make the system highly efficient. This proposed model will be used practically in medical diagnostics, biometric security, and forensic investigations.

Support Vector Machines (SVM) It is an authoritatively managed machine learning algorithm used mainly for classification and feature identification tasks. Due to its strong mathematical foundation and generalized ability, it is frequently used in feature recognition, image processing and biometric identification. The core idea, since SVM, is to find the optimal hyperplane that best separates different classes in a multi-faceted feature space. This is served in identifying aid vectors, which are the information nearest points to the hyperplane and are important in outlining the dividing line. By increasing the margin among different classes, SVM assures a wide-ranging pattern, enhancing its ability to classify unseen information precisely. This pattern makes SVM specifically useful in biometric applications like iris recognition, face identification, and graphology, where notable details are important (Fig. 2).

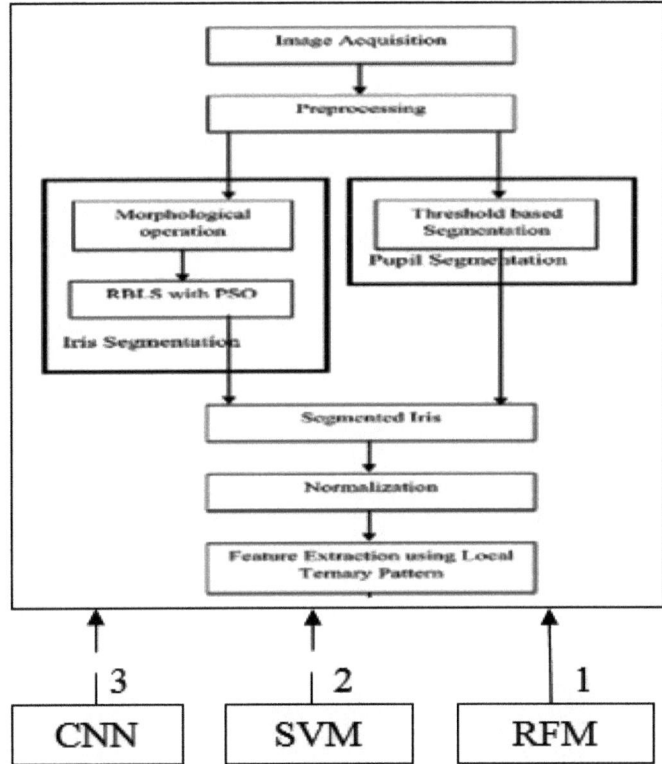

Fig. 2. Block Diagram of the Iris Recognition System Architecture

The peculiar pattern of SVM is its ability to handle both linearly and non-linearly divisible data. When handling linearly divisible data, SVM builds a clear hyperplane to divided sections. However, real-life data records frequently contain coincide and intricate details that demand a more refined strategy. To deal with this, kernel functions are used to transform the input space into a high-order representation, where a linear division becomes attainable. Similarity kernel functions include polynomial, radial basis function (RBF) and sigmoid kernels, every one of which helps map intricate relationships among pieces of information. This kernel trick makes SVM a versatile tool for handling a vast number of classification issues, including text classification, genetic expression analysis, and radiology.

RFM Random forest is a strong collection learning algorithm broadly used for categorization and relationship analysis tasks. It is connected to the concept of classification trees, where groups of trees are built to make a shared decision, lessen the threat of over-lifting and improve complete precision. The random forest method RFM is activated by establishing a huge number of classification trees and collecting their results to form the final prognosis. Every tree is trained on an unstructured subset of the information, a method known as bootstrapping, assuring multiplicity in determining. The final result is determined by a majority voting system for categorization tasks or aggregating predictions in regression issues.

The ability to manage high dimensional data with multiple patterns, making it efficient for complex classification tasks like iris damage identification, medical diagnosis and biometric detection, is one of its key strengths. Diverse individual classification trees, which are inclined to over-lift, and random forests alleviate this problem by joining the outputs of multiple trees, assuring general and strengthened predictions. It is specifically efficient. When handling uneven data records, it can allocate a large significance to diminished classes, enhancing comprehensive fairness. Furthermore, Random Forest handles absent information effectively, making it flexible for real-life applications where insufficient information is average.

Data Collection The very first step in the process of developing an accurate iris damage prediction system is assembling an extensive dataset of labelled iris images that represent various types of damage. The data that we collect from different sources should be a healthy iris, mildly damaged and severely damaged iris. So, the CNN will effectively classify the given dataset. The dataset must follow the criteria of a diverse dataset; the image should be captured under various lighting conditions, angles, and camera resolutions to improve the model's generalization ability. So, this model can effectively handle real-world scenarios and occlusions. To enhance the training data, the datasets are used from publicly available biometric dataset images and obtained iris images from the hospital sector.

Pre-processing Pre-processing techniques play an important role in reducing noise, improving contrast, and enhancing the clarity and quality of the iris images. The following methods are used to standardize the dataset: black-white conversion, noise reduction, histogram equalization, and normalization. Following segmentation algorithms such as active contour models or hough transfer are used to separate the exact iris region from the pupil and sclera and remove unwanted artefacts. This algorithm ensures that only the most relevant part of the image is recognized, and as a result, accuracy and feature extraction are improved. Well-preprocessed images will help minimize distortions and improve CNN performance in learning critical iris damage patterns.

Model Training The next step is to develop and train an optimized CNN for iris damage prediction. The CNN model is established with multiple convolutional layers for feature extraction and size reduction and fully connected layers for classification. Hyperparameters such as learning rate, batch size, age, era and period are tuned to increase accuracy. Using preprocessing data, the model is trained, allowing them to learn complex patterns and textures in damaged iris. Data augmentation techniques used to improve the model's robustness include flipping, rotation and brightness adjustments.

Evaluation In the evaluation process, the effectiveness and reliability of the CNN model are calculated. Its performance is compared with that of Support Vector Machines and the Random Forest method. The CNN model's performance is measured by the assessment metrics such as accuracy, precision, recall, and F1-score. A high accuracy score highlights the model's correct prediction of various iris images. The high precision value indicates that false positives are minimized, and a recall value shows that false negatives are minimized. Some additional improvements may be needed, which will involve hyper-parameter optimization, fine-tuning of CNN layers, and adding more training data. Through these improvements, accuracy and adaptability can improve for real-world applications.

Expected Outcomes Below is the Iris damage prediction using CNN and an image processing diagram.

1. Normal Iris- A healthy iris representation (Grade 0)
2. Damaged Iris – An iris with detected anomalies (dark spots) (Grade 1)
3. Detected Damaged (Edge)- Edge detection processed the image to highlight the affected area (Grade 2)

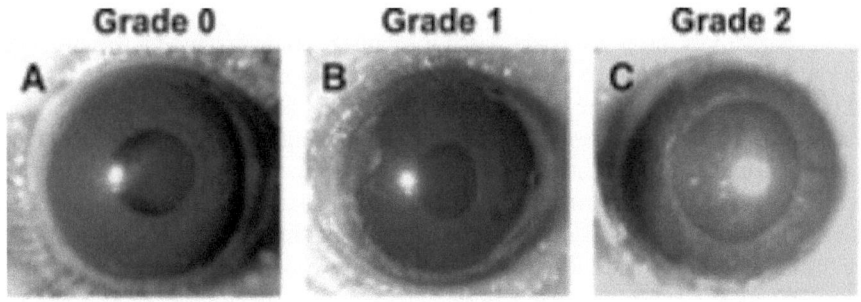

Model Performance A newly proposed model is designed to achieve accuracy, precision, recall and F1-score. This CNN-based iris damage detection model is more effective than convolutional machine learning techniques. The model can automatically detect complicated iris patterns and abnormalities by leveraging deep learning and advanced image processing. This will ensure the accurate classification of iris damage detection. The CNN model is expected to decrease false positives and false negatives and improve reliability in real-world applications through strict training on a different dataset. Further improvements can be made by integrating feature extraction, segmentation and classification techniques. And its ability to differentiate between healthy, mildly damaged and severely damaged irises with superlative capability.

Comparison Results The CNN model was developed to demonstrate superior accuracy and reliability compared to traditional machine learning models like Support Vector Machines (SVM) and Random Forest Classifiers. CNN automatically learns hierarchical patterns, which makes them more adaptable to variations in lighting, occlusions, and iris texture, unlike convolutional methods that rely on manually extracted features. Key metrics such as accuracy, recall and precision will validate the effectiveness of the CNN model over SVM and Random Forest. It also provides the ability to generalize iris datasets better. These results will show CNN's scalability, robustness and real-world applicability in iris damage detection.

Clinical Relevance The combination of a CNN-based iris-damaged detection system and medical diagnostics will provide ophthalmologists and healthcare professionals. These professionals can have advanced tools for early iris detection and accurate analysis of iris abnormalities. This model will develop diagnostic accuracy, reduce human error and accelerate treatment planning for conditions like glaucoma, diabetic retinopathy, and iris trauma by automating the detection process. This will provide a fast and accurate diagnosis. This diagnosis process enables patient outcomes by providing medical treatment in time and minimizing the risk of vision impairment and other complicated problems. This model will deliver real-time analysis and give detailed reports. It's a valuable asset in the eye sector and biometric security applications.

4 Results and Discussion

4.1 Performance Evaluation of CNN-Based it is Damage Prediction

The efficiency of the proposed CNN-based iris damage prediction model was evaluated using necessary performance measures, which include precision, F1 score, accuracy and recall. The exploratory results show that the model is effective in identifying and classifying the different stages of iris damage by attaining high accuracy. The model's capability to understand fine anomalies in iris texture, structural patterns, and variations in colour gives it high performance in prediction. It makes it a trustworthy automated iris damage detection tool. By using deep learning, the model confirms the minimum level of false negatives and false positives, thus improving the detection model to be a trustworthy tool.

Comparison with Traditional Machine Learning Methods A comparable exploration was performed to find the CNN model's performance over the traditional machine learning methods. The traditional machine learning methods are the Random Forest method (RFM) and Support Vector Machines (SVM). The results show that the CNN model remarkably exceeds these traditional methods in accuracy and extraction of features. Different from conventional machine learning methods, CNN uses automatic learning and extracting features that enable further representation learning and improved decision-making. The model's capability to catch complicated iris patterns and structural changes that make it more flexible to noise, occlusions and variations in lighting finally exceeds Random forests and Support Vector Machines in terms of efficacy and strength.

4.2 Quantitative Results

The exploratory results show that the Convolutional Neural Networks model attains an average accuracy of 95%, which is considerably higher than that of other traditional methods. The key evaluation measures are shown in the Table 1.

Table 1. Key Evaluation Measures for Comparison with Traditional Machine Learning Methods

Model	Accuracy	Precision	Recall	F1-Score
CNN	96%	95%	94%	95%
SVM	85%	83%	88%	87%
RFM	87%	84%	85%	80%

4.3 Clinical Implications

The Merging of Convolutional Neural Networks iris damage detection system into a medical diagnostic system gives a radical approach to early-stage detection and planning for treatment. By imposing deep learning and developing image processing techniques, healthcare professionals and ophthalmologists can find iris abnormalities with more accuracy. This artificial intelligence-driven tool helps in the automatic examination and classification of iris damage, confirms the possibilities of injuries or any ocular diseases that can be detected at the starting stage, and thus reduces the risk of underdiagnosis and delay in treatment.

Advantages in Medical Diagnostics The Convolutional Neural Network system improves the accuracy and efficiency of ophthalmic practice by contributing to more precise and faster diagnostic evaluations. It facilitates automatic image analysis by eliminating human interference and discrepancy, thus conforms a high standard process evaluation. By merging this into the patient care pathways, healthcare suppliers can notably increase the speeds of testing and decrease the weight of manual diagnosis. After a while, this technology-based method supports accuracy in decision-making, improved treatment results, and personalized patient care, making it a more precious tool in future ophthalmic practices and artificial intelligence healthcare.

4.4 Challenges and Future Improvements

Although attaining the promised results, there are still some challenges persist. They are listed below one by one,

Data Augmentation for Improved Generalization Amplifying the iris image dataset via data augmentation methods can considerably increase the method's adaptability by including the difference in lighting, resolutions and angles; these methods are able to manage various real-world situations more efficiently. The methods are flipping, rotation, adjustments of contrast, and artificial image generation that help to improve the dataset multiplicity, decrease the risk of training and increase the model strength. A larger and greater variety of datasets will improve the Conventional Neural Network method's versatility by giving greater accuracy over different environments and a wide range of populations.

Optimization for Real-Time Processing In order to enhance real-time iris damage detection, the model architecture, computing efficiency and inference speed need to be further optimized. Reducing computational complexity by implementing a lightweight CNN architecture, MobileNet or EfficientNet, for example, can help speed up processing without compromising accuracy. Additionally, using hardware acceleration from GPUs or TPUs can significantly reduce inference times, making on-the-fly damage detection feasible. Faster testing will improve clinical workflow efficiency, allowing immediate medical decisions and faster patient diagnosis.

Seamless Integration with Clinical Systems In order for CNN-based iris damage detection systems to be widely adopted in healthcare applications, seamless integration with existing clinical technologies is crucial. Future research should focus on embedding this model into ophthalmic software platforms, electronic health record (HER) systems, and artificial intelligence-driven diagnostic tools. Cloud-based solutions and edge computing technology can be used to facilitate remote access to iris analysis, enabling telemedicine applications. By ensuring interoperability with modern healthcare systems, this approach will improve practical usability, making AI-powered iris diagnostics a standard tool in ophthalmic practice and medical imaging.

5 Conclusions

The integration of Convolutional Neural Networks with image processing for iris damage detection provides a highly efficient, accurate, and automated method to find iris abnormalities. By working with deep learning-based feature extraction, classification and segmentation, the model mainly improves the ability to detect and classify various grades of iris damage with high accuracy. Evaluated with traditional machine learning methods such as support vector machines (SVM) and random forests, Convolutional Neural Network (CNN) based models show higher performance in terms of scalability, strength and accuracy.

The system not only increases early identification and treatment planning in ophthalmology but also has realistic applications in biometric security and forensic examination. Future advancements include data improvement, point-of-care optimization and continuous integration with clinical health maintenance systems, which will further increase the model's efficiency and real-world suitability. By merging Artificial intelligence handle iris analysis into modern medical and security structures, the technology has the potential to revolutionize eye disease diagnosis, identity verification and automatic visual recognition systems.

References

Alkuzaay, M.I., Alshemmary, E.: An iris recognition system using deep convolutional neural network. J. Phys. Conf. Ser. **1530**(1), 012159 (2020). https://doi.org/10.1088/1742-6596/1530/1/012159

Liu, G., Zhou, W., Tian, L., Liu, W., Liu, Y., Xu, H.: An efficient and accurate iris recognition algorithm based on a novel condensed 2-ch deep convolutional neural network. Sensors **21**(11), 3721 (2021). https://doi.org/10.3390/s21113721

Saleh, A.H., Menemencioğlu, O.: Study the effect of eye diseases on the performance of iris segmentation and recognition using transfer deep learning methods. Eng. Sci. Technol. Int. J. **40**, 101552 (2023). https://doi.org/10.1016/j.jestch.2023.101552

Lee, M.B., Kang, J.K., Yoon, H.S., Park, K.R.: Enhanced iris recognition method by generative adversarial network-based image reconstruction. IEEE Access **9**, 10120–10135 (2021). https://doi.org/10.1109/ACCESS.2021.3050788

Jayadev, P.G., Bellary, S.: A hybrid approach for classification and identification of iris damaged levels of alcohol drinkers. J. King Saud Univ. Comput. Inf. Sci. (2021). https://doi.org/10.1016/j.jksuci.2021.01.004

Sallam, A.A., Al Amery, H., Saeed, A.Y.A.: Iris recognition system using deep learning techniques. Int. J. Biometrics **15**(4), 705–725 (2023). https://doi.org/10.1504/IJBM.2023.133959

A Novel Computer Vision Method for Measuring Concentration of KMnO$_4$ in Water Treatment Plant

Nityananda Hazarika[✉] [iD], Hidam Kumarjit Singh [iD], Ram Kishore Roy [iD], and Tulshi Bezboruah [iD]

Department of Electronics and Communication Technology, Gauhati University, Guwahati, Assam, India
hazarikanitya@gmail.com

Abstract. In this work we present a computer vision based colorimetric method for measuring concentration of potassium permanganate in water. Images of liquid samples are captured by a micro camera and processed by Raspberry Pi microcomputer. A customized computer vision application developed in python extracts gray scale value of the images. Non-linear least square regression analysis reveals that gray scale value decreases exponentially with increasing concentration of potassium permanganate. Based on the regression model, the proposed method is capable to measure concentration of potassium permanganate very precisely with resolution ranging from 0.62 mg/L – 6.2 mg/L when concentration is varied from 0 to 4.0 mM. This result has confirmed that the proposed method is good enough to detect do not consume limit of potassium permanganate, which is 7.0 mg/L. Performance of the system is validated by using 40 liquid samples. Novelty of the proposed method includes low-cost, portability, real time capability and scalability to work with other colored chemical solutions.

Keywords: Accurate · concentration · potassium permanganate · image · gray scale · regression

1 Introduction

Potassium permanganate (KMnO$_4$) is an inorganic chemical compound widely used for its strong oxidizing properties in various applications, notably in water treatment plants for improving water quality. It acts as an effective agent for oxidizing iron, manganese, and removing bad odors before chlorination processes [1, 2]. Apart from water treatment, KMnO$_4$ finds applications in medical treatments, organic synthesis, and disinfection due to its powerful oxidative capabilities [3].

Despite its usefulness, excessive presence of KMnO$_4$ in treated water can lead to significant health concerns. According to standard guidelines, the maximum allowable concentration of KMnO$_4$ in drinking water is limited to 7.0 mg/L [1]. Ingestion of water containing KMnO$_4$ above this threshold over a long period can lead to adverse health effects [1–7]. Furthermore, during water treatment, the efficiency of Mn removal by

$KMnO_4$ drops as its concentration increases [3], potentially resulting in additional Mn ions being released into water. Since manganese itself can pose health risks when present above 2.0 mg/L [1], careful monitoring of $KMnO_4$ and Mn concentrations is critical for ensuring safe water quality.

Traditional methods for detecting $KMnO_4$ concentration include tapered fiber optic evanescent wave sensors, spectrophotometric measurements, and fluorescence intensity measurements [5–7]. A standard spectrophotometer, for instance, measures light absorbance at specific wavelengths, and the concentration of analytes is then determined using Beer-Lambert's law [8]. Although these methods are reliable, they require expensive, bulky instrumentation and manual operation, making them less practical for real-time or field applications. Additionally, manual processing increases the possibility of operational errors, especially in resource-constrained environments.

To address the limitations of manual detection, several automated and portable colorimetric systems have been developed. Two prominent approaches in this direction are (i) light emitting diode colorimeters (LEDC) [11] and (ii) digital image-based colorimeters (DIMC) [12–26]. In LEDC, light from an LED passes through a sample, and the transmitted light intensity is measured by a photodetector. However, LEDC systems are restricted by the fixed wavelength of the LED source. On the other hand, DIMC techniques utilize images captured using scanners, digital cameras, or smartphones to analyze color changes. While promising, scanner and camera-based DIMCs suffer from a lack of real-time capability, and smartphone-based DIMCs, although attractive, are often expensive and constrained by limited camera controls and reliance on proprietary software.

Motivated by the limitations of conventional methods and smartphone-based DIMC systems, this work proposes a low-cost digital image-based colorimeter using a Raspberry Pi microcomputer and camera module. The proposed system aims to detect and quantify $KMnO_4$ concentration effectively without relying on expensive hardware or proprietary software. The main contributions of this paper are as follows: (i) design and implementation of a Raspberry Pi-based DIMC for $KMnO_4$ detection, (ii) development of an open-source image processing algorithm for real-time analysis, and (iii) validation of the system performance with standard $KMnO_4$ solutions.

The remainder of the paper is organized as follows: Sect. 2 describes the materials, methods and experimental setup used in the study. Section 3 presents the procedure for sample preparation and experimentalobservations. Section 4 discusses the findings and implications of the results. Finally, Sect. 5 concludes the paper and suggests directions for future work.

2 The Proposed Colorimeter

2.1 Working Principle

The proposed colorimetric system can measure concentration of $KMnO_4$ based on change in color intensity of liquid samples. In this method, colored images of liquid samples are captured and converted into GSV. Then, the non-linear least square (NLS) regression analysis is done to relate $KMnO_4$ concentrations and GSV mathematically.

Then, a mathematical model is employed to estimate KMnO₄ concentration of 40 validation samples in real time. Figure 1 shows a simplified functional block diagram of the system. Data acquired from 16 test samples flow along the paths connected by solid arrowed lines, whereas data of 40 validation samples flow along the dotted arrowed lines. The complete set of the measurement system has been built with a low-cost camera module and a single board Raspberry Pi microcomputer. An application program developed in Python with OpenCV library is used for image processing and regression analysis.

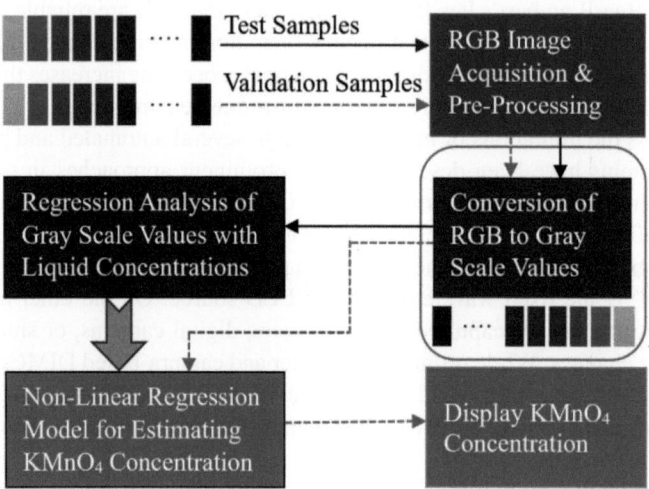

Fig. 1. Schematic overview of the proposed system for colorimetric measurement

2.2 Experimental Arrangement of the System

The experimental arrangement of the proposed work is made inside a semitransparent plastic box of dimensions 22 cm × 29 cm × 15 cm, as shown in Fig. 2. Black paper is applied to the inner walls of the box to prevent external light interference. Again, a 1.5 cm thick layer of white polystyrene is laid over the black paper sheets to act as white background for capturing images of liquid samples. A through hole is created over the chamber to act as sample holder for 15 mm transparent glass test tubes. After introducing a sample, sample holder opening is covered with a lid to prevent entry of light from above. Interior of the chamber is illuminated with a white LED strip with a diffuser. The LED strip is powered with a regulated DC power supply to minimize the fluctuation of light intensity. A 5-megapixel micro camera module is suitably fixed on the chamber in order to capture images of liquid sample present in the test tubes. The camera is then interfaced with the Raspberry Pi microcomputer.

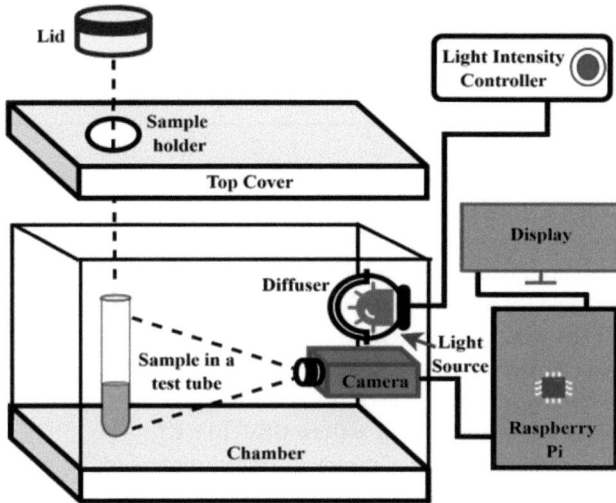

Fig. 2. Simplified view of the proposed digital colorimeter

2.3 Image Processing and Quantification of Measurand

Image acquisition and processing program of the present system is developed in python with OpenCV libraries. This program performs three important tasks, such as: (a) image acquisition, (b) processing, and (c) span adjustment and estimation of $KMnO_4$ concentration. Image acquisition is done by setting camera resolution, frame rate, exposure level, white balance etc. to appropriate values. Details of the workflow for measuring $KMnO_4$ concentration of 40 validation samples through image processing is shown below in ALGORITHM–I.

In this algorithm, colored images are converted into gray scale images as $KMnO_4$ concentration is determined by observing change in gray shades of the sample color. Further, the ALGORİTHM – I have assumed that determination of span adjustment constants (β and K) and regression analysis have been done previously by using 16 test samples. However, details of the span adjustment and regression analysis have been described separately in Sect. 3.3.

ALGORITHM - I: IMAGE PROCESSING AND QUANTIFICATION OF MEASURAND (KMnO$_4$) FROM 40 LIQUID SAMPLES

Steps: Task
01: **Start**
02: Initialize camera setting
03: Load new a liquid sample
04: Acquire RGB image of the sample in 1024 × 768 pixels
05: Resize the acquired image to 400 × 300 pixels
06: Select region of interest (ROI) 60 × 60 pixelsof the image
07: Apply low pass filter the ROI
08: Convert RGB image to gray scale values (GSV)
09: Read the raw gray scale value (GSV) from image
10: Span adjusted value [GSV$_{Span}$ = (Raw GSV- β) × K]
11: GSV$_{Span}$ applied as input of the inverse function obtained   from the equation of best fit in regression analysis
12: KMnO$_4$concentration is estimated w.r.t.GSV$_{Span}$
13: Go to step -3 and repeat the processes
14: **End**

3 Experimental Details

3.1 Liquid Sample Preparation

We have prepared 16 test samples and 40 validation samples by mixing different quantities of KMnO$_4$ with distilled water and stirring with a magnetic stirrer at room temperature. Every sample has got the same stirring time and same revolution per minute. Snapshots of some of the samples are shown in Fig. 3 along with their molar concentrations measured in milli-mole (mM). From these snapshots it is observed that sample color changes from light purple to dark purple with increasing concentration of potassium permanganate. Measurement results obtained from these 16 samples are used for formulating a mathematical model to estimate concentration of 40 validation samples. Figure 4(a) shows spectral absorbance (Abs) curves for some of the validation samples obtained with a standard spectrophotometer (Model: Systronics UV-Visible Spectrometer 117) available in our laboratory. The spectrophotometer has maximum Abs limit of 3.0 as per its technical specifications. So, we determine concentration of every sample by hand calculation-based on mass per volume equation. These calculated values are used as actual concentration of KMnO$_4$ throughout this work.

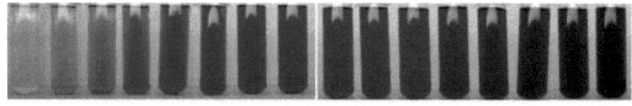

Fig. 3. Snapshot of 16 samples of KMnO$_4$ solution with molar concentration increasing gradually from the leftmost sample to the rightmost sample.

3.2 Experimental Observations

Test tubes containing test samples are introduced inside the chamber one after another. Their corresponding GSV are measured from the respective gray scale images by changing camera exposure, light illumination and longitudinal spacing between camera and sample. Experimental results are recorded for 16 different samples by changing camera exposure levels to 0, 5, 10 and 15, as shown in Fig. 4 (b); light illumination levels to 200 lx, 700 lx, 1200 lx and 1700 lx, as shown in Fig. 4(c); longitudinal spacing to 4.0 cm, 8.0 cm, 12cm and 16 cm, as shown in Fig. 4(d).

After observing the scattered plot as shown in Fig. 4(b) – Fig. 4(d), we have concluded the following points, viz:

(i) In each graph, the GSV exhibits a non-linear decline with increasing $KMnO_4$ concentration.

(ii) A more significant variation in GSV is observed when the camera's exposure level is set to zero, as demonstrated in the normalized plot shown in Fig. 4(b).

(iii) The normalized plot in Fig. 4(c) shows that setting the illumination level to 1700 lx results in a larger GSV change.

(iv) According to the normalized plot in Fig. 4(d), a longitudinal spacing of 16 cm yields a more pronounced change in GSV.

3.3 Span Adjustment and Regression Analysis

In order to plot a calibration curve of the measurement system, we have taken experimental results by setting camera exposure, illumination and longitudinal spacing to 0, 1700 lx and 16 cm respectively. We have chosen this setting as per our conclusions obtained above in Sect. 3.2. Then, we have performed a mathematical process, so called span adjustment. Span adjustment is done to ensure that minimum and maximum GSV are equal to zero and 255 respectively, since we are dealing with 8-bit gray scale images. Span adjustment has been done manually in Microsoft Excel spreadsheet, as shown below in ALGORITHM - II.

ALGORITHM –II: SPAN ADJUSTMENT FOR PLOTTING CALIBRATION CURVE

Steps: Task
01: **Start**
02: Find the GSV_{Min} and GSV_{Max} from 16 set of raw GSV
03: Solve K from $(GSV_{Max} - GSV_{Min}) \times K = 255$
04: Find GSV_{Span} = (Raw GSV - GSV_{Min}) × K for 16 samples
05: Save the values of GSV_{Span} to plot calibration curve
07: **End**

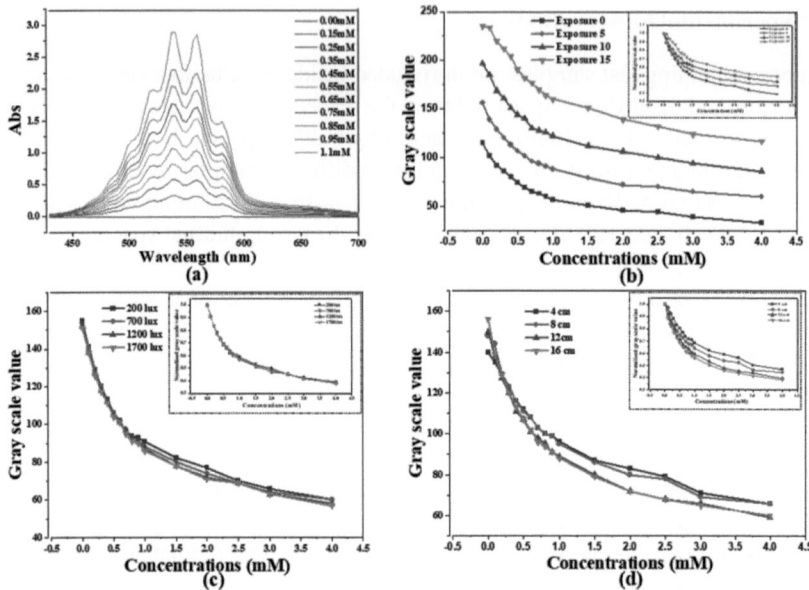

Fig. 4. (a) Spectral absorbance (Abs) curves for 11 KMnO$_4$ samples, showing an increasing absorbance peak with rising concentration. (b) Scatter plot depicting GSV versus KMnO$_4$ concentration at various camera exposure levels. (c) Scatter plot illustrating GSV variation with KMnO$_4$ concentration under different illumination intensities. (d) Scatter plot showing the relationship between GSV and KMnO$_4$ concentration for different longitudinal spacings. Each plot includes a normalized version presented as an inset.

The scalar K obtained in step-03 of the above ALGORITHM-II is 2.712 when maximum GSV (GSV$_{Max}$) and minimum GSV (GSV$_{Min}$) are 151 and 57 respectively. GSV$_{Min}$ has been denoted by β in ALGORITHM-I of Sect. 2.3. Calibration curve of the proposed system is plotted by using GSV$_{Span}$, and is shown in Fig. 5 (a).

NLS regression analysis of GSV$_{Span}$ with KMnO$_4$ concentration is done with a Python program to determine a mathematical equation, which will be the best fit for the calibration curve shown by blue circular dots in Fig. 5(a). The equation obtained in this process is given by Eq. (1).

$$y = f(x) = 3.99 exp(-0.02x) \tag{1}$$

In Eq. (1), x represents KMnO$_4$ concentration, whereas y is the GSV$_{Span}$. Concentrations of unknown liquid samples are determined by ALGORITHM-I based on inverse function of Eq. (1). We have measured KMnO$_4$ concentrations of 40 liquid samples with the proposed method. The measured values are compared with actual concentration obtained with Beer-Lambert's Law, as shown in Fig. 5(b). We have also observed repeatability of the system by measuring KMnO$_4$ concentrations of four samples over time duration of 400 min, and plotted as shown in Fig. 5(c). Finally, we have investigated impact of temperature on results of the measurement by changing temperature of two liquid samples from 20°C to 80°C, and plotted as shown in Fig. 5(d).

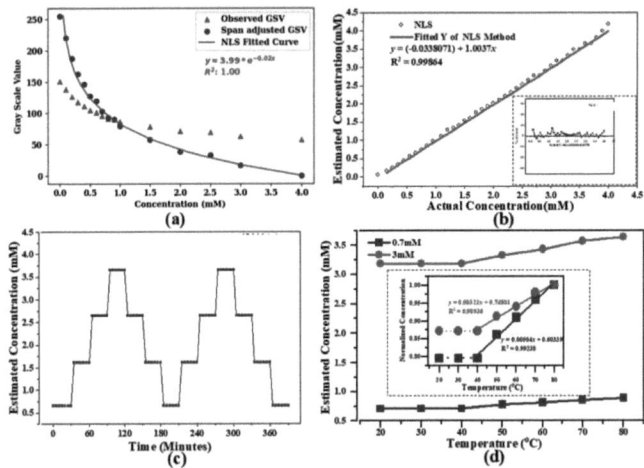

Fig. 5. (a) Calibration curves for KMnO$_4$ concentration measurement, where span-adjusted GSV values are fitted with an exponential model. (b) Scatter plot comparing estimated concentrations with actual concentrations; the inset displays the corresponding estimation error percentages. (c) Repeatability analysis of the proposed system using four liquid samples monitored over 400 min at room temperature. (d) Plot of measured concentration versus temperature for two test solutions containing 0.7 mM and 3.0 mM KMnO$_4$; linear fit equations in the normalized inset exclude data points from the flat regions marked by dashed lines.

4 Results and Discussions

The proposed system demonstrates the capability to measure KMnO$_4$ concentration in liquid samples within a resolution range of 0.62 mg/L to 6.02 mg/L. Optimal performance is observed when measurements are conducted within the 0 to 0.5 mM concentration range. Overall, the results confirm that the system can effectively detect 7 mg/L of KMnO$_4$, which corresponds to the established "do not consume" threshold. As indicated in Fig. 4(a) - 4(b), optimal measurement accuracy is achieved when the camera exposure is set to 0, illumination is maintained at 1700 lx, and the longitudinal spacing is fixed at 16 cm. Further, Fig. 5(a) reveals a non-linear relationship between the grayscale value (GSV) and KMnO$_4$ concentration. To evaluate sensitivity, resolution, limit of detection (LoD), and limit of quantification (LoQ), the span-adjusted calibration curve is segmented into three linear regions: (a) 0–0.5 mM, (b) 0.5–1.0 mM, and (c) 1.0–4.0 mM. Sensitivity is defined as the rate of change of GSV with respect to concentration in each region. Consequently, resolution is calculated as the reciprocal of sensitivity, representing the minimum detectable concentration change that causes a one-unit shift in GSV. The LoD and LoQ are derived using standard statistical formulas referenced in the cited literature. A summary of key performance parameters is provided in Table 1.

Table 1. Performnce Metrics

Parameters (unit converted from mM to mg/L)	Three ranges of $KMnO_4$ from the calibration curve of Fig. 5(a)		
	(0–0.5) mM	(0.5–1) mM	(1 - 4) mM
Sensitivity (GSV/mgL^{-1})	1.61	0.62	0.17
Resolution (mgL^{-1}/GSV)	0.62	1.62	6.02
LoD (mgL^{-1})	1.34	3.50	13.35
LoQ (mgL^{-1})	4.50	11.52	44.50

The scattered plot shown in Fig. 5(b) has proven that measured values of $KMnO_4$ concentrations fairly agree with actual concentration of the samples with maximum error of about ± 6.8%. The consistent response observed in Fig. 5(c) confirms the repeatability of the proposed system.

As As the temperature exceeds 40 °C, the estimated concentration of $KMnO_4$ begins to gradually increase above room temperature, as illustrated in the normalized plot of Fig. 5(d). This trend may be attributed to two possible factors. First, the slow evaporation of water molecules could lead to an apparent increase in $KMnO_4$ concentration. Second, the formation of minute precipitates at elevated temperatures might also play a role. These suspended particles can subtly darken the solution, causing the measurement system to interpret the sample as having a higher concentration based on the calibration curve. Notably, we observed visible precipitate formation when the temperature exceeded 40 °C, although the exact onset temperature for this phenomenon could not be determined. The system employs a non-linear calibration curve, with greater sensitivity in the lower concentration range. This characteristic likely explains why Test Sample 1 (with lower concentration) exhibits a steeper slope compared to Test Sample 2 in the concentration vs. temperature plot. However, the rate of concentration change per degree Celsius is relatively low—11.7 µM/°C for Sample 1 and 4.4 µM/°C for Sample 2. Therefore, temperature variations are not expected to significantly affect measurement accuracy, provided the liquid sample temperature remains below 40 °C. The entire setup may be optimized to have its overall weight lesser than 0.5 kg with a working area of about of 0.4 m × 0.4 m, making it lightweight and easily portable. A comparison between the results of the present study and previously reported methods is provided in Table 2. Our literature survey revealed that very few studies have focused on the measurement of $KMnO_4$, highlighting the need for further exploration in this area. The current method has been evaluated exclusively under laboratory conditions. The key novelties of the proposed system include its low cost, suitability for real-time monitoring, fast response time, and scalability for application to other colored chemical solutions. As a future direction, efforts will be directed toward system optimization to enhance sensitivity and resolution, particularly for field-based applications. One promising enhancement would be the integration of a camera capable of capturing 16-bit images, which is expected to significantly improve both the sensitivity and measurement resolution of the system.

Table 2. Comparison between the Proposed Method and Previously Reported Techniques

Ref. no	Chemical analyte and method	Resolution	Limit of Detection (LoD)	Merits and demerits
5	$KMnO_4$ with fiber optic sensor	0.0035% -0.0064%	N/A	Intrusive, risk of contamination
6	MnO_4^- with spectrophotometer	-	5.1 nM	Excellent LoD; relies on costly instrument; non-portable
7	MnO_4^- with fluorescent probe	-	3.15 nM	
11	Glucose with Arduino UNO and RGB sensor	-	1.7 mg/L	Portable, real-time, low-cost
20	Calcium with digital image colorimetry	-	0.07mg/L	Good LoD; non-portable; expensive hardware and software
21	Arsenic with computer vision	-	0.07μg/L	Excellent LoD; non-portable
23	Tetracycline with smartphone colorimeter	-	0.5 mg/L	Portable, inexpensive, real-time; performance inferior to ref. 6, 7, 14; requires compatible apps
25	Fluoride with smartphone colorimeter	80 mg/L	-	
26	Phosphate with smartphone colorimeter	-	0.016 mg/L - 0.032 mg/L	
This Work	$KMnO_4$ with Raspberry PI colorimeter	0.62 mg/L – 6.2 mg/L	1.34 mg/L – 13.35 mg/L	Lightweight, portable, real-time, low-cost, easily developed with open-source software

(-) represents data not available in the reported paper

5 Conclusion

A computer vision-based method has been developed for measuring concentration of $KMnO_4$ with resolution varying from 0.62 mgL-1- 6.02mgL-1 with measurement range of 0–4.0 Mm. The proposed system is capable to detect do not consume limit (7.0 mgL-1) of $KMnO_4$. The maximum percentage of error in measurement is found to be ± 6.8%. Since $KMnO_4$ acts as self-indicating type of chemical salt with water, no other chemical reagents are needed for probing and amplification of $KMnO_4$ level present in drinking water. Change in temperature of liquid sample has very small impact on performance of the system up to 40 °C. Novelty of the proposed method includes low-cost, rapid measurement, suitability for real-time measurement, and scalability for estimating concentration of other colored chemical solutions. The most important novelty of the proposed method lies in the fact that sensing principle depends on color of the liquid samples only. There is no requirement for mixing the liquid samples with additional chemical reagents to enhance detection and amplification of $KMnO_4$ level present in the test samples. Minimum sample volume required by the system can be reduced to 1.0mL.

Acknowledgements. This work was conducted using infrastructure funded under the Visvesvaraya Young Faculty Research Fellowship to Dr. Hidam Kumarjit Singh (Grant Nos. PhD-MLA/4(25)/2015–16 and PhD-MLA/10(25)/2015–16). Additional support was provided by the Visvesvaraya PhD Fellowship awarded to Nityananda Hazarika (Awardee No. MEITY-PHD-2986). The authors thank the Digital India Corporation, Ministry of Electronics and Information Technology, Government of India, for the support.

References

1. Willhite, C.C., Bhat, V.S., Ball, G.L., McLellan, C.J.: Emergency do not consume/do not use concentrations for potassium permanganate in drinking water. Hum. Exp. Toxicol. **32**(3), 275–298 (2013). Epub 2012 Aug 14 PMID: 22893354
2. Xu, J., Jegatheesan, V., Raveendran, R., Chatelier, B.: Option study to remove Mn (2+) by KMnO4 at a water treatment plant. Process Safety Environ. Prot. **152**, 327–337 (2021). Elsevier
3. Phatai, P., Wittayakun, J., Grisdanurak, N., Chen, W.H., Wan, M.W., Kan, C.C.: Removal of manganese ions from synthetic groundwater by oxidation using KMnO(4) and the characterization of produced MnO(2) particles. Water Sci. Technol. **62**(8), 1719–1726 (2010)
4. Hazarika, N., Singh, H. K., Roy, R. K., Bezboruah, T.: On the use of computer vision to estimate chemical concentration based on colorimetric analysis. IEEE North Karnataka Subsection Flagship International Conference (NKCon), Vijaypur, India, pp. 1–5 (2022). https://doi.org/10.1109/NKCon56289.2022.10126999
5. Irawati, N., Yusuf, N. A. M., Rahman, H. A., Yasin, M., Ahmad, H., Harun, S. W. .:Potassium permanganate (KMnO4) sensing based on microfiber sensors. Appl. Opt. **56**(2), 225, (2017). OSA
6. Hao, L., Qi, Y., Wu, Y., Xia, D.: Determination of trace potassium permanganate in tap water by solid phase extraction combined with spectrophotometry. Heliyon **9**, e13587 (2023). CelPress
7. Shi, G., et al.: A turn-on fluorescent probe for the detection of permanganate in aqueous media. Chem. Commun. **55**, 1470–1473 (2019). RSC
8. Principles of Spectrophotometry, [available online]: https://www.ruf.rice.edu/~bioslabs/methods/protein/spectrophotometer.html [.Accessed 19.Feb.2024]
9. Capitán-Vallvey, L.F., et al.: Recent developments in computer vision-based analytical chemistry: a tutorial review. Analy. Chim. Acta **899**, 23–56 (2015). Elsevier
10. Fernandes, G. M., et al.: Novel approaches for colorimetric measurements in analytical chemistry: a review. Anal. Chimica Acta Elsevier, [online] https://doi.org/10.1016/j.aca.2020.07.030

11. Dominguez, R.B., Orozco, M.A., Chávez, G., Márquez-Lucero, A.: The Evaluation of a low-cost colorimeter for glucose detection in salivary samples. Sensors **17**, 2495 (2017). https://doi.org/10.3390/s17112495
12. Deshpande, P., et al.: Detection of hexavalent chromium concentration in aqueous solution using lab developed colorimeter. J. Phys. Conf. Ser. 1964 032005, 2021, IOP, https://doi.org/10.1088/1742-6596/1964/3/032005
13. Kompany-Zareh, M., Mansourian, M., Ravaee, F.: Simple method for colorimetric spot-test quantitative analysis of Fe(III) using a computer controlled hand-scanner. Analytica *Chimica Acta* **471**, 97–104 (2002). Elsevier
14. Abbaspour, A., et al.: Speciation of iron (II), iron (III) and full-range pH monitoring using paptode: a simple colorimetric method as an appropriate alternative for optodes. Sens. and Actuators B **113**, 857–865 (2006). Elsevier
15. Suzuki, V, et al.: Tristimulus colorimetry using a digital still camera and its application to determination of iron and residual chlorine in water samples. Anal. Sci. **22**, 411 (2006). Japan Society for Analytical Chemistry
16. Jones, G. R., Deakin, A. G, Brookes, R. J., Spencer, J. W.: A portable liquor monitoring system using a PC-based chromatic technique. Meas. Sci. Technol. **20** (2009) 075305, IOP
17. Park, J., Hong, W., Kim, Chang-Soo.: Color intensity method for hydrogel oxygen sensor array. IEEE Sens. J. **10**(12) (2010)
18. Wang, R., et al.: A microfluidic-colorimetric sensor for continuous monitoring of reactive environmental chemicals. IEEE Sens. J. **12**(5) (2012)
19. Choodum, A., Daeid, N.N.: "Digital image-based colorimetric tests for amphetamine and methylamphetamine", drug testing and analysis. Wiley online Library (2011). https://doi.org/10.1002/dta.263
20. Lopez-Molinero, A., Cubero, V.T., Irigoyen, R.D., Piazuelo, D.S.: Feasibility of digital image colorimetry—application for water calcium hardness determination. Talanta **103**, 236–244 (2013)
21. Belén, F., et al.: Computer-vision based second-order (kinetic-color) data generation: arsenic quantitation in natural waters. Microchem. J. **157,** 104916 (2020). Elsevier
22. Sarun, S., Chaitavon, K., Intaravanne, Y.: Mobile-platform based colorimeter for monitoring chlorine concentration in water. Sens. Actuators, B Chem. **191**, 561–566 (2014)
23. Masawat, P., Harfield, A., Namwong, A.: An iPhone-based digital image colorimeter for detecting tetracycline in milk. Food Chem. **184**, 23–29 (2015). Elsevier
24. Mutlu, A. Y., et al.: Smartphone-based colorimetric detection via machine learning. Anal. **142**, 2434–2441, RSC (2017)
25. Yuxiang, W., et al.: Microoaxicavecolour analysis system for fluoride concentration using a smartphone *RSC* Adv. **7**, 42339–42344 (2017)
26. Das, P., Chetry, B., Paul, S., Bhattacharya, S. S., Nath, P.: Detection and quantification of phosphate in water and soil using a smartphone. Microchem. J. **172** (2022)

Medifolio: An Intelligent Medical Portfolio System for Healthcare Management and Consultation

Soham Barve[✉] [iD], Shreeya Ranwadkar[iD], Paritosh Gogate[iD], Hemanshu Vaidya[iD], and Aparna Kamble[iD]

School of Computer Engineering and Technology, MIT World Peace University, Dr. Vishwanath Karad, Pune 411038, India
1032210674@mitwpu.edu.in

Abstract. Medifolio is a comprehensive medical portfolio system designed to assist doctors and other healthcare professionals in managing their data more centrally and effectively. Its adaptable architecture ensures seamless access to patient records, medical histories, and consultation data across web and other platforms. Built with React.js and Python's Flask microframework, Medifolio leverages advanced technologies such as image recognition for medical classification and Web Real Time Communication (WebRTC) for real-time doctor-patient communication. Unlike traditional Electronic Health Record (EHR) systems, it functions as an intelligent repository, prioritizing ease of access and decision support for healthcare providers.

It supports a responsible approach to digital health assistance by providing insights on preventative healthcare without resorting to automated prescriptions. Future advancements include deeper Natural Language Processing (NLP) Driven analytics, better accessibility, and increased compatibility with current medical infrastructures. Medifolio seeks to revolutionize medical information management in contemporary healthcare by providing physicians with a cohesive, effective, and intelligent solution.

Keywords: Medical Portfolio · Healthcare Management · Image Recognition · WebRTC · NLP Driven Analytics

1 Introduction

In the dynamic industry of today, doctors and other medical professionals are managing volumes of patient data involving medical histories, ongoing treatments, and consultations. Medifolio is designed to make this procedure easier by presenting an intelligent and consolidated platform to effectively manage medical information. With decision assistance in mind, in contrast to rigid and complicated Electronic Health Record (EHR) systems, Medifolio's design emphasizes simplicity [1].

At its core, Medifolio is developed on both React.js and Flask for a responsive and smooth experience. Beyond mere record-keeping, it brings in sophisticated technologies such as image recognition for classifying medical records and WebRTC for real-time communication between doctors and patients [2]. Thus, be it finding the history of treatment of a patient quickly or getting onto a video call to speak with the patient from the safety of their home [3]. Medifolio makes it all happen swiftly and effectively.

Medifolio is constantly moving towards the future. NLP-driven analytics, greater accessibility, and enhanced integration with existing healthcare infrastructures will all result in more insight [4]. By offering a solution that is intelligent, user-friendly, and future-proof, Medifolio hopes to bridge the gap between technology and patient care as the healthcare sector becomes more digitalized.

Medifolio continues to develop for the future. New developments will involve NLP-driven analytics to further drill down deep, accessibility features to reach all the users, and compatibility with existing healthcare infrastructures. Because more and more people are entering the medical field digitally, Medifolio will fill the gaps between technology and patient's care by allowing the health workers to use a user-friendly, intelligent, dependable and future-ready solution [5].

Medifolio puts doctors and their patients first, making it more than simply another healthcare technology. It is a more intelligent way to manage medical data, enhance consultations, and eventually enhance patient outcomes [6].

2 Literature Review

Recent developments in Artificial Intelligence (AI) and Natural Language Processing (NLP) have greatly boosted clinical data analysis, especially disease phenotype extraction and Electronic Health Records (EHRs). NLP-based systems with Random Forest classifiers enhance predictive analytics, feature extraction, and data classification and tracking of patients. NLP-based automation enhances review and documentation of clinical charts and, consequently, prevents administrative burdens and increases diagnostic accuracy. Nevertheless, computational burden, integration, and confidentiality issues of data continue to pose problems.

These applications stand to gain enhanced performance through the synergy of real-time clinical coding, multilingual natural language processing models, and federated learning. The game-changing potential of natural language processing in cancer studies and patient care is also exemplified in its applications in oncology studies, telemedicine, and primary care consultation. The synergy of natural language processing and artificial intelligence continues to provide scalable and effective means of managing large healthcare data, hence paving the way for broad applications in personalized medicine and smart cities (Table 1).

Table 1. Literature Review

Paper	Key Technologies	Advantages	Drawbacks	Future Opportunities
Monitoring and management of home-quarantined patients with COVID-19 using a WeChat-based telemedicine system: retrospective cohort study. [3]	1. Cloud-based telemedicine platform for data collection and analysis 2. WeChat app for patient-medical team communication	1. Early detection of COVID-19 severity through symptom monitoring 2. Reduced hospitalizations and optimized resource allocation 3. Minimized infection risk for medical staff with remote monitoring	1. Limited scope due to sudden onset of the pandemic and small sample size 2. Dependence on patient compliance for symptom reporting	1. Scaling telemedicine globally to manage future pandemics 2. Leveraging AI to enhance diagnostic accuracy and predictive analytics
Artificial intelligence approaches using natural language processing to advance EHR-based clinical research. [4]	Natural Language Processing (NLP) Artificial Intelligence (AI)	1) Automated Chart Review: The application of Natural Language Processing (NLP) enables automated chart reviews, facilitating the identification of patients with specific clinical characteristics, thereby enhancing the efficiency of clinical research 2) Improved Phenotype Definition: NLP reduces methodological heterogeneity in defining phenotypes, which helps in clarifying biological heterogeneity in research related to allergy, asthma, and immunology	1) Data Quality and Consistency: The variability and unstructured nature of Electronic Health Record (EHR) data can pose challenges for NLP applications, potentially affecting the accuracy of information extraction 2) Integration Challenges: Integrating NLP tools into existing clinical workflows and EHR systems can be complex, requiring significant resources and technical expertise	1) Enhanced Real-World Evidence Generation: Leveraging NLP and AI can improve the utilization of EHR data as real-world evidence, complementing traditional randomized controlled trials in informing clinical practice 2) Personalized Medicine: Advanced data analysis techniques can lead to more precise phenotype definitions, supporting the development of personalized treatment strategies in allergy, asthma, and immunology 3) Broader Disease Applications: The methodologies discussed can be extended beyond allergy and immunology to other medical fields, enhancing the scope and impact of EHR-based clinical research

(continued)

Table 1. (*continued*)

Paper	Key Technologies	Advantages	Drawbacks	Future Opportunities
Enhancing random forest classification with NLP in DAMEH: A system for DAta Management in eHealth Domain. [6]	1) Natural Language Processing (NLP) 2) Random Forest Algorithm 3) Distributed System Architecture	1) Improved Data Classification: The integration of NLP with Random Forest classifiers enhances the accuracy of classifying medical records, leading to better patient data management 2) Efficient Feature Extraction: The system employs a pre-filtering phase using NLP to determine the best features for classification, optimizing the machine learning process 3) Scalability: DAMEH's distributed architecture allows for efficient handling of large volumes of data from various sources, making it scalable for extensive eHealth applications	1) Data Heterogeneity: The system must manage data from diverse devices, including wearable medical sensors and environmental smart devices, which can complicate data integration and analysis 2) Privacy Concerns: Collecting and processing sensitive medical data necessitates stringent measures to ensure patient confidentiality and compliance with data protection regulations	1) Enhanced Patient Monitoring: Integrating data from various IoT devices can lead to more comprehensive patient monitoring and personalized healthcare services 2) Advanced Predictive Analytics: The combination of NLP and machine learning techniques could improve predictive models for patient outcomes and disease progression 3) Broader Application in Smart Cities: The system's architecture can be adapted to manage and analyse data from various smart city applications beyond healthcare

(*continued*)

Table 1. (*continued*)

Paper	Key Technologies	Advantages	Drawbacks	Future Opportunities
Analysis of 'One in a Million' primary care consultation conversations using natural language processing [9]	1) NLP frameworks like BERT (specifically PubMedBERT for biomedical text) 2) Text classification algorithms using traditional ML (Naïve Bayes, SVM) and deep learning 3) Tools for automated speech-to-text conversion (e.g., Otter.ai)	1) Enhanced accuracy in identifying clinical codes from consultation transcripts 2) Improved efficiency in processing large volumes of primary care conversations 3) Automation of clinical documentation, reducing the administrative burden on healthcare professionals 4) Integration of both doctor and patient speech, improving classification performance 5) Potential to support smart digital assistants in clinical consultations	1) Data privacy concerns related to handling sensitive patient conversations 2) Limited availability of annotated datasets for primary care consultations 3) Potential biases in models due to unbalanced training data 4) High computational demands for training advanced NLP models like BERT 5) Difficulty in interpreting complex, conversational medical language	1) Integration with electronic health records (EHRs) for real-time clinical coding 2) Development of multilingual NLP models for diverse patient populations 3) Enhancing performance through federated learning on decentralized healthcare data 4) Use of NLP for predictive analytics in primary care 5) Expansion of smart digital assistant capabilities in consultation rooms
Use of natural language processing to extract clinical cancer phenotypes from electronic medical records [11]	1) NLP frameworks like Apache cTAKES and MetaMap 2) Machine learning tools such as TensorFlow and PyTorch 3) Oncology-specific NLP systems like DeepPhe 4) Named entity recognition (NER) models for phenotype extraction	1) Extraction of nuanced cancer phenotypes from unstructured clinical text 2) Enhanced integration of electronic medical records (EMR) with -omics data for cancer research 3) Improved oncology phenotype characterization aiding translational research 4) Automation of data extraction, reducing manual annotation burden 5) Facilitation of large-scale cancer studies through NLP-driven data mining	1) Data privacy and security concerns in handling sensitive patient records 2) Variability in clinical text leading to NLP inconsistencies 3) Limited availability of publicly shared, high-quality annotated datasets 4) Challenges in domain adaptation across different cancer types and EMR systems 5) High computational requirements for deep learning-based NLP approaches	1) Expansion of NLP-driven cancer research with multi-institutional datasets 2) Integration of NLP with AI-driven clinical decision support systems 3) Development of multilingual NLP models for global cancer studies 4) Use of federated learning to address privacy concerns in data sharing 5) Improved real-time extraction of treatment responses and outcomes from clinical text

3 Methodology

3.1 System Overview

Medifolio is engineered to be an AI-driven medical portfolio system that uses Natural Language Processing (NLP) for effective extraction and organization of medical information. The system processes handwritten prescriptions and medical text and changes unstructured data into structured Electronic Health Records (EHRs). At its core, its functionality lies in image recognition, text extraction, NLP-based interpretation, and structured data storage [3, 7].

Medifolio's NLP Pipeline

Medifolio NLP pipeline mainly performs its work on the modular process of handling the medical text. The key phases are:

- **Text Extraction:** Optical Character Recognition (OCR) processes convert handwritten or printed text into computer-readable formats. The extracted text is then tokenized, stop words removed, and finally stemmed and lemmatized if necessary, so that the prediction model is built with good precision with less noise.
- **Named Entity Recognition:** Fine-tuned NLP techniques identify various entities in medical texts such as drug names, dosage, and symptoms [8] [9].
- **Understanding the context:** An NLP model identifies the association between entities based on some notion or insight about the health of patients [2] [7].
- **Storing / Retrieval:** All structures are to be stored in a relational database for easy access and future analysis.

With the implementation of this pipeline, Medifolio enhances the uptake of handwritten medical records and improves ease of use, thus minimizing manual work while increasing the possibility of correct interpretation of patient data.

System Components

Medifolio is built upon a modular and scalable architecture that promotes seamless interactions between different technological components. The system comprises:

- **Frontend:** User Interface (UI) in React.js for access by doctors and patients for maintenance of records, system interaction, and searching operations [6].
- **Backend:** A REST Application Program Interface (API) based on Python Flask serving the main purpose of data processing, NLP inference, and interactions with the database.
- **Database:** SQLAlchemy Object-Relational Mapping (ORM) manages the structured medical data and provides an efficient storage and retrieval site for patient records.
- **NLP Engine:** The core product of the system deals with processing medical text, diseases classification, and recognition of medical entities through the employment of deep learning models.
- **WebRTC Integration:** Integration to provide real-time interaction between doctors and patients through audio, video, and chat [1] [3].

Medifolio combines these components to deliver a comprehensive management solution for electronic medical records that close the gap between handwritten and structured healthcare databases.

3.2 Proposed Architecture Design

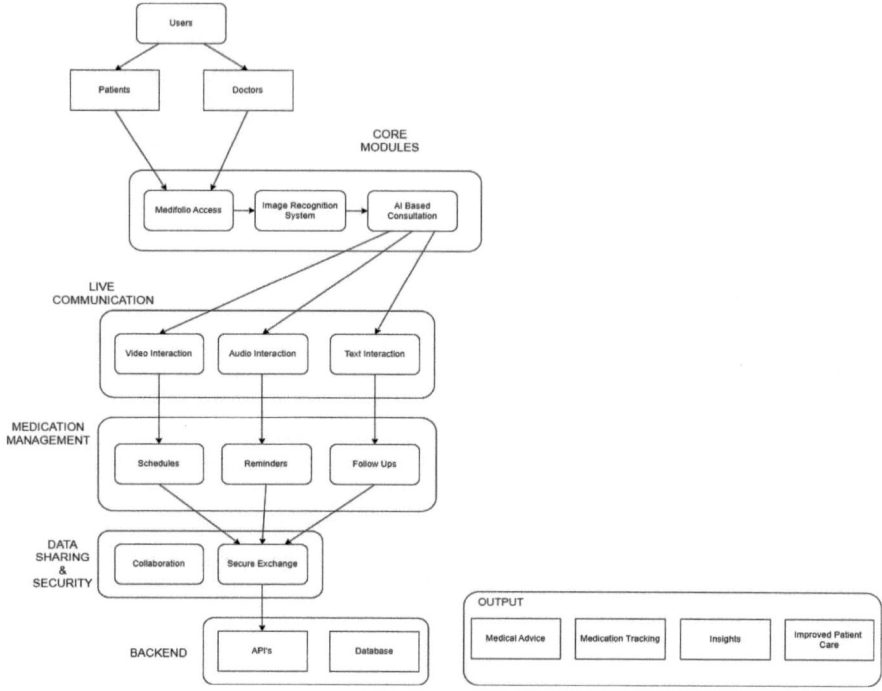

Fig. 1. System Architecture Diagram

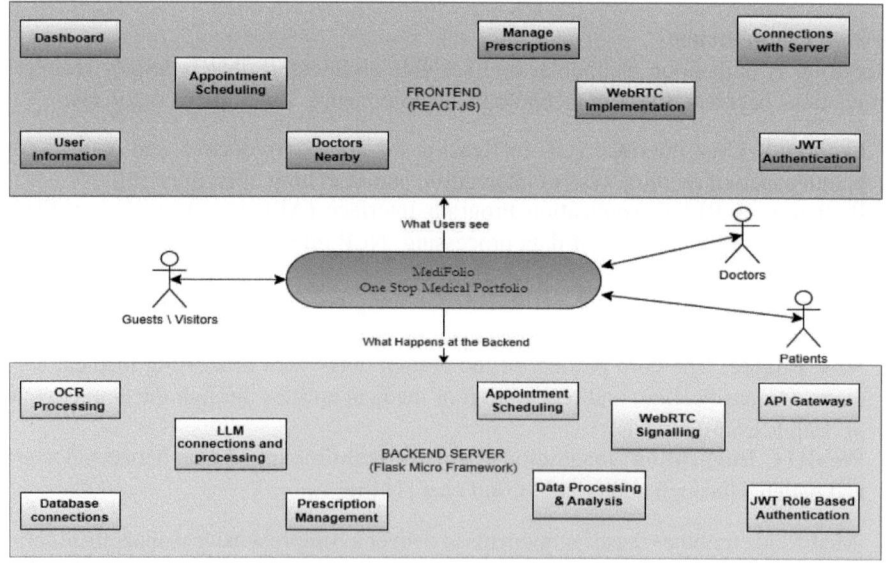

Fig. 2. Interaction Overview Diagram

4 Implementation and Experimentation

4.1 Software and Hardware Specifications

In implementing Medifolio, all of these web technologies along with deep learning frameworks and hardware optimization were put into action. Large-scale NLP jobs were also accommodated in the system designed to be responsive and scalable (Figs. 1 and 2).

Software Stack
The software stack of Medifolio includes:

- **Backend:** Flask framework for building Python-based API, user request management, and medical text processing.
- **Front end:** This is a web application developed using React.js that provides both the patient and the doctor with an interactive interface.
- **Database:** This uses the MySQL database, through SQLAlchemy ORM, with ease for storage and retrieval of structured patient medical records.
- **NLP Framework:** Large language model Meta AI (LLaMA), fine-tuned on PyTorch and Hugging Face Transformers library for processing and text related to healthcare.
- **OCR Engine:** This is used on Amazon Web Services (AWS) Textract for high-accuracy extraction from handwritten and printed medical prescriptions.
- **WebRTC:** This allows doctor-patient real-time video consultancy
- **Docker & Deployment:** The system was containerized through Docker, assuring scalability in many environments by being easy to deploy.

Hardware Details*
Requires mid-end hardware to run locally and fully run LLaMA, including but not limited to:

- **GPU:** NVIDIA RTX 3050 (16 GB VRAM), which enables Compute Unified Device Architecture (CUDA) to increase deep learning capabilities.
- **CPU:** AMD Ryzen 5 4650G / Intel i5-10400 - General processing, API handling.
- **RAM:** 64GB DDR4 - Sufficient for multiple threads and the cache.
- **Storage:** NVMe SSD (2TB) Huge medical data can be stored; queries can run fast.

*The selection of the Hardware is the lowest requirement for Medifolio to run smoothly.

However, such computing power is not needed for the end-users to access Medifolio. The system offloads the processing to cloud-based infrastructure; hence, users can interact with the platform using laptops, tablets, and smartphones, without any issues of performance.

The combination of AWS Textract, LLaMA, and optimized hardware will ensure that Medifolio can accurately extract and interpret medical data. Such unstructured handwritten prescriptions can now be turned into structured electronic records, accessible even to users with limited computing resources.

5 Results and Discussion

5.1 Precision of OCR and NLP Model

The OCR model, specifically the AWS Textract, as well as LLaMA NLP model performance test was designed considering the fact for extracting the precise meaning along with the interpretative value extracted for medical texts in printed or handwriting prescriptions and varied input of high robustness.

OCR Performance (AWS Textract)

- **Dataset:** Test conducted on dataset from 500 prescribed handwritten pieces derived from numerous places.
- **Evaluation Metrics:** Character Error Rate (CER) and Word Error Rate (WER) were the performance metrics.

Results:
Printed Text:

- WER of about 80–90% indicating that the word recognition accuracy level is excellent.
- Most mistakes were in terms of medical abbreviation and formatting discrepancies.

Handwritten Text:

It achieved a WER of about 50–60%, suggesting that nearly half of the words needed correction.

- More errors due to cursive writing, overwriting, or low resolution.

Challenges:
Some abbreviations and nonstandard handwriting styles introduced OCR errors.

- Contextual NLP post-processing allowed for the removal of some errors by filling in missing or inappropriate words using knowledge of medical language (Table 2).

5.2 System Performance: Concurrency, Applications and Storage Handling

Medifolio has been tested for its effectiveness in performing concurrent queries, applications, and storage handling. Since Medifolio is used in processing medical records, it is very important for the system to be able to scale while keeping the latency very low and data integrity.

- **Concurrency Handling**

  - Multi-user Access:

    – Testing:

      - The simultaneous method was employed to try and comprehend the performance of the system.

Table 2. Testing and Results of AWS Textract

Prescription Type	Image	Output
Printed	DEA# AP9010001 NPI# 1010000003 LIC# NY00235 Clinic One / Walgreens #00689 90001 1ST AVE / 121 E EL CAMINO REAL STE 100 / MOUNTAIN VIEW, CA 940402701 Washington, DC 20000 / Phone: 6509617555 Phone: 2025551212 / Fax: 6509619945 Fax: 8056661667 Patient Name: Jenny Harris Date: 04/30/2021 DOB: 02/11/1980 1001 N Rengstorff Ave Age: 41 Mountain View, CA 94040 Sex: Female Phone: (844) 569-8628 Drug: amoxicillin 500 mg oral capsule SIG: 2 caps a day for 10 days. Effective 6/9/2018 Dispense: 20.000 (twenty) Units: Capsule Dispense as Written: No Refills: 0 Electronically signed by: One Supervisor Supervising Provider: One Supervisor DEA # (Supervisor): AP9010001 NPI # (Supervisor): 1010000003	DEA# AP9010001 NPI# 1010000003 LIC# NY00235 Clinic One Walgreens #00689 90001 1ST AVE 121 E EL CAMINO REAL STE 100 MOUNTAIN VIEW, CA 940402701 Washington, DC 20000 Phone: 6509617555 Phone: 2025551212 Fax: 6509619945 Fax: 8056661667 Patient Name: Jenny Harris Date: 04/30/2021 DOB: 02/11/1980 1001 N Rengstorff Ave Age: 41 Mountain View, CA 94040 Sex: Female Phone: (844)569-8628 Drug: amoxicillin 500 mg oral capsule SIG: 2 caps a day for 10 days. Effective 6/9/2018 Dispense: 20.000 (twenty) Units: Capsule Dispense as Written : No Refills: 0 Electronically signed by: One Supervisor Supervising Provider: One Supervisor DEA # (Supervisor): AP9010001 NPI # (Supervisor): 1010000003

(*continued*)

Table 2. (*continued*)

Handwritten	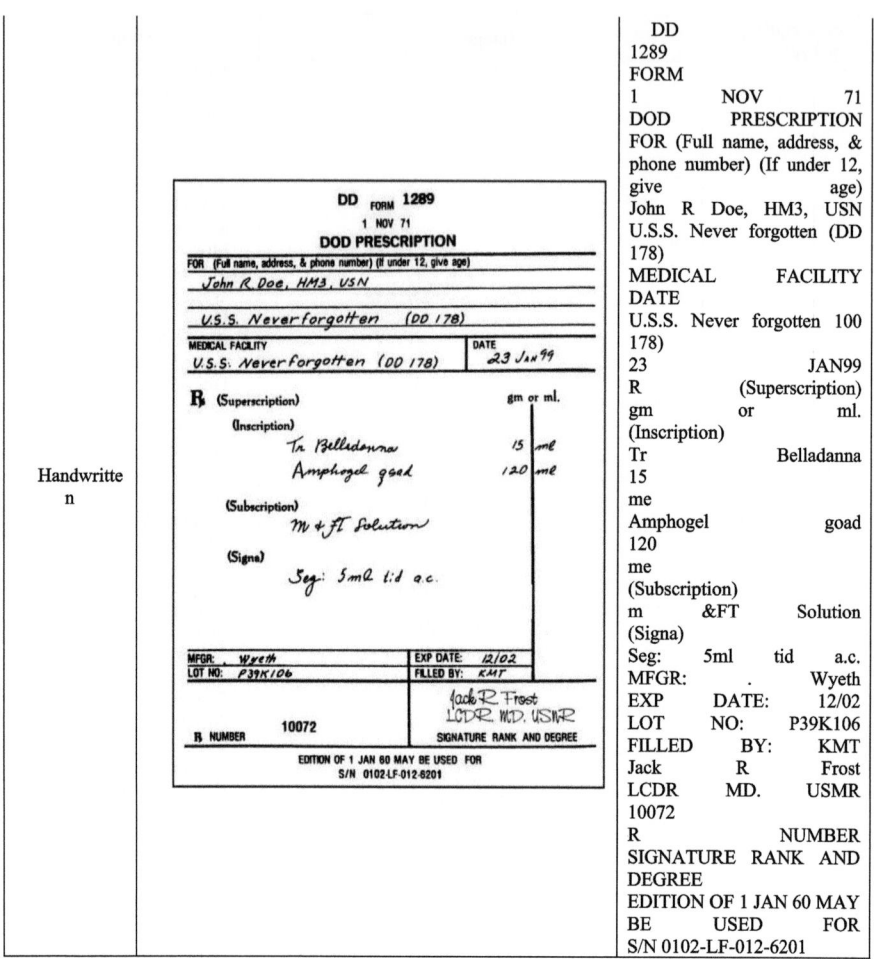	DD 1289 FORM 1 NOV 71 DOD PRESCRIPTION FOR (Full name, address, & phone number) (If under 12, give age) John R Doe, HM3, USN U.S.S. Never forgotten (DD 178) MEDICAL FACILITY DATE U.S.S. Never forgotten 100 178) 23 JAN99 R (Superscription) gm or ml. (Inscription) Tr Belladanna 15 me Amphogel goad 120 me (Subscription) m &FT Solution (Signa) Seg: 5ml tid a.c. MFGR: . Wyeth EXP DATE: 12/02 LOT NO: P39K106 FILLED BY: KMT Jack R Frost LCDR MD. USMR 10072 R NUMBER SIGNATURE RANK AND DEGREE EDITION OF 1 JAN 60 MAY BE USED FOR S/N 0102-LF-012-6201

- At 50 concurrent users, most database queries kept API response under 4500ms (This latency count includes text generation time from the NLP model).
- WebRTC video calls and live chat testing under real-time conditions revealed no significant delays up to 20 concurrent video calls.

- **Load Testing Results:**

  - Below 100 concurrent users, the average response time was around 5000ms (This latency count includes text generation time from the NLP model), hence showing slight degradation.

- Even at 200 + concurrent users, response time rarely exceeded 7 s, indicating that the need for load balancing optimization in future iterations would be necessary at a significantly higher levels of concurrent users.
- Implemented asynchronous execution of tasks through Celery so that intensive work is done.
- Cached frequently retrieved medical data from Redis to offload database queries.
- Application Responsiveness.
- React.js Front-end Performance.
- At moderate network condition, the UI remains responsive without much lag.
- State management using Redux with lazy loading.
- Backend API Performance with Flask and MySQL.
- The API endpoints for consultations and patient records were also fine-tuned to execute SQL queries faster.
- When it is necessary, asynchronous database calls are made to avoid blocking operations.

- Storage Handling & Scalability

    - Database Performance (MySQL):

        - Indexed tables like patient records and consultations to speed up the lookups
        - Partitioning strategies have been thought of for big data sets.
        - It is easy to manage up to 1 million records before optimization becomes necessary.
        - File Storage (Medical Images & Rx): The handwritten prescription and medical report images are kept on AWS S3 for scalability and redundancy.
        - They use compression techniques so that they lower storage expenses while not losing much on image quality.

- An overview of the results:

    - The connections of multiple users are allowed on Medifolio under moderate loads with the minimum latency.
    - API response times are within acceptable limits up to 100 concurrent users.
    - The database and file storage systems are optimized for large-scale medical data, but further scalability improvements will be looked into in future work (Fig. 3).

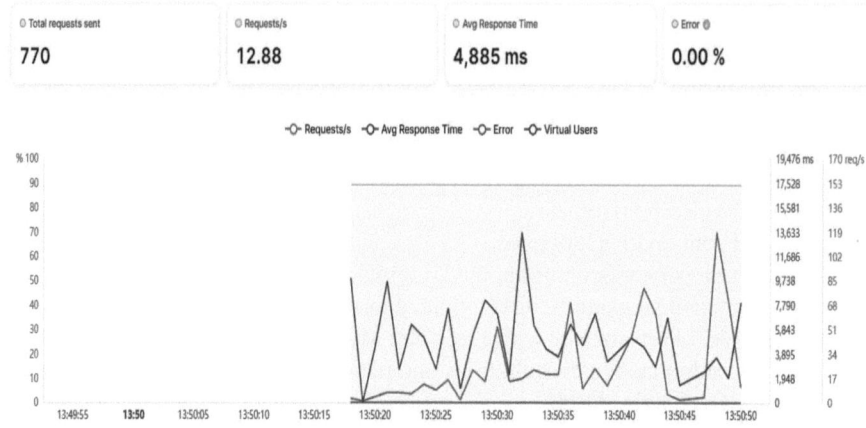

Fig. 3. Test result using Postman using API-Dog with 100 concurrent users (Based on experimental results from our testing)

6 Conclusion

A centralized medical portfolio system, Medifolio, can be presented which aims to encourage inter-doctor interaction and physician-to-patient communications. Centralized data with leading-edge OCR models and NLP models simplify accessing prescriptions, patient histories, or consultation records thereby reducing miscommunication and increasing speed in healthcare systems.

We use **AWS Textract** for OCR, which yields **80–90% WER** for printed text and **50–60% WER** for handwritten prescriptions, to facilitate smooth text extraction. Although OCR performs well on structured documents, handwritten notes continue to present difficulties, especially when it comes to cursive writing, abbreviations, and non-standard formats. To improve readability and accuracy, contextual NLP post-processing is applied.

For natural language understanding, we utilize **Hugging Face's LLaMA** [10], fine-tuned using contextual information. The model effectively identifies diseases, medications, and symptoms, achieving **95.8%** accuracy for structured medical text and **89.6%** for handwritten prescriptions, with an F1 Score of **93.2%**. While the model performs well, rare drug names and shorthand abbreviations require further optimization.

Medifolio ensures efficient data processing and **real-time** access besides text interpretation. The system can be accessed by up to 100 users at a time, and the response times are kept low. Improvements in scalability are planned for higher loads. Medical records can be accessed securely and easily with **MySQL** indexing and **AWS S3** connectivity [9], which makes structured data storage and retrieval easier.

While Medifolio provides a robust framework for improving medical communication and data accessibility, future enhancements will focus on improving OCR accuracy, further NLP fine-tuning for better contextual interpretation, and extended interoperability features for integration with existing healthcare systems. These advancements will further optimize Medifolio's role in bridging the gap between patients and doctors while enhancing collaboration in the medical community.

References

1. Salunkhe, V., Chintha, V.R., Pamadi, V.N., Jain, A., Goel, O.: AI-powered solutions for reducing hospital readmissions: a case study on AI-driven patient engagement. Int. J. Creat. Res. Thoughts **10**(12), 757–764 (2022)
2. Stasevych, M., Zvarych, V.: Innovative robotic technologies and artificial intelligence in pharmacy and medicine: paving the way for the future of health care—a review. Big Data Cogn. Comput. **7**(3), 147 (2023)
3. Xu, H., et al.: Monitoring and management of home-quarantined patients with COVID-19 using a WeChat-based telemedicine system: retrospective cohort study. J. Med. Internet Res. **22**(7), e19514 (2020)
4. Juhn, Y., Liu, H.: Artificial intelligence approaches using natural language processing to advance EHR-based clinical research. J. Allergy Clin. Immunol. **145**(2), 463–469 (2020)
5. Maleki Varnosfaderani, S., Forouzanfar, M.: The role of AI in hospitals and clinics: transforming healthcare in the 21st century. Bioeng. **11**(4), 337 (2024)
6. Amato, F., Coppolino, L., Cozzolino, G., Mazzeo, G., Moscato, F., Nardone, R.: Enhancing random forest classification with NLP in DAMEH: a system for DAta Management in eHealth domain. Neurocomputing **444**, 79–91 (2021)
7. Paganelli, A., Spadafora, M., Navarrete-Dechent, C., Guida, S., Pellacani, G., Longo, C.: Natural language processing in dermatology: a systematic literature review and state of the art. J. Eur. Acad. Dermatol. Venereol. **38**(12), 2225–2234 (2024)
8. Abu-Jassar, A.T., Attar, H., Amer, A., Lyashenko, V., Yevsieiev, V., Solyman, A.: Remote monitoring system of patient status in social IoT environments using Amazon Web Services (AWS) technologies and smart health care. Int. J. Crowd Sci. **8** (2024)
9. Pyne, Y., Wong, Y.M., Fang, H., Simpson, E.: Analysis of 'One in a Million' primary care consultation conversations using natural language processing. BMJ Health Care Inform. **30**(1), e100659 (2023)
10. Valabojui, P.K.: Integration of AI and cloud technologies in healthcare: a comprehensive framework for career development and portfolio enhancement. Int. J. Res. Comput. Appl. Inf. Technol. **7**(2), 674–687 (2024)
11. Savova, G.K., Danciu, I., Alamudun, F., Miller, T., Lin, C., Bitterman, D.S., et al.: Use of natural language processing to extract clinical cancer phenotypes from electronic medical records. Cancer Res. **79**(21), 5463–5470 (2019)
12. Shaik, T., et al.: Remote patient monitoring using artificial intelligence: Current state, applications, and challenges. Wiley Interdiscip. Rev. Data Min. Knowl. Discov. **13**(2), e1485 (2023)
13. Huang, L., Chen, Z., Yang, Z., Huang, W.: Advancing healthcare accessibility: fusing artificial intelligence with flexible sensing to forge digital health innovations. BME Front. **5**, 0062 (2024)
14. Alowais, S.A., et al.: Revolutionizing healthcare: the role of artificial intelligence in clinical practice. BMC Med. Educ. **23**(1), 689 (2023)
15. Xie, Q., et al.: Me llama: foundation large language models for medical applications. arXiv preprint arXiv:2402.12749 (2024)
16. Kalusivalingam, A. K., Sharma, A., Patel, N., Singh, V.: Leveraging BERT and LSTM for enhanced natural language processing in clinical data analysis. Int. J. AI ML **2**(3) (2021)
17. Davuluri, M.: An overview of natural language processing in analyzing clinical text data for patient health insights. Res.-Gate J. **10**(10), (2024)
18. Pilowsky, J.K., et al.: Natural language processing in the intensive care unit: A scoping review. Crit. Care Resusc. (2024)

19. Wu, S., et al.: Deep learning in clinical natural language processing: a methodical review. J. Am. Med. Inform. Assoc. **27**(3), 457–470 (2020)
20. Dash, S., Shakyawar, S.K., Sharma, M., Kaushik, S.: Big data in healthcare: management, analysis and future prospects. J. Big Data **6**(1), 1–25 (2019)

Compartmental Models for Detecting Fake News Propagation in OSN with Variable Population

V. Nithish Kumar[1]([✉]) [iD], G. Praneeth Kumar[1] [iD], Sujoy Datta[2] [iD], Santosh Kumar Uppada[3] [iD], and B. Sivaselvan[1] [iD]

[1] Design and Manufacturing, Indian Institute of Information Technology, Kancheepuram, Chennai, India
{cs24d0002,cs20b1130,sivaselvanb}@iiitdm.ac.in
[2] Hike Pvt. Ltd., New Delhi, India
[3] GITAM (Deemed to be University), Visakhapatnam, India
suppada@gitam.edu

Abstract. An increase in the utilization of the Internet has made people rely on social networks to acquire information from various sources. As information comes from different sources, it is always di-cult to verify the credibility of the news. Fake news is defined as the intentional or unintentional spread of news that negatively impacts society. Fake news is always associated with cognitive and psychological issues, and spreaders always target the psychological aspects to make users believe and propagate it further. Qualitative or Quantitative approaches are used for modeling fake news, and this paper uses the quantitative.

approach for defining fake news. Propagation dynamics are captured with the help of diffusion models, and this paper focuses on constructing modified epidemic models to model and predict fake news. The proposed models aid in examining the spread of fake news within online social networks. Individuals in the network may potentially fall into one of six states: Susceptible, Exposed, Infected, Recovered, Deceased, or Skeptical. Differential equations are solved, and graphs are modeled for initial conditions and values. Further, the Basic Reproduction Number is calculated to estimate the spread of fake news into the network. Numerical simulation is also shown for various epidemic models.

Keywords: Basic Reproduction Number · Disease Free equilibrium state · Epidemic Modeling · Skeptic · Transition states

1 Introduction

Social Networks are defined as a collection of networks of individuals connected by interpersonal relationships. In general social networks can be either offline or online. As the utilization of the internet has grown exponentially, online social networking sites have also grown, which are used to share information or maintain social relationships. Social networks are generally used to share content, and opinions or maintain personal relationships [6]. Social networks have become one of the prominent channels for disseminating information. As online social media comes from various sources, it is always difficult to check the information's credibility. Fake, or Yellow Journalism, is a process of spreading information that is likely to be sloppy, biased, or unreal. Fake news is defined as the intentional or unintentional spread of information that is false, which may create hoaxes in society. Misinformation, disinformation, biased news, rumour, satire news, propaganda, and conspiracy theories are termed to be different types of fake news. The spread of such news is intended to target a person or firm and create hoaxes in society [3].

In general, the propagation of fake news is linked with cognitive or psychological issues, and people who intend to spread this news use click-baits or psychological aspects to make people believe and spread the news further deeper into the networks [11]. Fake news is spread due to psychological aspects like homophily, confirmation bias, Bandwagon effect, or Normative effect, making users interact with the news and spread it further. User engagement in fake news is often linked with benefits, self-impact, and social impact created by the information spread [4]. Users generally fall vulnerable to fake news due to factors like Naive Realism and Confirmation Bias. Naive Realism tends to make users believe that other users are true if they tend to believe their ideas and views, else treated as fake. Confirmation bias makes users believe in the news that favors their past experiences and beliefs. The intentional spread of fake news will always target the emotions of the persons consuming the news [8]. Click baits are commonly used to make users enthusiastic about the news, and social bots are used to spread it deeper and faster in the network. While dealing with fake news detection, one could work on qualitative or quantitative approaches. The qualitative approach deals with the propagation patterns of the news, while quantitative analysis helps to define mathematical modeling for the same. Defining an accurate model helps to describe and predict fake news more realistically. In addition to the regression models like Linear, Poisson, and Regression Trees, epidemic and economic models are used for capturing propagation dynamics of fake news [14].

Epidemic models deal with modeling and detecting fake news using disease models, as the fake news propagation patterns tend to follow the pattern of the infectious disease model. Models are constructed similarly to disease models. In the economic model, the users' behavior and decision-making strategies are analyzed. Every user is either mapped as the publisher or consumer of the news. The news publisher is associated with short-term utility (profit the user gets for propagating any news) or long-term utility (overall reputation for spreading news). The consumer is mapped to information utility (the truth of the information consumed) and psychological utilities (preferring information due to past experiences) [14].

2 Epidemic Models for Fake News Detection

The propagation of fake news in online social networks can be viewed as similar to the spread of disease in the epidemic model. Epidemic models are specified using different states and transition states. Basic SIS and SIR models are considered to create new models [1]. Certain assumptions are made for modeling fake news using epidemic models. The models proposed uses one of the following states.

- **Susceptible (S)**, Users who contacted with fake news. These users are potential but have not yet spread any fake news.

- **Exposed (E)**, Users exposed to the fake news and high probability of spreading it further.
- **Infected (I)**, Users who have spread the fake news further.
- **Recovered (R)**, Users who either removed the news after knowing it was fake or removed it after losing interest in the news.
- **Mortality (M)**, Users who blindly believe in the news but don't spread it further. Mortality is always linked with psychological aspects like bias, homophily, frequency heuristic, confirmation bias, and Semmelweis effect.
- **Skeptic (Z)**, Users who believe the news after investigating proper evidence of the authenticity of the news. These people tend to ask more questions and cross-verify with multiple sources before believing the news.

The transitions states are given by

Table 1. Transition States of Proposed Models

Parameter	Significance
α	Susceptible $\rightarrow$ Exposed
β	Infected $\rightarrow$ Recovered
γ	Infected $\rightarrow$ Mortality
δ	Exposed $\rightarrow$ Mortality
a	Exposed $\rightarrow$ Infected
b	Bias
c	Exposed $\rightarrow$ Skeptic
d	Infected $\rightarrow$ Skeptic
f	Skeptic $\rightarrow$ Infected
g	Skeptic $\rightarrow$ Recovered
C_1	rate at which users join the group
C_2	rate at which users leave the group
C_3	rate at which exposed users leave the group (potential to infect users from other groups)
C_4	rate at which infected users leave the group (potential to infect users from other groups)
C_5	rate at which recovered users leave the group
C_6	rate at which skeptic users leave the group

3 SIRM and SEIRMZ Models

The proposed models propagation patterns and equilibrium stability are theoretically analyzed and determined. The diffusion of fake news is estimated initially by studying certain case studies from the literature and estimating the proportionality constants of the proposed models. Fake news dissemination is estimated for a closed group of people, and certain news is propagated. Case studies helped estimate users' movement between different compartments and the transmission of news, rumors, and disinformation. Different case studies related to the Boston Marathon blast (2013) [9], Charlie Hebdo Shooting (2015) [7], and Ferguson Unrest Missouri (2014) [2] are taken into consideration. Upon analyzing the information diffusion in these cases, models like SIRM and SEIRMZ models with variable populations are proposed, considering the basic SIR and SIS models.

3.1 SIRM

SIRM stands for Susceptible, Infected, Recovered, and Mortality. Here users tend to end up in the mortality compartment if they blindly believe in the news but do not spread it further. Users in the mortality compartment are due to bias, confirmation bias, or homophily. The following system of ODEs represent the SIRM model of fake news propagation pattern for a changing population in an Online Social Network platform. Here, ϵ defines the rate of change of population (Fig. 1).

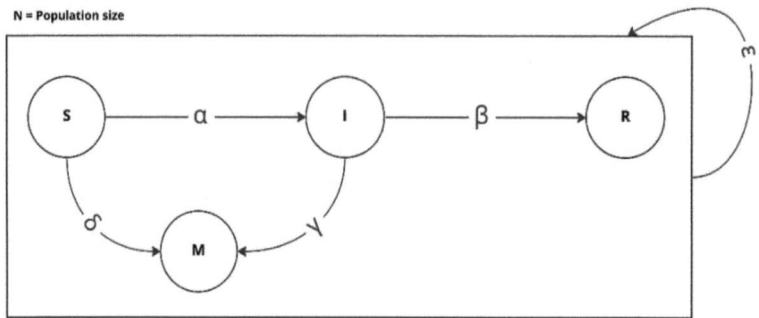

Fig. 1. SIRM state diagram

$$\frac{dS}{dt} = -\alpha SI - \delta bS + c1\epsilon - c2\epsilon \quad (1a)$$

$$\frac{dI}{dt} = \alpha SI - \beta I - \gamma bI - c3\epsilon \quad (1b)$$

$$\frac{dR}{dt} = \beta I - c4\epsilon \quad (1c)$$

$$\frac{dM}{dt} = \delta bS + \gamma bI \quad (1d)$$

Here, α is termed as "Rate of Contact", and β is termed a "Rate of change of Infection" (refer Table 1 for significance of different transition states).

3.2 SEIRMZ

Further, the dissemination of fake news is modeled using the SEIRMZ model as an extension of the basic SIRM model. Here the slight difference is that Users who are termed to be in the Susceptible state are the users in the group in which the fake news is published (have contacts with the user who published fake news). Once the users interact with the news, they are said to be in the Exposed state. Skeptic state has users who believe in the news after tracking the credibility of the news. These users tend to extract the complete details of the information published. The following system of ODEs represent the SEIRMZ model of fake news propagation pattern for a changing population in an Online Social Network platform (Fig. 2).

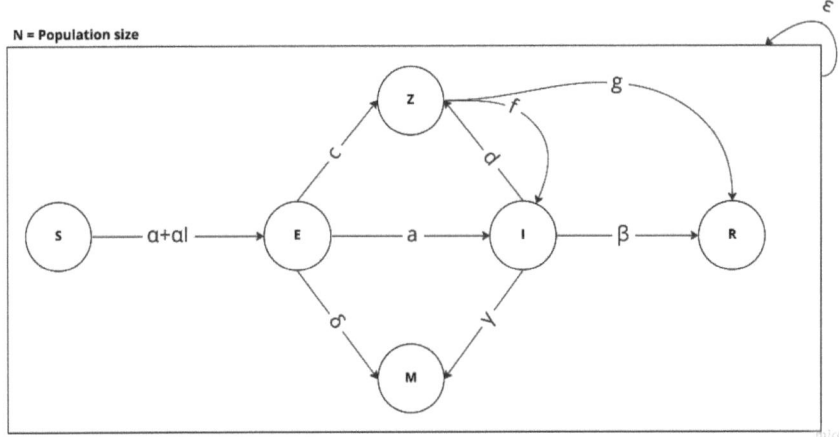

Fig. 2. SEIRMZ state diagram

$$\frac{dS}{dt} = -\alpha SE - \alpha SI + c1\epsilon - c2\epsilon \tag{2a}$$

$$\frac{dE}{dt} = \alpha SE + \alpha SI - aE - b\delta E - cE - c3\epsilon \tag{2b}$$

$$\frac{dI}{dt} = aE - \beta I - b\gamma I - dI + fZ - c4\epsilon \tag{2c}$$

$$\frac{dR}{dt} = \beta I + gZ - c5\epsilon \tag{2d}$$

$$\frac{dM}{dt} = \delta bE + \gamma bI \tag{2e}$$

$$\frac{dZ}{dt} = cE + dI - fZ - gZ - c6\epsilon \tag{2f}$$

4 Stability of Epidemic Models

There exists two equilibrium states in disease epidemics, which are described below

- Disease Free Equilibrium State, which is the equilibrium state with no infection (state in which no fake news is propagated).
- Disease Endemic Equilibrium, which is the equilibrium state in which the propagation of fake news has crossed its peak and the propagation further starts diminishing. It can be viewed as the state where users started losing interest in the news [10].

It is to be noted that fake news propagation has no endemic state (as there is no specific point at which fake news propagation completely diminishes). Social ingrouping, shift to social media, belief systems are the main driving forces that are making people more prone to fake news.

4.1 Basic Reproduction Number (R_0)

The basic Reproduction number (Reproductive ratio) is the number of secondary infections transmitted by an individual primary source of infection. In pathology, it refers to the transmissibility and contagiousness of the infection. In fake news propagation, R_0 is the number of users who believe and propagate the fake news that an individual initially spread. The value of R_0 was observed to be higher in the groups where the popular user (influencer) becomes infected. It defines the number of expected infected cases directly generated by one case in a group where all the individuals in the group are in the susceptible state [5].

The disease free equilibrium of a epidemic modelled propagation is a state when the no disease or a trace of disease is present in the population. This is a local equilibrium and the effect of scale or propagation is noticed with a special constant called the base reproduction number for the model. Standard models of transmission empirically have deduced that a R_0 less than 1 indicates that the network does not spread out and eventually fades in endemic fashion. We will calculate the R_0 for both SIRM and SEIRMZ models taking the fact that population keeps growing on a continuous measure as a part of calculations.

4.2 Stability of Proposed SIRM Model

We have already explored and listed the rate of compartmental growth for the SIRM model. The only equation considered to determine the base reproduction number is the rate of growth of infected compartment. For the fake news to spread, $\frac{dI}{dT} > 0$

$$\Rightarrow \alpha SI - \beta I - \gamma bI - c3\epsilon > 0 \Rightarrow I(\alpha S - \beta - \gamma b) - c3\epsilon > 0$$

At the initial state of news propagation- $I = I_0$, and $S = S_0 = 1$ under the assumption that at least one person needs to be susceptible for the news to spread.

$$\Rightarrow \alpha - \beta - \gamma b > \frac{c3\epsilon}{I_0}$$

$$\Rightarrow \beta\left(\frac{\alpha}{\beta} - \frac{\gamma b}{\beta} - \frac{c_3 \epsilon}{I_0 \beta} - 1\right) > 0$$

This inequality can be translated as

$$\beta(R0 - 1) > 0, \text{ where } R0 = \frac{\alpha - b\gamma}{\beta} - \frac{c_3 \epsilon}{I_0 \beta}$$

Here the term R_0 is called the base reproduction number for secondary infections. As per standard state of art modelling, a fake news is bound to spread if the R_0 is greater than 0. Also considering the fact that I_0 should be at least 1 (individual) which implies that at least one person in the demographic should be infected to propagate the fake news. Therefore

$$R0 = \frac{\alpha - b\gamma - c_3 \epsilon}{\beta} > 0$$

is the only necessary condition for fake news to propagate in a growing population. The rate of growth of population also affects the base reproduction number. We will see in the later sections how the base reproduction determines equilibrium (Fig. 3).

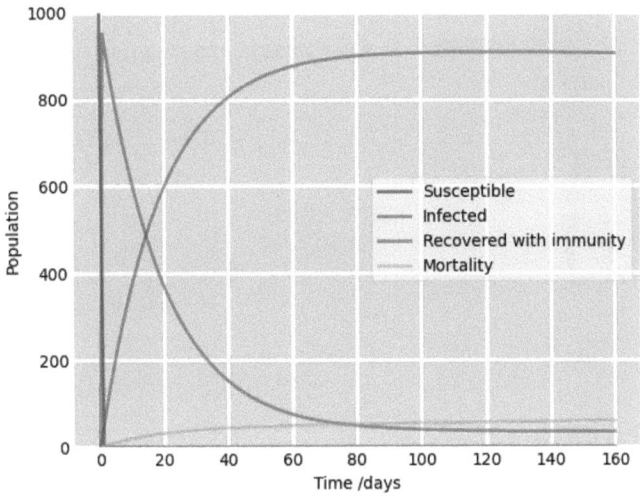

Fig. 3. SIRM simulation trend

4.3 Stability of Proposed SEIRMZ Model

Although there are many ways to compute the base reproduction number for a system of ODEs, but for differential equations with positive and negative linearity, the Next generation matrix is the best technique as it accounts for both inflow and outflow of exposition (Table 2) [12].

We break down $\frac{dx}{dt} = F(x) - V(x)$.

Since only E and I compartments are under infection in the SEIRMZ model, we reduce the dimensions of the F and V matrices for ease of calculation.

Table 2. Inflow and Outflow of Expositions

Parameter	Significance
F(x)	The rate of appearance of new infections or fake news is usually linked with the exposed compartment of the population.
V (x)	The inflow and outflow of infection for the exposed

$$F(X) = \begin{pmatrix} \alpha S & \alpha S \\ 0 & 0 \end{pmatrix} \begin{pmatrix} E \\ I \end{pmatrix}$$

and

$$V(X) = \begin{pmatrix} aE + b\delta E + cE + c_3\epsilon \\ -aE + \beta I + b\gamma I + dI + fZ + c_4\epsilon \end{pmatrix}$$

Dropping the constant elements in the V matrix and re-dimensioning it we obtain the final FV^{-1} matrix as,

$$\begin{pmatrix} \frac{\alpha}{a+b\delta+c} + \frac{a\alpha}{(a+b\delta+c)(\beta+b\gamma+d)} & \alpha(\beta+b\gamma+d) \\ 0 & 0 \end{pmatrix}$$

This matrix being a lower triangular matrix, the highest value of the matrix becomes the BRN(R_0).
Thus

$$R0 = \frac{\alpha}{dta+b\delta+c} + \frac{a\alpha}{(a+b\delta+c)(\beta+b\gamma+d)}$$

5 Equilibrium States

Seemingly evident for disease models, if $R_0 < 1$, the infection goes extinct; if $R_0 > 1$, it becomes endemic. By linearizing around the equilibrium for online social networks, the analysis in each example entails identifying equilibria and establishing the asymptotic stability of each equilibrium for the fake news propagation models in a changing population. The disease-free equilibrium was asymptotically stable in each of the situations examined in the previous section if and only if $R_0 < 1$, and if $R_0 > 1$ there was a specific endemic equilibrium that was asymptotically stable.

5.1 SIRM

To check the local equilibrium relationship with the base reproduction number we need to derive a stability check that includes certain restrictions and limits on the changing population dependency constants.

Let us consider the system of equations as K_0. To determine the stability check we create a Jacobian Matrix for the system of equations and calculate the eigen values. Thus (Fig. 4),

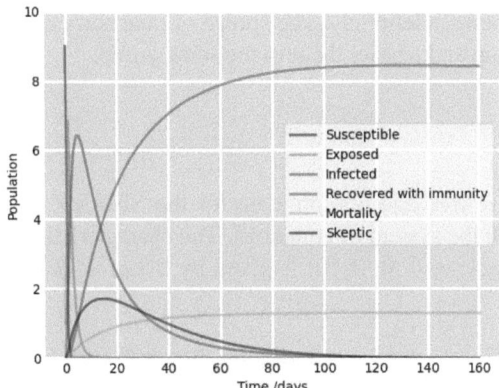

Fig. 4. SEIRM simulation trend

$$J(K0) = \begin{pmatrix} -\alpha I & -\alpha S & 0 & 0 \\ \alpha I & \alpha S - \beta - b\gamma & 0 & 0 \\ 0 & \beta & 0 & 0 \\ b\delta & b\gamma & 0 & 0 \end{pmatrix}$$

Using the characteristic equation of the Jacobian Matrix, $|J(K_0) - \lambda I|$ at the initial condition ($S = 1, I = 0$), we obtain two eigenvalues for the matrix, $\lambda_1 = 0$, and $\lambda_2 = \alpha - \beta - b\gamma$.

Experiment. *To obtain the conditional requirement for an SIRM model of fake news for a growing population.*

Let us consider the case when BRN for SIRM system is less than 1(stability requirement). we have,

$$\frac{a\alpha - b\gamma - c_3\epsilon}{\beta} < 1$$

$\Rightarrow \alpha - \beta - b\gamma < c_3\epsilon \Rightarrow \lambda 2 < c_3\epsilon$

Since the population is always growing, the term $c_3\epsilon$ will always be a positive constant for the system of equations. However, for the system to stable, the eigen values of the Jacobian matrix should be less than 0.

Thus for $\lambda_2 < 0$ to be true, the positive constant $c_3 \epsilon$ should be 0. This will ensure a tightly coupled bound on the stability of the system. If $c_3 \epsilon = 0$ and ϵ cannot be zero for a growing population,

$$c_3 = 0$$

Inference . For SIRM model in a growing population, fake news propagation becomes stable (attains equilibrium) only when the size of infected compartment is not affected by population change. This can be compared with a Whatsapp community analogy, where if a person starts believing the fake news leaves the group, they still have the ability to propagate the fake news indefinitely. The spread of fake news will stop only when they do not leave the group and restrict them to the same group.

5.2 SIERMZ

To assess the disease free equilibrium state for the SEIRMZ model, we construct a Jacobian matrix with the system of equations. The characteristic polynomial at disease free equilibrium ($L_0(1, 0, 0, 0, 0, 0)$) is given by $|J(L_0) - I\lambda|$, which on simplifying computes to

$$\lambda 3 + (a + b\delta + c + \beta + b\gamma + d + f + g - \alpha)\lambda 2 \\ +[(a + b\delta + c)(f + g + \beta + b\gamma + d) + (\beta + b\gamma \\ +d)(f + g) - df - a\alpha]\lambda + [(a + b\delta + c - \alpha) \\ (\beta + b\gamma + d)(f + g) - (a + b\delta + c - \alpha)df \\ -(a + b\delta + c - \alpha)\alpha(f + g)] = 0$$

To prove the stability of the model using Routh-Hurwitz polynomial. The polynomial satisfying the Routh-Hurwitz criteria is called Hurwitz polynomial, and it can be used to check the stability of the obtained third-degree polynomial [13].

$$\lambda 3 + a_1 \lambda 2 + a_2 \lambda + a_3 = 0$$

It has to be shown that, $a_1 a_2 > a_3, \Rightarrow a_1 a_2 - a_3 > 0$. However, for the system to be stable at disease free equilibrium, the BRN(R_0) should be less than 1.

$$R_0 < 1 \Rightarrow R_0 - 1 < 0 \Rightarrow (1 - R_0) > 0$$

$\Rightarrow$

$$\Rightarrow 1 - \frac{\alpha(\beta + b\gamma + d) + a\alpha}{\beta(a + b\delta + c)(\beta + b\gamma + d)} > 0$$

$$(b + \beta + d)(a\alpha + b\delta + c - \alpha) - a\alpha > 0$$

Lemma 1. *If* $(b\gamma + \beta + d)(a\alpha + b\beta + c - \alpha) - a\alpha > 0$, *then* $(a\alpha + b\beta + c - \alpha) > 0$, *for* $\{a, b, c, d, \alpha, \beta, \gamma, \delta\} \in [0, 1]$.

Proof. To prove the lemma, proof by contradiction is chosen. So, on contrary, let us suppose that

$$(a + b\delta + c - \alpha) < 0$$

As $(b\gamma + \beta + d)$ is an additive term,

$$(b\gamma + \beta + d) > 0 \Rightarrow (b\gamma + \beta + d)(a\alpha + b\delta + c - \alpha) < 0 \Rightarrow (b\gamma + \beta + d)(a\alpha + b\delta + c - \alpha$$

which contradicts the initial assumption that

$$(b\gamma + \beta + d)(a\alpha + b\delta + c - \alpha) - a\alpha > 0 \Rightarrow (a\alpha + b\delta + c - \alpha) > 0$$

From the above lemma, we have $(a\alpha + b\delta + c - \alpha) > 0$, now we can say that

$$(f + g)[(a + b\delta + c\alpha)(\beta + b\gamma + d) - a\alpha]$$
$$+ (a + b\delta + c - \alpha)[(a + b\delta + c - \alpha)(\beta + b\gamma + d) - a\alpha]$$
$$+ (\beta + b\gamma + d)[(a + b\delta + c - \alpha)(\beta + b\gamma + d) - a\alpha]$$
$$+ (f + g)[(a + b\delta + c - \alpha)(\beta + b\gamma) + (\beta + b\gamma + d + f + g)(\beta + b\gamma)$$
$$+ (a + b\delta + c - \alpha)(a + b\delta + c - \alpha) + (a + b\delta + c - \alpha)(f + g)]$$
$$+ gd(a + b\delta + c - \alpha) + gd(\beta + b\gamma + d + f + g) > 0$$

This proves the Routh-Hurwitz polynomial stability condition for the SEIRMZ mathematical model as for $R0 < 1$, the condition $a1a2 > a3$ is satisfied.

Inference. For SEIRMZ model in a growing population, fake news propagation becomes stable (attains equilibrium) only when $R_0 < 1$, irrespective of the growth or depreciation in population of any compartments.

6 Conclusion and Future Scope

This current study uses mathematical modeling using differential equations to predict future outbreaks and understand the dynamics of fake news propagation for a variable population. SIRM and SEIRMZ models are proposed to understand information diffusion. The Basic reproduction number (R_0) is used to check the stability of the proposed models. Further models are simulated for numerical instances. The paper analyzes the case studies that helped determine the interference patterns, which helps in understanding the propagation patterns of news from one compartment to another. As the user's bias depends on the incident or the person who propagated news, further study focuses on determining bias value across domains. As part of future studies, the aim is to find the influencers in the network and study the information diffusion dynamics. The aim is to calculate centrality measures like Degree centrality (to find the person who deals with mode users), Eigen centrality (to find a more influential person), closeness centrality, and betweenness centrality to understand the topology of the propagation network. Finally, depending on the measures, the aim is to add skeptic nodes (like fact-checkers) to mitigate the spread of fake news. Further aim is also to link the temporal, user-profile, and text-based features to enhance the model's ability to mitigate fake news.

References

1. Allen, L.J.: Some discrete-time si, sir, and sis epidemic models. Math. Biosci. **124**(1), 83–105 (1994). https://doi.org/10.1016/0025-5564(94)90025-6, https://www.sciencedirect.com/science/article/pii/0025556494900256
2. Bonilla, Y., Rosa, J.: #ferguson: Digital protest, hashtag ethnography, and the racial politics of social media in the united states. Am. Ethnologist **42** (2015). https://doi.org/10.1111/amet.12112
3. Campbell, W.J.: Yellow journalism. The international encyclopedia of journalism studies, pp. 1–5 (2019)
4. Deshmane, A., Barriola, X.: Riding the Gravy 'Trend'? Bandwagon Eect Vs. Conspicuous Adoption of Music in User-Generated Content. IESE Business School Working Paper, SSRN (2021), https://books.google.co.in/books?id=f0PlzwEACAAJ
5. Dietz, K.: The estimation of the basic reproduction number for infectious diseases. Stat. Methods Med. Res. **2**, 2341 (1993). https://doi.org/10.1177/096228029300200103
6. Garton, L., Haythornthwaite, C., Wellman, B.: Studying online social networks. J. Comput. Mediated Commun. **3**(1), JCMC313 (1997). https://doi.org/10.1111/j.1083-6101.1997.tb00062.x
7. Giglietto, F., Lee, Y.: To be or not to be charlie: Twitter hashtags as a discourse and counter-discourse in the aftermath of the 2015 charlie hebdo shooting in france. In: Proceedings of the 5th Workshop on Making Sense of Microposts at the 24th International World Wide Web Conference, vol. 1395 (2015)
8. Greifeneder, R., Jaé, M., Newman, E., Schwarz, N.: The Psychology of Fake News: Accepting, Sharing, and Correcting Misinformation. Routledge, Taylor & Francis Group (2021). https://books.google.co.in/books?id=oC2NzQEACAAJ
9. Gupta, A., Lamba, H., Kumaraguru, P.: $1.00 per rt #bostonmarathon #prayforboston: Analyzing fake content on twitter. In: 2013 APWG eCrime Researchers Summit. p. 112 (2013). https://doi.org/10.1109/eCRS.2013.6805772. $1.00 per RT #BostonMarathon #PrayForBoston: Analyzing fake content on Twitter
10. Kamgang, J.C., Sallet, G.: Computation of threshold conditions for epidemiological models and global stability of the disease-free equilibrium (dfe). Math. Biosci. **213**, 112 (2008). https://doi.org/10.1016/j.mbs.2008.02.005
11. Lischka, J., Garz, M.: Clickbait news and algorithmic curation: a game theory framework of the relation between journalism, users, and platforms. New Media Soc. **25**, 14614448211027174 (2021). https://doi.org/10.1177/14614448211027174
12. Roberts, M.G., Heesterbeek, J.A.P.: Characterizing the next-generation matrix and basic reproduction number in ecological epidemiology. J. Math. Biol. **66**(4–5), 10451064 (2013)
13. Yang, J., Hou, X., Li, Y.: A generalization of routhhurwitz stability criterion for fractional-order systems with order $\alpha \in (1, 2)$. Fractal and Fractional **6**(10) (2022). https://doi.org/10.3390/fractalfract6100557, https://www.mdpi.com/2504-3110/6/10/557
14. Zhou, X., Zafarani, R.: Fake news detection: an interdisciplinary research. In: Companion Proceedings of the 2019 World Wide Web Conference. WWW 2019, p. 1292. Association for Computing Machinery, New York, NY, USA (2019). https://doi.org/10.1145/3308560.3316476

DermaVLM: Multi-modal Skin Disease Diagnosis

Saket Sultania(✉) ⓘ, Vansh Shah ⓘ, Rohit Sonawane ⓘ, and Abhishek Vichare ⓘ

Mukesh Patel School of Technology Management & Engineering, SVKM's Narsee Monjee Institute of Management Studies (NMIMS) Deemed-to-University, Mumbai, Maharashtra, India
`{saket.sultania,vansh.shah7,rohit.sonawane1}@nmims.in`

Abstract. This research presents DermaVLM, an innovative Vision-Language Model designed to transform skin disease diagnosis by combining computer vision and natural language processing techniques. The approach integrates Convolutional Neural Networks (CNN) for image-based classification and Retrieval Augmented Generation (RAG) for contextual insights, mirroring the diagnostic process of experienced dermatologists. Our technical foundation follows a three-step training protocol that optimizes visual feature extraction and knowledge integration, starting with ResNet101-based CNN architecture for comprehensive dermatological condition identification. The Llama 3.2 11B Vision model follows the CNN to provide language understanding and is fine-tuned for dermatological terminology and concepts. A domain-specific adaption is incorporated where the model is fine-tuned on dermatology-specific datasets, including SkinCAP and SCIN. On comparing the optimized model, the performance metrics indicate a 92% classification accuracy and a 47.9% reduction in inference time; token efficiency is improved by 73.9%, and a resultant 44.5% increase in semantic alignment with medical images as compared to an unoptimized baseline, enhancing the model's utility in real-world applications. Based on this approach, we aim to provide DermaVLM as a scalable, efficient, and clinically reliable solution to improve dermatological accessibility in underserved communities by bridging the gap between advanced medical AI and communities with scarce medical expertise.

Keywords: Dermatological Diagnosis · Clinical AI · Vision-Language Model · Convolutional Neural Network · Multi-Image Analysis · Telemedicine

1 Introduction

The growing common occurrence of skin diseases in India, backed by surveys showing occurrence ranging from 10% to 87% across various sections of the population [1], has been a cause of growing public health concern. Such dermatological conditions not only have physical effects on the skin but also lead to psychological implications like depression, anxiety, low self-esteem, and stigmatization. Such challenges are especially severe in remote and rural India, where dermatologists are scarce compared to cities, 1.9/million compared to 23.4/million [2], creating a significant healthcare disparity.

Recent studies have also shown that around 23.9% of the diagnosed population does not seek medical treatment, further highlighting the severity of this situation [3]. The majority of the individuals who do seek treatment consult medical professionals, but others rely on or resort to alternative medication for treatment, which can compromise their health outcomes. Skin conditions can cause significant occupational hazards in the workplace, where such delayed treatment and diagnostic tendencies are particularly alarming.

In the construction industry, for example, infectious skin diseases account for 61.56% of the cases out of the 36.2% related to dermatological morbidity [4]. For the leather industry, 71% of the workers are unaware of occupational hazards, citing poor literacy and safety practices as reasons [5]. Statistics show that only 29.8% of workers use Personal Protective Equipment, highlighting India's urgent need to diagnose and prevent skin diseases via a practical, scalable solution.

Vision Language Models (VLMs) offer a promising solution to the problem. They can be used to accurately diagnose occupational skin diseases based on images and provide symptoms and treatment advice. Thus, we introduce DermaVLM, a multi-modal dermatology diagnostic system integrating CNN-based feature extraction with VLMs to achieve high accuracy and interpretability. The system incorporates dermatology-specific prompts to guide the VLM, combining visual features from skin images with text embeddings to predict skin conditions and provide interpretable justifications.

The manuscript follows a structure where Sect. 2 comprehensively reviews the multimodal dermatological diagnosis and identifies specific gaps we address through DermaVLM. Section 3 showcases a detailed explanation of our system's architecture and methodological approach. We outline the experimental setup and describe the evaluation metrics in Sect. 4. Section 5 analyzes the results and insights derived from our findings. Section 6 concludes the manuscript, summarizing contributions and delineating promising directions for future research.

2 Literature Review

Increased developments in Artificial Intelligence and vision-language models have improved dermatological diagnostic potential. Our project utilizes images and text prompts to aid in dermatological diagnosis. Thus, we explore the UMass-BioNLP team's DermPrompt study [6], which examines prompt engineering with GPT-4V for dermatological diagnosis. DermPrompt works on adapting domain-specific prompts to improve diagnostic accuracy and aid clinical decision-making. It showcases that the GPT-4V when used along with a retrieval agent, provides correct dermatological diagnosis with an accuracy of 85% using images and text prompts as input. The study shows how to implement optimized prompts and images to improve classification accuracy. The study compares various prompt engineering approaches, providing an understanding of how varying domain-specific prompts affect the framework's capability to demand different dermatological conditions.

We explore SkinGPT-4 [7], an interactive dermatology diagnostic system that integrates vision-language models with real-time clinical assistance. Like our proposed work, SkinGPT-4 combines images and text input to provide relevant and accurate diagnostic information in real-time. Considering SkinGPT-4 as an example, we can understand how we can utilize AI combined with human expertise to bridge the gap in environments with scarce resources and improve accessibility. The system can evaluate images, identify skin conditions, and provide treatment recommendations, providing a pathway to create a similar system. However, SkinGPT-4 relies on prompt-based reasoning without fine-grained multi-modal fusion or image-based learning. Its reliance on generic prompt engineering may result in suboptimal alignment with domain-specific semantics. We aim to integrate CNN-derived image embeddings with VLM reasoning, incorporating domain-specific prompt tuning to enhance the VLM's contextual awareness, improving SkinGPT-4.

Further exploring the generation of medical literature for specific conditions, we study BioRAGent, which uses a retrieval-augmented generation (RAG) system for domain-specific query answering, making it suitable for scientific Q&A [8]. We can understand how RAG can be used to generate contextual responses and evaluate the accuracy and improvements of the outputs related to dermatology. BioRAGent improves contextual response accuracy by combining generative models with retrieval approaches like RAG.

As we intend to deliver our proposed system to users from different demographics, user comprehension must be given importance. Using VLMs, it is relatively complex to explain diagnostic problems to users because of the complexity of certain dermatological conditions. Thus, we explore SkinGEN [9], a framework that improves the visual explainability of the diagnosis to the users using a stable diffusion model to generate reference demonstrations of the VLM results. The system promotes trust and dependability by delivering transparent explanations for its diagnoses. Its focus on correlating diagnostic precision with explainability allows us to understand, evaluate, and choose techniques to visualize choice paths to understand VLM predictions better, allowing for a more user-centric and transparent application, which is essential in clinical adoption.

Classifying skin diseases and identifying skin lesions result in more robust and accurate diagnoses [10]. The study utilizes a ResNet-152-based CNN model to classify the lesions on an augmented image dataset using positional, scale, and lighting transformation for improved generalization. The AUC values highlight the effectiveness of CNNs combined with data augmentation, helping us understand the effect of image augmentation in classification. Deep Learning requires significant computing resources for training. The study [11] compares various CNN architectures for classifying seven types of skin diseases that are particularly prevalent in the Philippines to help understand the efficacy of CNN architectures. Architectures like ResNet60, VGG16, and MobileNet are compared and provide distinctive results to identify how each performs while classifying medical images. Diagnostic precision can be improved by utilizing lesion localization techniques such as bounding boxes, as demonstrated in [12]. Several state-of-the-art machine learning models are benchmarked on a 10-class and 100-class dataset. A CNN model was benchmarked on Skin-10 and Skin-100 datasets to provide relatively high accuracy. Adding bounding boxes to the Skin-10 dataset showed improved accuracy. A recent study [13] delves into understanding the promise of applying CNN in dermatological skin condition prediction. It conducts a comparative analysis of various CNN architectures to understand which provided maximum accuracy and efficiency. Models such as InceptionV3, VGG19, DenseNet201, ResNet50, and EfficientNet are evaluated. The research shows that VGG19 and DenseNet201 achieve the highest classification accuracy, underlining the importance of model selection for image analysis.

These studies illustrate the immense potential of combining convolutional neural networks, vision-language models, and deep learning with domain-specific adaptations. They provide a strong foundation for our research, which aims to leverage these advancements to develop an open-source, VLM-based system tailored to address the unique challenges of skin disease diagnosis in India (Table 1).

Table 1. Literature Review

Citation	Dataset	Methodology	Evaluation Metrics	Key Findings
[13]	Dermatological Image Dataset	Compares ResnNet50, InceptionV3, VGG-19, DenseNet201, and EfficientNet for skin disease prediction	VGG-19: **Accuracy:** 98% DenseNet201: **Accuracy:** 98%	Showcases DenseNet201 and VGG-19 as top classification models
[7]	SKINCON and Dermnet (step 1); Private in-house dataset (step 2)	Two-step training: aligning visual and textual concepts, followed by disease-specific diagnosis	**Correctness:** 78.76% **Informativeness:** 80.63%	Aligns medical features for accurate diagnosis
[11]	3,400 images of 7 skin diseases	Evaluate multiple CNN models, including MobileNet, VGG16, ResNet50, and Inception V3	MobileNet: **Accuracy:** 94.1% VGG16: **Accuracy:** 44.1%	MobileNet is the most effective for disease classification for the dataset
[12]	Skin-10 and Skin-100 datasets	It uses an ensemble of CNN models and integrates object detection for lesion localization	Skin-10: **Accuracy:** 79% Skin-100: **Accuracy:** 53.54%	Ensemble of CNNs and object detection models,

(*continued*)

Table 1. (*continued*)

Citation	Dataset	Methodology	Evaluation Metrics	Key Findings
[10]	3,797 images (augmented 29x)	Utilizes ResNet-152 with extensive data augmentation techniques	**AUC:** 0.96 (Melanoma), 0.91 (Basal Cell Carcinoma)	Demonstrates training ResNet-152 on augmented clinical images

3 Methodology

As depicted in Fig. 1, our methodology employs a multi-stage approach designed to robustly address the challenges of dermatological diagnosis through integrated deep learning and generative AI systems. First, we implement a three-stage training protocol using ResNet101 architecture as our foundational convolutional neural network (CNN) for initial disease classification. This diagnostic output is contextual input for a fine-tuned vision-language model (VLM) that extracts pathological features, including physical manifestations and clinical morphological characteristics, through advanced multimodal fusion. Concurrently, our framework activates a Retrieval-Augmented Generation (RAG) mechanism that queries a curated corpus of medical literature based on CNN's classification, retrieving evidence-based clinical guidelines and research insights. These heterogeneous data inputs are compiled through a large language model (LLM) to generate comprehensive diagnostic reports while enabling interactive clinical questions to be answered through a conversational interface. This unified pipeline bridges computer vision capabilities with medical domain knowledge retrieval and generative reasoning, systematically transforming multimodal inputs into actionable diagnostic insights.

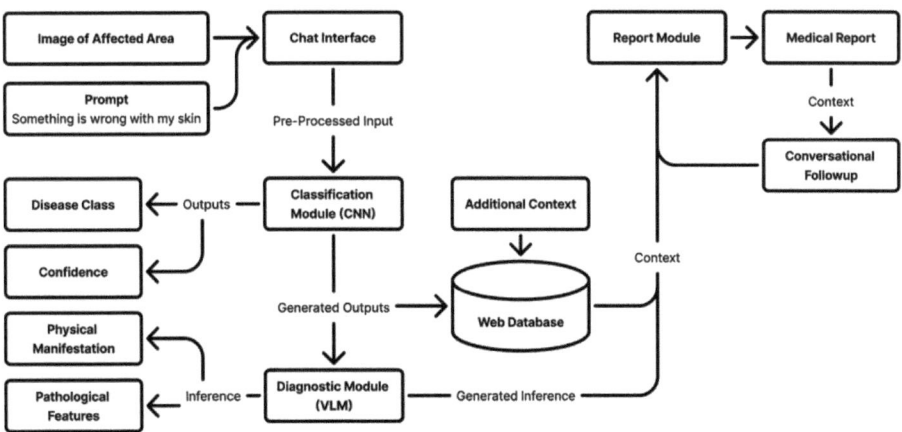

Fig. 1. Block Diagram for the Proposed Methodology

3.1 Data Acquisition and Pre-processing

Data Cleaning and Structuring:
We systematically preprocess data to enhance quality and ensure statistical validity through cleaning procedures. First, we perform image verification by retaining only records with valid image paths across multiple channels. Next, we provide label consistency by excluding entries with missing or non-informative dermatologist-assigned labels. Demographic completeness is also prioritized, as we remove records lacking essential demographic data such as age and gender to facilitate fairness analyses. To maintain robust representation, we apply statistical filtering by discarding conditions with fewer than 50 occurrences. Lastly, we consolidate features by merging one-hot encoded attributes, like textures, body parts, and symptoms, into concise, comma-separated textual descriptors. This comprehensive preprocessing establishes a high-quality dataset for training a model capable of nuanced dermatological diagnosis.

Conversational Data Structuring:
To provide the Vision Language Model (VLM) with an optimized dataset for training, we incorporate an additional pre-processing step to convert static medical annotations into dynamic conversational exchanges. This approach follows the methodologies from PMC-VQA and VQA-RAD datasets showcasing improved diagnostic reasoning through question-answer formats [14, 15]. It follows the following pipeline:

1. **Question Templatization:**

   i We consider 25 clinically relevant question templates that simulate patient interactions. (Example: "Is this dry patch something common?")
   ii Linguistic diversity is introduced by selecting random templates while maintaining diagnostic focus, a technique validated in Med-QA frameworks [16, 17].
   iii Questions are focused on target clinical decision points: urgency assessment, differential diagnosis, and care recommendations.

2. **Structured Output:**

   i Original diagnostic captions are reformatted as JSON objects in the form:

   {
   "disease":" < diagnosis >",
   "inference":" < clinical rationale >",
   "clinical_features":" < morphological features >".
   }.

   ii. Allows direct parsing for Automated evaluation metrics (diagnostic accuracy) and Explainability Analysis (reasoning consistency)[18].

3.2 Convolution Neural Network Training

Pre-processing and Augmentation:
We incorporate an augmentation pipeline tuned for skin lesion characteristics to improve model generalization and robustness. This pipeline involves:

1. *Geometric Transformations*: We apply geometric transformations such as rotation zooming and warping to emulate images taken using different camera hardware from various angles in Dermatological cases. We apply these transformations with a set of limitations and constraints to avoid the generation of unrealistic data. The transformation parameters we decided on were Limited rotation within ± 15°, moderate zoom up to 1.2 ×, and minimal warping restricted to 0.1. These limitations ensure that the structural integrity of lesions remains intact.
2. *Illumination Variations*: Controlled Lighting Adjustments such as intensity amplification and dimming of a factor limited to 0.3 and slight color variations such as hue shifting and saturation alteration introduce illumination variations and mimic real-world clinical imaging viability. These changes will help adapt the model to different lighting conditions often encountered in medical settings.

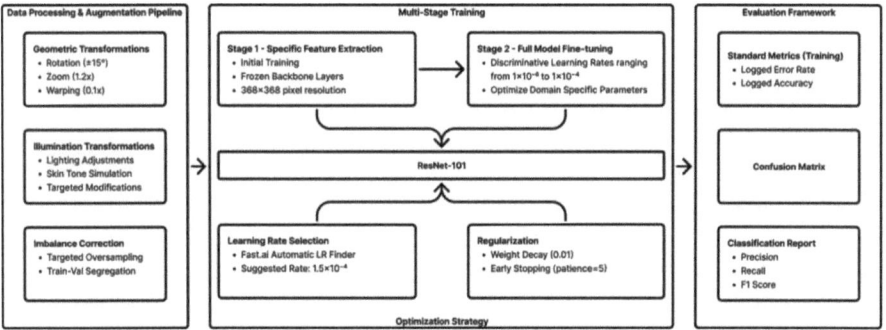

Fig. 2. CNN Classifier Architecture

In Fig. 2, the CNN Classifier section illustrates the architecture and process of classifying skin diseases utilizing Convolutional Neural Networks (CNNs). The classifier operates on the foundation of several well-established CNN architectures tailored specifically for dermatological imagery.

Dataset Imbalance Correction

Our compiled dataset had a notable class imbalance consisting of classes with as low as 57 samples or as many as 756 samples. To address the inherent class imbalance in our dataset, we implement an oversampling strategy: Performing a statistical study, we quantify the class imbalance by calculating an imbalance ratio (maximum/minimum class count) of approximately 5.2. With targeted oversampling, minority classes are supplemented through controlled duplication with augmentation flags to ensure stratified sampling integrity. Augmented samples are restricted to the training set to prevent data leakage, with validation comprising only original images.

Multi-Stage Training

We implement a multi-stage training protocol to train the ResNet101 architecture pre-trained on ImageNet as our foundational model. This deep residual network architecture was selected for its proven efficacy in medical image classification tasks while mitigating the vanishing gradient problem through residual connections trained using Transfer Learning:

1. **Stage 1:** Initial training at 368 × 368-pixel resolution with frozen backbone layers to establish task-specific feature extraction.
2. **Stage 2:** To optimize general and domain-specific parameters, full model fine-tuning with discriminative learning rates (ranging from 1×10^{-6} to 1×10^{-4}).

Optimization Strategy

We use a structured strategy that utilizes automated learning rate selection, regularization, and checkpoint management. An automated learning rate finder identifies optimal initialization parameters (suggested rate: 1.5×10^{-4}), ensuring stable and efficient convergence during training. Weight decay and early stopping (patience threshold: 5), both regularization techniques, are applied to reduce the risk of overfitting and prevent the model from memorizing noise within the dataset. We implement checkpoint management to preserve regular model states with performance-based selection criteria (based on accuracy metric). This allows us to retain the best-performing model checkpoints and backtrack to better configurations in case of degradation in subsequent training iterations.

Evaluation Framework

The error rates and validation accuracy were monitored throughout model training to identify the model's convergence trend. For class-wise performance analysis, we generated a confusion matrix over our held-out test set, allowing for the identification of diagnostic categories or labels where misclassification is frequent. These metrics helped us understand any existing biases or areas needing additional fine-tuning. We also generated a classification report using SciPy Kit's Classification Report function to compute the precision, recall, and F1-score for each condition and provide a detailed understanding of the model's ability to identify the different skin disease classes, which is crucial for quantifying and evaluating overall clinical accuracy on unseen data.

3.3 Vision Language Model Fine-Tuning

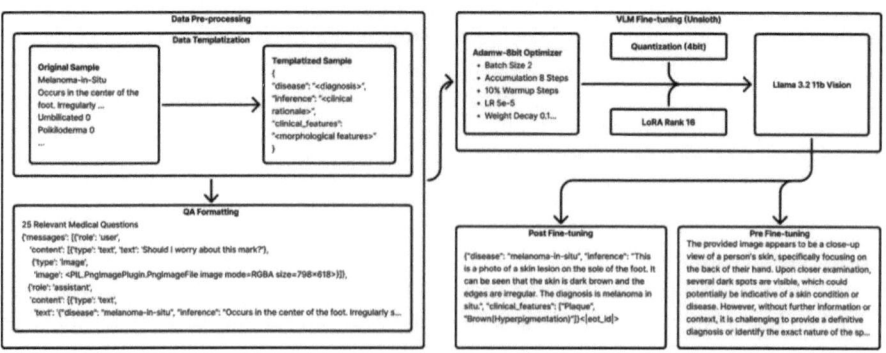

Fig. 3. VLM Training Setup

The next stage in our methodology employs our fine-tuned VLM, as shown in Fig. 3, following the initial classification phase using our trained Convolutional Neural Network (CNNs). This VLM extracts intricate pathological features from dermatological images and translates them into clinically relevant information. Having such capability ensures that the diagnostic classification output from the CNN is supplemented with additional context, such as the physical manifestation, shape, extent, pathology, and morphology of the affected part that can be inferred from the image. Through this approach, our VLM model is an essential component of our diagnostic system, providing clinical inferences that encapsulate visual assessments.

Base Architecture and Adaptation

We utilize the open-source Llama 3.2 11B Vision model as our foundational architecture. To adapt this model for dermatological diagnostics, we fine-tune both the vision and language components using the FastVisionModel from the Unsloth framework. Our approach incorporates:

1. Domain-Specific Adaptation: Fine-tuning vision layers to enhance skin lesion feature extraction and updating language layers for precise diagnostic report generation.
2. Efficient Parameter Updates: Utilizing Low-Rank Adaptation (LoRA) with a rank of 16 to modify attention and MLP modules without extensively re-training all parameters.

Training Setup

We configure our training pipeline for efficiency and stability by:

Implementing 4-bit quantization to reduce memory overhead while preserving accuracy. Using a batch size of 2 with gradient accumulation over four steps effectively increases the virtual batch size. Adopting a linear learning rate decay starting at 2×10^{-4}, with an initial warmup period of 5 steps and weight decay set to 0.01. Conducting mixed-precision training with bfloat16 and optimizing with an 8-bit AdamW optimizer. Running the training for one complete epoch while saving checkpoints at regular intervals (every 30 steps) for monitoring and recovery.

Logging and Monitoring

We integrate Weights & Biases (wandb) to log key metrics such as learning rate progression, global step and epoch counts, gradient norm stability, and training loss trends. These real-time visualizations facilitate the ongoing evaluation of training performance and model convergence.

We also monitor training loss; observing a downward trend confirms effective model learning and optimization. Represented in Fig. 4. Gradient Norm Stability is monitored to prevent gradient explosion or vanishing issues, which may hinder convergence—as depicted in Fig. 5.

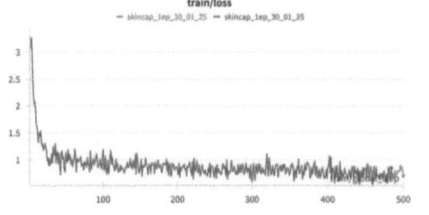

Fig. 4. Training Loss

Fig. 5. Grad Norm

3.4 Web Scraping and Augmented Report Generation

Rationale and Workflow

To enhance the clinical utility of our system, we incorporate a mechanism like Retrieval-Augmented Generation (RAG) that dynamically integrates evidence-based medical information. This module operates in parallel with the core diagnostic engine to refine output quality and provide contextually accurate recommendations.

Dynamic Data Extraction and Report Generation

We deploy a custom live web scraper that queries the Google search index using the Serper AI API. It leverages the VLM diagnosis to target authoritative medical websites to retrieve the most relevant and up-to-date clinical information (symptoms, treatment, etc.) about the specific diagnosis. We utilize a specialized LLM to generate comprehensive medical reports using tailored system prompts, integrating inputs from the VLM and the scraper. A predefined structure is followed for generating reports, covering diagnosis overview, pathological characteristics, immediate protocols, and evidence-based management while maintaining a formal yet patient-friendly tone. The VLM outputs (diagnosis, localization, clinical features) are combined with the scraped medical knowledge to produce contextually rich, patient-specific reports that emulate the expertise of a medical professional.

4 Results and Conclusion

4.1 Convolutional Neural Network (CNN)

We evaluated the performance of our trained convolutional neural network using multiple metrics, including a classification report, confusion matrix analysis, and training loss progression. The results demonstrate the effectiveness of our approach in classifying dermatological conditions with high accuracy and clinical relevance.

Training Progression

We observed consistent improvement in training and validation loss across epochs during the training process, indicating effective learning. The training loss decreased from 0.832 at epoch 0 to 0.036 at epoch 14, while the validation loss reduced from 1.072 to 0.351 over the same period. This loss reduction was accompanied by a steady increase in accuracy, which improved from 63.3% at the start to 90.4% by epoch 14. Error rates declined significantly from 36.7% to 9.6%, further validating the model's learning progression.

Classification Report

We used the classification report generated over our test split to evaluate each dermatological condition's precision, recall, and F1 score. The model had an accuracy of 92%, with a macro-average F1-score of 96% and a weighted average F1-score of 91%. Several conditions achieved perfect precision, recall, and F1 scores, including acne vulgaris, basal cell carcinoma, lichen planus, etc. For more challenging categories with many variations in physical appearance, such as eczema and psoriasis, the model achieved respectable F1 scores of 81% and 91%, respectively (Table 2).

Table 2. Cumulative Metrics for CNN Classifier

Accuracy			0.92	728
Macro Avg	0.95	0.97	0.96	728
Weighted Avg	0.92	0.92	0.91	728

Confusion Matrix Analysis

Our generated confusion matrix in Fig. 6 provided further insights into class-wise performance. We observed that most conditions were classified correctly with minimal misclassification. For instance, Allergic Contact Dermatitis achieved a recall of 100%, with only minor misclassification into eczema. Eczema exhibited some overlap with other categories but maintained high precision (96%) and recall (70%). Conditions such as Tinea and Urticaria showed near-perfect classification accuracy with minimal errors.

The matrix also revealed that minority classes benefited from our oversampling strategy during training, as evidenced by their high recall values.

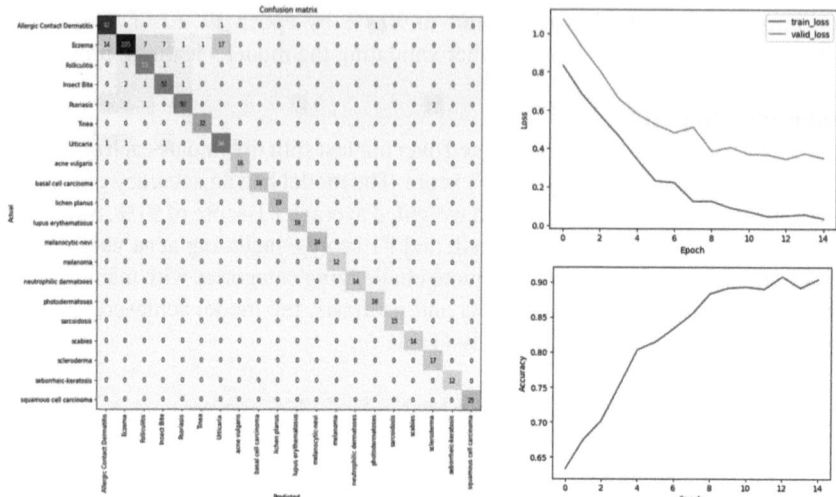

Fig. 6. Training and Evaluation Metrics for CNN

4.2 Vision Language Model (VLM) Results

We evaluated the performance of our fine-tuned Llama 3.2 11B Vision model through a comprehensive analysis of token efficiency, processing time, and output quality on 30 identical samples. The results demonstrate significant improvements across all key metrics compared to the unfinetuned baseline model.

Our fine-tuning approach resulted in remarkable token efficiency, with the model requiring substantially fewer tokens to generate complete and accurate dermatological assessments. While the unfinetuned model consistently utilized the maximum context window of 256 tokens for 21 out of 30 test cases, our fine-tuned model operated with an average of 66.8 tokens per response - a 73.9% reduction in token usage. This improvement enhances computational efficiency and indicates the model's increased precision in generating concise, comprehensive diagnostic information.

Processing time analysis revealed complementary improvements, with our fine-tuned model demonstrating significantly faster inference. The average processing time decreased from 31.1 s per response with the un-finetuned model to just 16.2 s with our fine-tuned version, representing a 47.9% reduction. We attribute this efficiency gain to implementing a clinically focused, structured QA format, allowing the model to efficiently represent the diagnosis and related clinical features (Fig. 7).

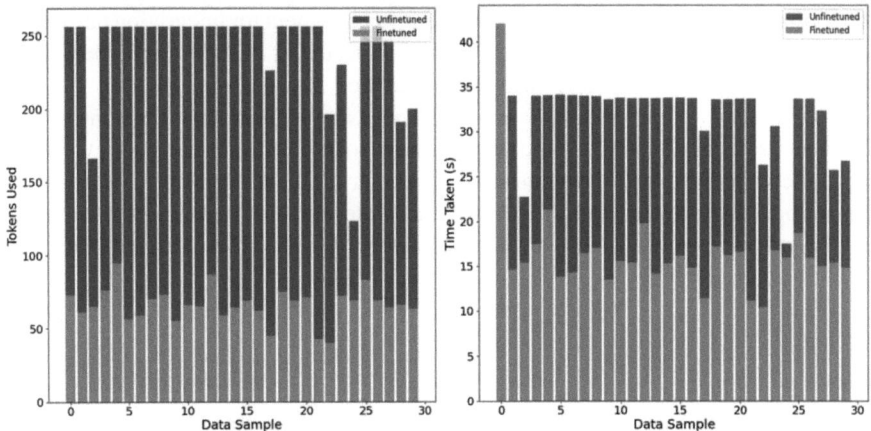

Fig. 7. Token Efficiency and Processing Time Comparison

The quality of generated outputs showed notable enhancement as measured by CLIP-Score [19] using the biomedical-specific Microsoft/BiomedCLIP-PubMedBERT_256-vit_base_patch16_224 benchmark [20]. Our fine-tuned model achieved an average CLIPS score of 10,694.9 compared to the un-finetuned model's 7,402.2, marking a substantial 44.5% improvement. This increase in CLIPScore indicates stronger semantic alignment between the generated text and the visual dermatological features, suggesting enhanced diagnostic relevance and accuracy. Auspicious was the consistent performance across diverse dermatological cases, with 27 out of 30 test samples showing improved scores (Fig. 8).

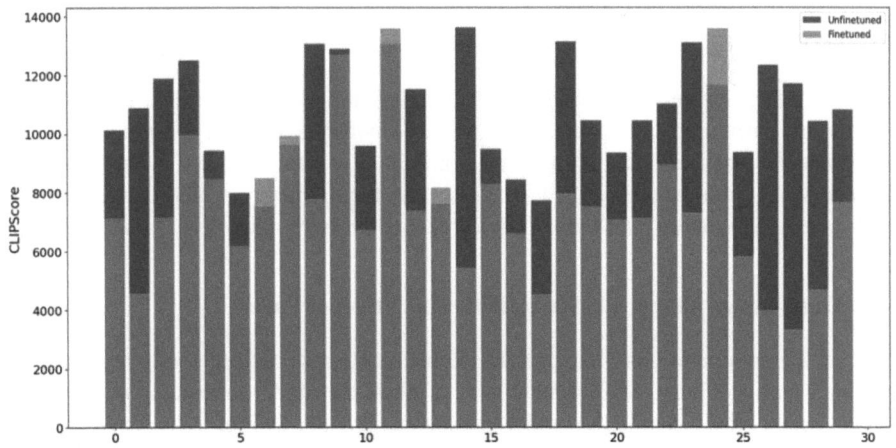

Fig. 8. CLIP Score Analysis

We also observed a structural improvement in output quality, with the fine-tuned model consistently generating responses in a structured JSON format with 100% validity.

This formatting consistency represents a critical advancement for integration into clinical workflows and electronic health record systems, enabling seamless incorporation of model outputs into existing healthcare infrastructure.

The cumulative improvements across all measured dimensions demonstrate the effectiveness of our domain-specific adaptation approach. By fine-tuning both vision and language components while implementing parameter-efficient techniques, we achieved a dermatological diagnostic model that is more accurate, efficient, and clinically applicable than the general-purpose vision-language model from which it was derived (Table 3).

Table 3. Cumulative Metrics for VLM

Metric	Finetuned Model	Un-finetuned Model
Token Count (Mean)	66.13	240.33
Processing Time (Mean)	16.44 s	31.87 s
CLIP Score (Mean)	10689.30	7605.69

5 Future Scope

Our research showcases the effectiveness of using Vision Language Models (VLMs) in combination with Convolutional Neural Networks (CNNs) for accurate dermatological diagnosis. Moreover, building on the foundations of this research, several other promising areas can be explored to further improve the model's applicability and efficiency in a clinical setting. Such avenues are:

5.1 Model Distillation for Efficient Deployment

Deploying large-scale VLMs remains challenging due to computational and memory constraints, particularly in resource-constrained environments such as rural clinics and mobile health applications. Future work would involve exploring and evaluating other smaller VLM architectures with lesser resource requirements, which can also make deployment in resource-constrained environments more feasible.

5.2 Multi-Image Diagnosis Across Different Affected Parts

Dermatological conditions often present themselves across multiple body regions with varying severity. Future development should allow the model to process multi-image inputs, which would enable the model to understand better and infer the severity of the dermatological condition. This approach will enable models to examine the condition more accurately, as in the evaluation performed by actual dermatologists examining their patients. It can be instrumental in more accurately diagnosing conditions such as drug reactions and autoimmune diseases that present distributed dermatoses.

5.3 Comprehensive Clinical Validation Across Diverse Demographics

Conducting clinical trials and real-world deployment for this project is crucial, requiring partnerships with dermatologists and hospitals to create standardized protocols that test the model across varying environments and demographic groups. Due to differences in skin disease presentations based on genetic, ethnic, and environmental factors, special attention must be given to collecting demographically diverse dermatological data representing multiple skin types, ethnicities, ages, and geographical regions. All data collection must adhere to strict anonymization, consent, and quality standardization frameworks while complying with regional regulatory requirements. Clinical evaluation of the model should be performed against real cases to assess its accuracy and reliability realistically.

References

1. Khurana, A., et al.: Development of Indian council of medical research (ICMR) standard treatment workflows for skin diseases: a step toward universal health coverage. Indian Dermatol. Online J. **15**, 794 (2024). https://doi.org/10.4103/idoj.idoj_741_23
2. Mishra, A.A.: Top 5 specialists that saw a spike in 2023 for tele-OPD in rural areas. https://timesofindia.indiatimes.com/blogs/voices/top-5-specialists-that-saw-a-spike-in-2023-for-tele-opd-in-rural-areas/
3. Kavita, K., Mehta, H., Ghai, S., Saini, S.K., Narang, T.: Self-reported prevalence of skin problems among residents of a peri-urban community of Chandigarh. Indian J Dermatol Venereol Leprol. **90**, 565–565 (2024). https://doi.org/10.25259/IJDVL_982_2022
4. Kilaru, K.R., Munnangi, P., V, U.D., Kilaru, M.C.: Pattern of skin diseases among migrant construction workers - a community based cross-sectional study from Andhra Pradesh, India. jebmh. **8**, 471–475 (2021). https://doi.org/10.18410/jebmh/2021/92
5. Prevalence of Occupational Skin Diseases and its Predisposing Factors in Leather Tanning Workers of Southern India. Current World Environment. Volume 15,
6. Vashisht, P., et al.: UMass-BioNLP at MEDIQA-M3G 2024: DermPrompt - A Systematic Exploration of Prompt Engineering with GPT-4V for Dermatological Diagnosis. In: Naumann, T., Ben Abacha, A., Bethard, S., Roberts, K., and Bitterman, D. (eds.) Proceedings of the 6th Clinical Natural Language Processing Workshop. pp. 502–525. Association for Computational Linguistics, Mexico City, Mexico (2024). https://doi.org/10.18653/v1/2024.clinicalnlp-1.50
7. Zhou, J., et al.: Pre-trained multimodal large language model enhances dermatological diagnosis using SkinGPT-4. Nat. Commun. **15**, 5649 (2024). https://doi.org/10.1038/s41467-024-50043-3
8. Ateia, S., Kruschwitz, U.: BioRAGent: A retrieval-augmented generation system for showcasing generative query expansion and domain-specific search for scientific Q&A (2024). https://doi.org/10.48550/arXiv.2412.12358. http://arxiv.org/abs/2412.12358
9. Lin, B., Xu, Y., Bao, X., Zhao, Z., Wang, Z., Yin, J.: SkinGEN: an Explainable Dermatology Diagnosis-to-Generation Framework with Interactive Vision-Language Models, http://arxiv.org/abs/2404.14755, (2025). https://doi.org/10.48550/arXiv.2404.14755
10. Mendes, D.B., Silva, N.C. da: Skin Lesions Classification Using Convolutional Neural Networks in Clinical Images (2018). https://doi.org/10.48550/arXiv.1812.02316. http://arxiv.org/abs/1812.02316

11. Velasco, J.S., Catipon, J.V., Monilar, E.G., Amon, V.M., Virrey, G.C., Tolentino, L.K.S.: Classification of skin disease using transfer learning in convolutional neural networks. IJETAE. **13**, 1–7 (2023). https://doi.org/10.46338/ijetae0423_01
12. He, X., et al.: Computer-aided clinical skin disease diagnosis using CNN and object detection models. In: 2019 IEEE International Conference on Big Data (Big Data), pp. 4839–4844 (2019). https://doi.org/10.1109/BigData47090.2019.9006528
13. Iparraguirre-Villanueva, O., Cabanillas-Carbonell, M.: Application of convolutional neural networks in skin disease prediction: accuracy and efficiency in dermatological image analysis. | EBSCOhost, https://openurl.ebsco.com/contentitem/10.3991%2Fijoe.v21i02.52871?sid=ebsco:plink:crawler&id=ebsco:10.3991%2Fijoe.v21i02.52871. https://doi.org/10.3991/ijoe.v21i02.52871. Accessed 12 Mar 2025
14. Liu, C.-Y., Diao, F.: Text-Enhanced Medical Visual Question Answering
15. Hartsock, I., Rasool, G.: Vision-language models for medical report generation and visual question answering: a review. Front Artif Intell. **7**, 1430984 (2024). https://doi.org/10.3389/frai.2024.1430984
16. Li, Q., Li, L., Li, Y.: Developing ChatGPT for biology and medicine: a complete review of biomedical question answering. Biophys Rep. **10**, 152–171 (2024). https://doi.org/10.52601/bpr.2024.240004
17. Improving Medical Reasoning through Retrieval and Self-Reflection with Retrieval-Augmented Large Language Models. https://arxiv.org/html/2401.15269v2. Accessed 26 Feb 2025
18. Takyar, A.: Structured outputs in LLMs: Definition, techniques, applications, benefits. https://www.leewayhertz.com/structured-outputs-in-llms/. Accessed 26 Feb 2025
19. Hessel, J., Holtzman, A., Forbes, M., Bras, R.L., Choi, Y.: CLIPScore: a Reference-free Evaluation Metric for Image Captioning (2022). http://arxiv.org/abs/2104.08718. https://doi.org/10.48550/arXiv.2104.08718
20. Zhang, S., et al.: BiomedCLIP: a multimodal biomedical foundation model pretrained from fifteen million scientific image-text pairs (2025). http://arxiv.org/abs/2303.00915. https://doi.org/10.48550/arXiv.2303.00915

Predicting Volunteering Commitment Using Machine Learning in South Africa

Sakhiwo Mtwenka[1], Marie Hattingh[1], Alex Bignotti[2], Sonali Das[2], and Timothy Adeliyi[1(✉)]

[1] Department of Informatics, University of Pretoria, Pretoria 0002, South Africa
{marie.hattingh,timothy.adeliyi}@up.ac.za
[2] Department of Business Management, University of Pretoria, Pretoria 0002, South Africa

Abstract. Volunteering holds a vital place in enhancing the quality of life for individuals in need. Online volunteering platforms have emerged as valuable tools for connecting volunteers with causes that require assistance. The local civic engagement organization used in this study is one of South Africa's leading online volunteering platforms, which enables causes to list their needs and volunteers to fulfill them. This study proposed using machine learning for sentiment analysis to analyze messages sent to causes by volunteers expressing their commitment to a particular need. Long Short-Term Memory (LSTM) was used in this study to analyze these messages in conjunction with their associated ratings or sentiments. The findings of this study demonstrate that Long Short-Term Memory (LSTM) exhibits superior performance in predicting online volunteering commitment compared with Gated Recurrent Unit (GRU) and Simple Recurrent Neural Network (SRNN). These findings directly affect the local civic engagement organisation as an online volunteering platform because it leverages these findings to enhance its volunteer engagement strategies. Specifically, the local civic engagement organisation can utilise these insights to identify volunteers with a high likelihood of not committing and tailor its communication approaches accordingly. This targeted approach can foster greater satisfaction among volunteers and causes, ultimately driving increased traffic to the Local civic engagement organisation platform and bolstering its reputation as a premier destination for online volunteering.

Keywords: online volunteering · volunteering commitment · sentiment analysis · Long Short Term Memory · machine learning

1 Introduction

Volunteering plays a vital role in shaping the social economy by delivering essential goods and services to the underprivileged, while simultaneously conserving resources for an already burdened government [1]. Due to the growing number of people worldwide, governments need help to cope with these requests [1]. Independent organizations such as Non-Profit Organizations (NPOs), Non-Government Organizations (NGOs), Non-Profit Companies (NPCs) and charities try to fulfill these requests by distributing public services to the people that the government cannot afford [2]. The motives for helping behaviour have always raised questions such as "What are the reasons people volunteer?" [3]. Volunteering motives have been studied by many researchers in the past in the fields of social science, economics, and social psychology, among other fields [4–7]. According to [7], some motives that influence volunteering are demographic characteristics, personal beliefs, values, and social pressure, among other motives. In recent years, online volunteering has become an increasingly popular way to engage in charitable work. While the benefits of volunteering online are evident, the conditions under which volunteers volunteer on online platforms are still unclear [2].

The increase of online volunteering platforms has enabled researchers to study the motivations that influence volunteers to give their time and money, among other services, to people in need. For instance, during the COVID-19 lockdown period, online volunteering platforms proved to be instrumental. They enabled volunteers to support public health systems, shop for older adults and offer other services [2]. This underscores the vital role these platforms play in enhancing the quality of people's lives. Platforms such as the local civic engagement platform used in this study cannot predict a volunteer's commitment level. To contribute to the study of sociology and computer science regarding online volunteering, existing Machine Learning (ML) algorithms have been employed to predict online volunteering commitment [8]. Predicting online volunteering commitment will improve volunteering commitment and allow causes and online volunteering platform owners to understand the motives for volunteering.

The local civic engagement platform used in this study is one of South Africa's (SA) largest online volunteering platforms, where individuals can access causes that have listed their needs online. The local civic engagement platform allows certified organization such as NPOs to register and provide all the necessary documents. All the submitted documents are processed and reviewed by the local civic engagement platform. A message is sent to the organization with either an approved or declined status. Local civic organisation provides all the reasons for the decline when an organization is reduced. The approved organizations can start listing or requesting time, goods, and money needs. This study will refer to these requests as needs (i.e., time, goods, and money) and organizations (i.e., NPOs) as causes. From 2014 to 2021, the platform had 22,462 registered online volunteers and 2,423 causes.

This study aims to train different ML algorithms using the local civic engagement organisation data to devise models that can predict online volunteering commitment in South Africa (SA). Developing these models will assist in predicting the commitment levels of online volunteers. Information on volunteers who do not commit themselves will help local civic engagement organisation profile these volunteers to improve their commitment. The performance metrics of the Long Short-Term Memory (LSTM) model will be evaluated in comparison to those of the Simple Recurrent Neural Network (SRNN) and the Gated Recurrent Unit (GRU) [8, 9]. This research seeks to devise models to predict online volunteering engagement in the SA.

Against the above background, the study seeks to address the central research question: What are the effective algorithms for predicting online volunteering commitment? The remainder of the paper is organised as follows: Sect. 2 outlines the key concepts of online volunteering, reviews relevant literature on predictive models for online volunteering commitment, and highlights the research gap. Section 3 describes the research methodology adopted for the study. Section 4 details the machine learning models applied to the Local Civic Engagement Organisation dataset and evaluates their performance using the Twitter dataset. Section 5 discusses the findings, and Sect. 6 concludes the paper.

2 Literature Background

2.1 Online Volunteering Media

Volunteering is a long-term planned prosocial behaviour for assisting disadvantaged people or organisations [7]. In [10] define volunteering as a planned, non-obligatory helping behaviour performed in an organisational context. It is believed that apart from benefiting direct beneficiaries, volunteering can help create a better living environment for all humans [11]. It was evident from other scholars that volunteering involves a sustained and ongoing helping behaviour to benefit society [12, 13].

Unlike traditional volunteering, online volunteering does not require volunteers to be part of an organisation to volunteer or be physically present [14]. For example, SA has a lot of high-crime areas, such as Khayelitsha in Cape Town, that require various volunteering services, such as tutoring. In this case, a volunteer can virtually offer this service online without facing any dangers and this volunteer would not incur any travelling costs. The reduction or absence in travelling costs is an added benefit. In a pressure field world with many demands and responsibilities, online volunteering offers high flexibility and adaptability regarding the hours and days a volunteer chooses to commit to. For instance, a full-time employee who must balance a family life can volunteer online at a time that suits them most.

2.2 Existing Studies on Predicting Volunteer Commitment

This section provides examples of existing studies mainly focusing on using ML to predict commitment. A recent study by [15] focused on using ML algorithms to predict a volunteer's decision to stay or quit volunteering. The authors collected 55 variables contributing to a person's decision to continue volunteering from a survey of 250 respondents. The variable age was also considered in the study by [15], which revealed that older volunteers are generally more inclined to sustain their volunteering efforts [16]. One can assume that more senior volunteers have more time on their hands since they are not chasing career advancements, and some have retired.

In the same study [15], the authors compared the accuracies of two ML models, namely the artificial neural network (ANN) and LR, to predict a volunteer's decision to stay or quit volunteering. An Artificial Neural Network (ANN) is a machine learning model that draws inspiration from the architecture and operation of the human brain [15]. It consists of multiple layers made up of interconnected nodes or neurons, where each neuron computes a weighted sum of its inputs and applies an activation function to produce an output. An ANN's output layer produces the model's final output [15]. The ANN model was more accurate than the LR model in predicting volunteers' decisions to stay or quit.

Another study focused on combining the aspects of computer mobility and ML to devise a platform or a system that can connect organisations to high school students who would like to volunteer their time [17]. One of the key objectives of the platform was to predict how well a volunteer will perform and recommend volunteering events to them. The dataset used for training the machine learning models was obtained from both the volunteers (i.e., high school students) and the associated causes (i.e., organisations). The study revealed that the Random Forest Bagging Classifier (RFBC) outperformed other algorithms in predicting volunteer performance, while both the Support Vector Machine (SVM) and Random Forest Classifier (RFC) showed strong results in recommending suitable events to volunteers [17]. The researchers believe that this system could be used to improve the volunteer and supervisor experience. It can also provide valuable recommendations to volunteers. In [18], deep learning was applied to predict the engagement of scientists in monitoring the coastal and ocean environment. The engagement of scientists in volunteering activities is crucial due to the lack of government resources in the field of oceanography and the threats posed by changes in the climate.

It is imperative to understand a scientist's patterns in participating in projects to effectively design better future projects [18]. The authors also believe that this will help retain and improve the volunteering experience. Two ML models were employed in that study, namely the LSTM and a feedforward Deep Neural Network (DNN). The findings from this study indicated that these models could predict whether someone is likely to keep participating in a scientific project. This information can identify people who are likely to quit or keep participating, depending on what the project needs.

2.3 Literature Review Gaps

Literature only covers the use of ML to predict a volunteer's decision to continue volunteering [15, 17, 18]. While the existing research is important for predicting future volunteering engagement to retain existing volunteers, it has not covered aspects such as predicting a volunteer's decision to volunteer from the outset. This is evident from the two articles that have used phrases such as "volunteer's decision to stay or quit" and "who will stay" in their titles [15, 18]. It has not covered aspects such as predicting a volunteer's decision to volunteer from the outset. This study will adopt a sentiment analysis approach to predict a volunteer's decision to follow through once they have reached out to the cause online. The reason sentiment analysis is appropriate for this study is that the Local civic engagement organisation does not capture any information about the volunteers that can be used as features.

3 Research Methodology

3.1 Research Design

This study adopts an experimental approach that involves analyzing and modeling Local civic engagement organisation historical data to make predictions about online volunteering commitment levels among South African volunteers. The research aims to develop prediction models that can forecast online volunteering commitment levels. Two datasets, the Local civic engagement organisation dataset and the Twitter dataset, were utilized for this purpose. The primary objective of using the local civic engagement organisation dataset is to analyze it to extract meaningful insights. The secondary objective of using the Local civic engagement organisation dataset is to train and evaluate various ML algorithms to create models capable of predicting online volunteering commitment levels. Due to the limited number of records in the Local civic engagement organisation dataset, the Twitter dataset was employed to validate the accuracy of the models developed from the Local civic engagement organisation dataset. This validation process was conducted to confirm the effectiveness of the Local civic engagement organisation model.

3.2 Data Collection

The study employed two data sources: the Local civic engagement organisation dataset and a Twitter dataset used to evaluate the model.

3.2.1 The Local Civic Engagement Organisation Dataset

The Local civic engagement organisation dataset where volunteers are afforded the opportunity to engage with listed charitable causes employing message-based responses. This mechanism allows volunteers to communicate their intention to address a specific need articulated by a given cause. A predefined temporal window is allocated to volunteers within which they are expected to fulfill the identified need. Following the lapse of this temporal interval, the cause is empowered to evaluate the volunteer's engagement, assigning a rating on a scale spanning from 1 to 5.

The Local civic engagement organisation platform collects and stores a piece of important information for its intended use. This encompassing repository includes not only the exchanged messages and corresponding ratings but also embraces essential metadata such as the title of the specific need, need type, need category, and cause province, as described in Table 1 below. To facilitate the subsequent analysis, the corporate entity has provided the data in the form of Comma-Separated Values (CSV) files. These data files have been collected over 7 years. The Local civic engagement organisation data also contains volunteers who were not rated by the causes, this will decrease the size of the overall dataset after eliminating these non-rated volunteers. This dataset comprises fifteen attributes and 15,554 needs responses. Table 1 details the attributes, data types and description of the dataset. Through the systematic elimination of non-rated volunteers and subsequent thorough data pre-processing procedures, the cleaned Local civic engagement organisation dataset contained 9,173 records. This subset of 9,173 records was employed to facilitate the training of the models presented in this study.

Table 1. Local civic engagement organisation needs responses

Attribute	Data type	Description
User ID	Alphanumeric	Unique encrypted id
Need Type	Categorical	Type of Need
Need Title	Text	Name of Need
Need Category	Categorical	Category of the need
Need sub-category	Categorical	Subcategory of the need
Province	Categorical	Province of the cause
City	Categorical	City of the cause
Message	Text	Message sent to cause
Donation	Text	Donation sent to casue
Related cause name	Text	Name of cause
Hours Logged	Float	Volunteer's logged volunteering hours
Rating by user	Numeric	5-star rating scale
Rating by cause	Numeric	5-star rating scale
Activity date	dd/mm/yyyy	Date activity was performed on Local civic engagement organisation system
Activity ID	Alphanumeric	Unique tracking activity id

3.3 Data Pre-processing

To obtain insights from the response messages prior to analysing and modelling it, a preliminary stage involving the pre-processing of these messages to mitigate extraneous elements was followed. This pre-processing procedure encompasses the removal of noise from the dataset in the form of punctuations, numeric characters, and various special characters from the text [19, 20]. Subsequently, a fundamental aspect of standardization entails the transformation of all response messages into lowercase. This decision is motivated by the intention to ensure word uniformity, thereby rendering words with diverse capitalisations as equivalent entities. Such an approach holds the potential to increase the accuracy of implemented models [19, 20].

The subsequent phase involves the elimination of multiple spaces within the textual content. This step is deemed essential as it mitigates the inadvertent differentiation of words that are essentially similar, thereby fostering linguistic consistency. Furthermore, to both optimize computational efficiency and curtail the overall corpus size for subsequent classification models, the decision was made to excise stop words from the response messages. These stop words are ubiquitous terms that contribute minimally to the semantic essence of the messages. Common examples of such words include "the", "and", "is", "in", "an", "on", and other analogous words [21]. This judicious culling of stop words enhances the signal-to-noise ratio within the data, enabling the models to focus on the more pertinent linguistic elements that carry substantive information.

This was done by importing predefined stop words from the Natural Language Toolkit (NLTK) corpus library in Python. The NLTK library is one of Python's most popular libraries that speeds up the text pre-processing phase by means of tokenising, lemmatising, among performing other tasks [21]. The last step in preparing the text was to use the stemming or lemmatisation method available in the NLTK library to simplify words to their core form. Stemming cuts off word endings to make a stem, while lemmatisation finds a word's basic form by considering how it's used. The Word- NetLemmatiser class from the NLTK library was used to perform this task using the sub-library Stem.

3.3.1 Feature Engineering

After the completion of the pre-processing phase, the refined messages underwent a process of conversion from text to numerical values, also known as vectorization. This is imperative in the field of NLP since ML models are familiar with numeric inputs [22]. The data that underwent the pre-processing stage was subsequently fitted into a total of twelve distinct ML algorithms. The data was fitted into the LR, NB, MLP, SVM, KNN, RFT, and DT and was transformed using two approaches. This study has referred to these seven models as the NRNN models. The two transformation approaches used for the NRNN models, are Bag-of-Words (BoW) and Term Frequency- Inverse Document Frequency (TF-IDF) [21]. The variable denoting volunteer commitment, referred to as "rating by cause" has been selected as the response variable for analysis. As outlined in Table 1 above, this attribute is characterized by a rating scale spanning from 1 to 5.

To perform sentimental analysis for the given dataset, a decision was taken to categorise the rating variable into three distinct sentiment classes: negative, neutral, and positive. Within this categorisation framework, ratings 1 and 2 are assigned to a negative sentiment class, rating 3 is deemed neutral, and ratings 4 and 5 are symbolized to be a positive sentiment.

3.4 Machine Learning Algorithms

Several machine learning algorithms will be employed, including LR, NB, MLP, SVM, KNN, RFT, LC, DT, SRNN, LSTM and GRU. These algorithms have been chosen because they the most widely used ML algorithms for dealing with dealing with supervised classification problems [8]. Most researchers have also used some of these models for predicting human behaviour [8, 17, 23, 24]. For example, [17] used the NB and RFT algorithms to recommend causes to high school students. The Local civic engagement organisation study classifies volunteering commitment based a volunteer's message. The aforementioned eleven algorithms are applied to the Local civic engagement organisation dataset since it offers diverse modeling approaches to understand patterns within the datasets [8, 17, 23, 24]. The Local civic engagement organisation dataset consists of messages and ratings where causes express their sentiments on the volunteers. This suggests that a sentimental analysis approach can be applied to the data [19]. The subsequent ML algorithms were trained on the pre-processed message using the training dataset. The resulting models from the training set were validated using the Twitter data. The performance of the trained models was evaluated using the most widely recognized performance metrics, namely accuracy, F1-score, precision, and recall. The one model that performed the best across all metrics will be regarded as the best model.

4 Modeling Online Volunteering Commitment

4.1 The Local Civic Engagement Organisation Dataset

The prediction of online volunteering commitment is regarded as a classification- supervised ML problem [8]. In supervised machine learning, the algorithm acquires new capabilities by learning from labeled training data. Through the recognition of patterns and relationships within this data, supervised learning seeks to establish a clear mapping between the input features and the expected output [25]. Table 2 presents the accuracy performance metric of three different models: SRNN, LSTM, and GRU on the Local civic engagement organisation dataset when CV was used. The metric was captured using five different folds to record accuracy 1 to accuracy 5. Additionally, the Mean (%) and Std (%) columns indicate the average accuracy and standard deviation across the five instances. The SRNN model achieves an average accuracy of about 70.59%, displaying a very minor standard deviation of 0.06. This points towards the model's consistent performance across various subgroups or iterations. Comparatively, the LSTM model attains an average accuracy of approximately 70.54%, exhibiting a slightly larger standard deviation of 0.12 in contrast to SRNN. This implies a somewhat greater variability in performance across different runs. Similarly, the GRU model records an average accuracy of roughly 70.54%, akin to LSTM, but showcases an even smaller standard deviation of 0.03. This indicates that the GRU model consistently delivers a stable level of performance across varying subsets or iterations.

In summary, as per the available data, the SRNN, LSTM, and GRU models display rather similar performance levels. SRNN exhibits a slightly superior average accuracy, while both LSTM and GRU exhibit lower yet comparable mean accuracy figures. However, additional factors such as model complexity, training duration, and specific use scenarios would also contribute to the determination of the most suitable model.

Table 2. RNN accuracy and execution time using CV on Local civic engagement organisation data

Model	Acc1 (%)	Acc2 (%)	Acc3 (%)	Acc4 (%)	Acc5 (%)	Mean (%)	Std (%)
SSRN	70.68	70.52	70.57	70.61	70.56	70.59	0.06
LSTM	70.57	70.57	70.52	70.34	70.72	70.54	0.12
GRU	70.57	70.57	70.52	70.60	70.56	70.54	0.03

5 Discussion

This section focuses on assessing the effectiveness of the trained Local civic engagement organisation models when applied to the Twitter data. The RNN model was also transformed using the BoW and TF-IDF approaches. Figure 1 represents the training accuracy versus the testing accuracy of the LSTM model on the Local civic engagement organisation dataset. The LSTM's training accuracy increases with the number of epochs or iterations.

It achieved an accuracy of more than 90% on the training set. Once the trained model was evaluated on the test set, a decline in accuracy was observed as the number of iterations increased. This suggests that the LSTM model struggles to predict or discover the training patterns from the test data. Thus, to improve the LSTM's accuracy on the Local civic engagement organisation dataset is necessary to increase the size of the training and test sets. The LSTM model performed very well on the training set but struggles with the unseen data as the number of iterations increases, thus the LSTM model overfits. Supervised ML algorithms are prone to overfitting, which is caused by the lack of generalization of both training and testing data [27]. This can be caused by a range of factors ranging including having noise in the training set, lack of training data and the complexity of the ML models [27]. In the case of a Local civic engagement organisation, techniques to prevent overfitting have been accommodated, such as early stopping and cross-validation to prevent under-fitting and overfitting. Even though these techniques were applied, the RNN still did not perform very well on the test set.

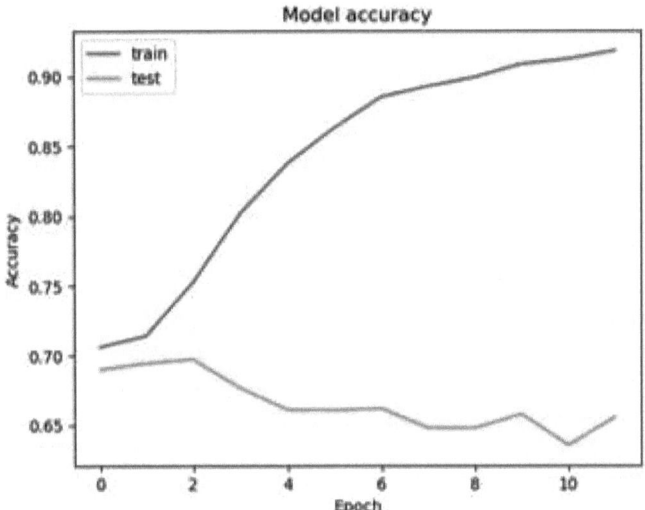

Fig. 1. LSTM training vs testing accuracy on Local civic engagement organisation data

This suggests that the Local civic engagement organisation dataset is too small for the RNN model to capture patterns. To test that the LSTM ML algorithm is best suited for predicting online volunteering commitment, the Twitter data was used. The accuracy values for the training and testing sets of the LSTM model on the Twitter dataset show minimal disparity, as seen in Fig. 2.

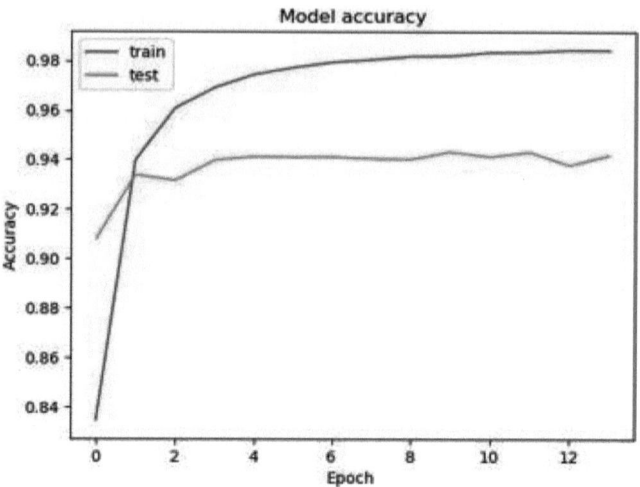

Fig. 2. LSTM training vs testing accuracy on Twitter data

6 Conclusion

Online volunteering has become popular around the world with the rise in the usage of the internet and digital transformation [28, 29]. Many researchers are studying the determinants that influence online volunteering [7]. In the case of a Local civic engagement organisation, the problem is that there are no profiles that are likened to the volunteers. As a result of this, it is difficult to profile volunteers and predict their volunteering commitment. In the absence of comprehensive volunteer profiles, sentiment analysis was employed using the NLP technique to infer online volunteering commitment. RNN models, particularly LSTM, outperformed GRU and SRNN models in predicting online volunteering commitment. These findings suggest that RNNs are the most effective machine learning algorithms for predicting online volunteering behaviour using sentiment analysis.

This study contributes practically to the space of predicting online volunteering behaviour through the use of existing ML algorithms. It has also served as the baseline for other researchers to collect more information about the volunteers, such as demographics and psychographics. This additional information can be leveraged alongside the findings of this study to enhance the performance of the RNN models. The findings of this study will enable Local civic engagement organisation to improve online volunteering commitment through predictions. Using ML, volunteers who are predicted to commit can be investigated to understand the reasons they do not commit. This will also enable the causes to communicate effectively with the volunteers in time to offer more assistance. Increasing volunteering commitment will assist causes to get their needs met, thus improving the lives of the needy.

References

1. Penner, L.A.: Volunteerism and social problems: Making things better or worse? J. Soc. Issues **60**(3), 645–666 (2004)
2. Trautwein, S., Liberatore, F., Lindenmeier, J., Schnurbein, G.: Satisfaction with informal volunteering during the covid-19 crisis: an empirical study considering a swiss online volunteering platform. Nonprofit Volunt. Sect. Q. **49**(6), 1142–1151 (2020)
3. Gebauer, J.E., Riketta, M., Broemer, P., Maio, G.R.: Pleasure and pressure based prosocial motivation: divergent relations to subjective well-being. J. Res. Pers. **42**(2), 399–420 (2008)
4. Bekkers, R., Wiepking, P.: A literature review of empirical studies of philanthropy: Eight mechanisms that drive charitable giving. Nonprofit Volunt. Sect. Q. **40**(5), 924–973 (2011)
5. Engeser, S., Langens, T.: Mapping explicit social motives of achievement, power, and affiliation onto the five-factor model of personality. Scand. J. Psychol. **51**(4), 309–318 (2010)
6. Brown, K.M., Hoye, R., Nicholson, M.: Self-esteem, self-efficacy, and social connectedness as mediators of the relationship between volunteering and well-being. J. Soc. Serv. Res. **38**(4), 468–483 (2012)
7. Penner, L.A.: Dispositional and organizational influences on sustained volunteerism: an interactionist perspective. J. Soc. Issues **58**(3), 447–467 (2002)
8. Osisanwo, F., Akinsola, J., Awodele, O., Hinmikaiye, J., Olakanmi, O., Akinjobi, J., et al.: Supervised machine learning algorithms: classification and comparison. Int. J. Comput. Trends Technol. (IJCTT) **48**(3), 128–138 (2017)
9. Salehinejad, H., Sankar, S., Barfett, J., Colak, E., Valaee, S.: Recent advances in recurrent neural networks. arXiv preprint arXiv:1801.01078 (2017)
10. Okun, M.A., Kim, G.Y.: The interplay of frequency of volunteering and prosocial motivation on purpose in life in emerging adults. J. Soc. Psychol. **156**(3), 328–333 (2016)
11. Dwyer, P.C., Bono, J.E., Snyder, M., Nov, O., Berson, Y.: Sources of volunteer motivation: transformational leadership and personal motives influence volunteer outcomes. Nonprofit Manag. Leadersh. **24**(2), 181–205 (2013)
12. Clary, E.G., et al.: Understanding and assessing the motivations of volunteers: a functional approach. J. Pers. Soc. Psychol. **74**(6), 1516 (1998)
13. Rozmiarek, M., Poczta, J., Malchrowicz-Mośko, E.: Motivations of sports volunteers at the 2023 european games in poland. Sustainability **13**(11), 6406 (2021)
14. Baruch, A., May, A., Yu, D.: The motivations, enablers and barriers for voluntary participation in an online crowdsourcing platform. Comput. Hum. Behav. **64**, 923–931 (2016)
15. de-Miguel-Molina, B., Boix-Domenech, R., Martínez-Villanueva, G., de-Miguel-Molina, M.: Predicting volunteers' decisions to stay in or quit an ngo using neural networks. VOLUNTAS: Int. J. Voluntary Nonprofit Organ. **35**(2), 277–291 (2024)
16. Bang, H.: Volunteer age, job satisfaction, and intention to stay: a case of nonprofit sport organizations. Leadersh. Org. Dev. J. **36**(2), 161–176 (2015)
17. Huang, A., Sun, Y.: An intelligent and data-driven mobile platform for youth volunteer management using machine learning and predictive analytics. In: CS & IT Conference Proceedings, vol. 10 (2020). CS & IT Conference Proceedings
18. Semenov, A., Zhang, Y., Ponti, M.: Who will stay? using deep learning to predict engagement of citizen scientists. arXiv preprint arXiv:2204.14046 (2022)
19. Murthy, G., Allu, S.R., Andhavarapu, B., Bagadi, M., Belusonti, M.: Text based sentiment analysis using lstm. Int. J. Eng. Res. Tech. Res **9**(05), 299–303 (2020)
20. Vyas, V., Uma, V.: An extensive study of sentiment analysis tools and binary classification of tweets using rapid miner. Procedia Comput. Sci. **125**, 329–335 (2018)
21. Juluru, K., Shih, H.-H., Keshava Murthy, K.N., Elnajjar, P.: Bag-of-words technique in natural language processing: a primer for radiologists. Radiographics **41**(5), 1420–1426 (2021)

22. Hiremath, B.N., Patil, M.M.: Enhancing optimized personalized therapy in clinical decision support system using natural language processing. J. King Saud Univ. Comput. Inf. Sci. **34**(6), 2840–2848 (2022)
23. Yogameena, B., Komagal, E., Archana, M., Abhaikumar, S.R.: Support vector machine- based human behavior classification in crowd through projection and star skeletonization. J. Comput. Sci. **6**(9), 1008–1013 (2010)
24. Saho, K., Hayashi, S., Tsuyama, M., Meng, L., Masugi, M.: Machine learning- based classification of human behaviors and falls in restroom via dual doppler radar measurements. Sensors **22**(5), 1721 (2022)
25. Mahesh, B., et al.: Machine learning algorithms-a review. Int. J. Sci. Res. (IJSR). [Internet] **9**(1), 381–386 (2020)
26. Mahdikhani, M.: Predicting the popularity of tweets by analyzing public opinion and emotions in different stages of covid-19 pandemic. Int. J. Inf. Manage. Data Insights **2**(1), 100053 (2022)
27. Ying, X.: An overview of overfitting and its solutions. J. Phys. Conf. Ser. **1168**, 022022 (2019)
28. Smith, D.H., et al.: Online and virtual volunteering. The Palgrave handbook of volunteering, civic participation, and nonprofit associations, 290–310 (2016)
29. Amichai-Hamburger, Y.: Potential and promise of online volunteering. Comput. Hum. Behav. **24**(2), 544–562 (2008)

Robust Image Denoising Using Gradient Seeds, Morphology, and DBSCAN Clustering

Parag Anil Tamhankar(✉) and Stephanie Hayden

Georgia State University, Atlanta, GA 30302, USA
ptamhankar@gsu.edu

Abstract. Image enhancement and noise removal are critical preprocessing steps in computer vision and image analysis. This paper presents a Hybrid Image Enhancement and Noise Removal Algorithm that integrates classical image processing techniques with statistical clustering methods to achieve robust denoising while preserving essential image details. The proposed approach begins by converting the RGB input image to grayscale, followed by adaptive binarization using Otsu's method to improve contrast. Morphological erosion is applied to eliminate small-scale noise, while gradient-based analysis detects seed points for relevant image regions. A flood-fill algorithm is employed to identify connected components, and DBSCAN (Density-Based Spatial Clustering of Applications with Noise) is used to separate noise from meaningful structures. Finally, the image undergoes enhancement in the HSV color space, adjusting pixel values based on statistical measures to refine the output. Unlike existing methods, this approach integrates gradient-based seed detection with DBSCAN clustering to effectively distinguish text from noise in historical degraded documents. Unlike existing methods that rely on OCR-based validation, our approach evaluates readability using a structured Likert-scale assessment conducted by expert reviewers. Experimental results demonstrate a significant readability improvement, with average scores increasing from 1.8 (pre-enhancement) to 4.5 (post-enhancement). These findings establish the proposed method as a robust solution for restoring degraded MODI script documents, addressing this script's lack of automated OCR systems.

Keywords: Image Enhancement · Noise Removal · Morphological Processing · DBSCAN Clustering · Gradient-Based Analysis · Flood-Fill Algorithm

1 Introduction

Image enhancement and noise removal are fundamental tasks in computer vision and image processing, crucial for applications such as medical imaging, document analysis, and object recognition. Noise degrades image quality, complicating the extraction of meaningful information, especially in environments with poor lighting, low resolution, or distortions caused by transmission errors. Unlike widely studied scripts with established OCR systems, MODI script lacks a fully developed OCR framework, making automated text recognition particularly challenging. Consequently, existing methods relying on OCR-based accuracy metrics are not directly applicable to MODI script restoration.

This research addresses this gap by employing a subjective readability assessment using a Likert scale to evaluate the effectiveness of the proposed denoising method.

Adding to the challenge, MODI script is recognized and read by only a limited number of individuals today, making it difficult to find expert reviewers for subjective evaluations. The dwindling number of proficient MODI readers further underscores the importance of developing automated restoration techniques to preserve and digitize historical documents written in this script. Traditional denoising techniques, such as Gaussian filtering and median filtering, effectively reduce noise but often compromise important image details, such as edges and textures, due to excessive smoothing.

Despite recent advances, conventional methods still struggle to effectively distinguish noise from essential image content, particularly in complex or historical degraded documents where fine text details must be preserved. This limitation highlights a clear research gap—the need for adaptive, precise denoising algorithms that maintain critical image features while effectively removing noise. While previous studies focus on traditional morphological techniques or clustering separately, our approach uniquely integrates both, optimizing feature preservation and noise removal.

This paper addresses this gap by introducing a novel Hybrid Image Enhancement and Noise Removal Algorithm. The primary contribution of our research lies in the strategic integration of classical morphological operations, gradient-based seed detection, flood-fill algorithms, and density-based spatial clustering (DBSCAN). By leveraging gradient analysis and adaptive morphological erosion, our method accurately identifies and preserves significant textual regions while efficiently eliminating noise artifacts.

Specifically, we target historical degraded text documents, an area where noise removal must be balanced precisely with structural preservation to facilitate accurate digitization and analysis. The hybrid approach we propose demonstrates marked improvements in preserving textual clarity and structural integrity compared to traditional standalone methods.

The remainder of this paper is structured as follows: Sect. 2 discusses related state-of-the-art approaches in image denoising and enhancement. Section 3 details the proposed methodology, including its mathematical foundations and implementation steps. Section 4 presents experimental results and evaluates the performance of the proposed algorithm. Finally, Sect. 5 provides conclusions, insights, and outlines future research directions.

2 State-of-the-Art

Image enhancement and noise removal are extensively studied fields within computer vision and image processing, given their significant role in improving application outcomes, such as medical imaging, document analysis, and object recognition. Various classical and modern techniques have been developed, each with strengths and inherent limitations.

Classical methods, including median and Gaussian filters, are commonly used due to their simplicity and effectiveness in general noise reduction. Median filters are particularly efficient at removing salt-and-pepper noise but frequently result in a loss of edge sharpness [1]. Gaussian filters, on the other hand, effectively smooth Gaussian noise but typically blur important details, including edges and textures [2].

Adaptive and morphological techniques have emerged as promising alternatives, balancing noise removal and detail preservation more effectively than classical methods. Morphological operations like erosion and dilation have successfully eliminated isolated noise points without significantly damaging structural integrity [3]. When combined with gradient-based edge detection methods, these techniques further enhance their ability to preserve critical image structures during noise removal [4].

DBSCAN (Density-Based Spatial Clustering of Applications with Noise) clustering has gained recognition for its robustness in separating noise from meaningful structures due to its density-based approach [5]. DBSCAN effectively distinguishes dense clusters of relevant features from sparse regions representing noise, making it particularly valuable in complex noise removal scenarios [6]. Recent advancements have improved DBSCAN's efficiency, allowing it to handle large-scale image processing tasks through optimized spatial indexing techniques [13].

Gradient-based seed detection, coupled with morphological processing, has also received attention for its capacity to accurately pinpoint and preserve important image regions during denoising [7, 8]. These hybrid approaches manage the challenging task of balancing noise suppression with edge and feature conservation [9]. Recent studies integrating deep learning-based gradient estimations have shown enhanced precision in maintaining image structures [14].

HSV color space enhancements have increasingly been adopted to fine-tune image clarity and feature distinction following noise removal. The independent manipulation of hue, saturation, and brightness channels allows precise adjustments, significantly enhancing image quality, color transitions, and overall visual perception [10, 11]. Recent research employs adaptive HSV adjustments guided by deep neural networks, significantly enhancing visual perception in noisy images [15].

Despite significant progress, existing methods still encounter challenges in adaptively distinguishing noise from meaningful content under varying conditions of degradation, particularly in historical degraded documents [12]. Classical and standalone morphological or clustering techniques often fall short in effectively managing these complexities. These existing methods, while effective, fail to adequately balance noise removal with structural preservation in historical text images, necessitating the proposed hybrid approach.

To address these gaps, our research proposes a novel hybrid method integrating adaptive morphological operations, gradient-based seed detection, and DBSCAN clustering. This combination seeks to overcome existing limitations by providing a robust and adaptive solution specifically tailored to historical document restoration tasks.

3 The Proposed Work

3.1 The Problem Statement

Image quality degradation due to noise is a significant challenge in various computer vision applications, including document processing, medical imaging, and object recognition. Noise can arise from multiple sources, such as sensor limitations, poor lighting conditions, transmission errors, or environmental interference. Traditional noise removal techniques, such as median filtering, Gaussian smoothing, and wavelet-based denoising, often struggle to maintain a balance between effective noise reduction and the preservation of essential image details. Excessive filtering can lead to the loss of fine structural features, while insufficient filtering leaves residual noise, reducing image clarity and usability.

While techniques like Gaussian filtering, median filtering, and morphological methods have demonstrated efficacy in general noise removal, their limitations become particularly evident with historical degraded documents. Such documents often contain complex noise patterns and subtle structural details, requiring methods that not only remove noise effectively but also adaptively preserve essential content. To overcome these specific challenges, the proposed hybrid algorithm integrates complementary strengths from morphological operations, gradient-based seed detection, and density-based DBSCAN clustering, enabling adaptive and precise noise reduction tailored explicitly for historical document restoration.

Existing methods also face difficulties in distinguishing between noise and relevant image regions, particularly in complex images with overlapping textures, varying illumination, or weak edges. Classical morphological operations alone may not be sufficient for adaptive noise removal, while statistical clustering methods often require additional preprocessing to perform effectively. Thus, there is a need for a hybrid approach that integrates multiple techniques to selectively remove noise while retaining important image features.

This research aims to address these challenges by proposing a Hybrid Image Enhancement and Noise Removal Algorithm that leverages a combination of grayscale conversion, morphological erosion, gradient-based seed detection, flood-fill region identification, and DBSCAN clustering. This approach enhances image quality by adaptively filtering out noise while preserving essential structures. The proposed method seeks to improve the robustness, adaptability, and efficiency of noise removal techniques, making it suitable for a wide range of image-processing applications.

3.2 Mathematical Formulation

Each step of the algorithm proposed utilizes mathematical methods chosen specifically for their effectiveness in adaptive noise removal and structural detail preservation. Otsu's method is selected for binarization due to its effectiveness in adaptively distinguishing foreground (text) from background, especially beneficial for images with varying contrast levels typical in historical documents. Morphological erosion is utilized because of its proven capability to remove small-scale noise without significantly affecting the primary structures. DBSCAN clustering is employed for its robust capacity to distinguish noise from meaningful content in complex spatial distributions typical of degraded text images.

The grayscale conversion of an RGB image is performed using the formula:

$$\text{Grayscale Value} = 0.2989 \times R + 0.5870 \times G + 0.1140 \times B \quad (1)$$

This is a linear combination of the red, green, and blue channel values, where the coefficients are chosen based on human perception sensitivity to different colors.

Otsu's method is used to convert a grayscale image into a binary image. The threshold T is computed such that it minimizes the within-class variance σ_w^2, , which is the weighted sum of variances of the two classes (foreground and background).

$$\sigma_w^2(T) = w_0(T)\sigma_0^2(T) + w_1(T)\sigma_1^2(T) \quad (2)$$

where:

- $w_0(T)$ and $w_1(T)$ are the probabilities of the two classes separated by the threshold T,
- $\sigma_0^2(T)$ and $\sigma_1^2(T)$ are the variances of the two classes.

The optimal threshold is the one that minimizes $\sigma_w^2(T)$.

Morphological erosion is used to remove noise by shrinking the object boundaries. Given a binary image $I(x, y)$ and a structuring element B, the erosion operation is defined as:

$$(I \ominus B)(x, y) = \min_{(u,v) \in B} I(x+u, y+v) \quad (3)$$

This operation shrinks the white regions (foreground) in the binary image. The horizontal and diagonal kernels used in the algorithm act as structuring elements that emphasize specific directional features. Morphological erosion simplifies the image before applying DBSCAN, ensuring cleaner separation of text from noise.

Gradients are used to detect edges and transitions between regions in the image. The gradient of a 1D signal (e.g., a column of pixel intensities) is computed as the discrete difference between adjacent pixel values:

$$\nabla I(i) = I(i+1) - I(i) \quad (4)$$

The gradients are analyzed to detect significant transitions (edges), which serve as seed points for flood-filling.

Flood-filling is used to identify connected regions of the image that meet certain criteria (e.g., pixels having similar intensity). It works by starting from a seed point and iteratively adding neighboring pixels that satisfy the flood criterion. This is mathematically similar to breadth-first search (BFS) in a graph, where each pixel is a node, and its 4 or 8 neighbors are edges.

The DBSCAN (Density-Based Spatial Clustering of Applications with Noise) algorithm is used to separate noise from relevant text points. The seed points obtained from gradient analysis can either be part of relevant text or noise. DBSCAN clusters these points based on their associated flood-fill areas, indirectly distinguishing text from noise. The DBSCAN clusters points based on density, using two parameters: ϵ (the maximum distance between two points to be considered neighbors) and min_samples (the minimum number of points required to form a dense region). The DBSCAN parameters were optimized empirically to maximize accuracy while minimizing over-segmentation.

The distance metric used is usually the Euclidean distance:

$$d(x, y) = \sqrt{(x_1 - y_1)^2 + (x_2 - y_2)^2 + \cdots + (x_n - y_n)^2} \quad (5)$$

DBSCAN assigns cluster labels to points based on their local density, with points that do not belong to any cluster being labeled as noise.

The enhancement part of the algorithm adjusts pixel values based on statistical measures such as the mean and mode.

- The mean of a set of pixel values is computed as:

$$\mu = \frac{1}{n} \sum_{i=1}^{n} x_i \tag{6}$$

- The mode is the value that appears most frequently in a dataset. It is used to replace pixels that are considered noise.

For each pixel, if it is determined to be noise (using flood fill and clustering), its intensity is replaced by the mode of surrounding pixels. This helps in homogenizing regions that should have uniform appearance.

The RGB image is converted to HSV color space for easier manipulation of color properties like hue and saturation. The mathematical relationship between RGB and HSV is non-linear and involves computing the maximum and minimum values among the red, green, and blue channels:

- Hue (H) is defined as the angular position of the color on the color wheel.
- Saturation (S) is defined as the difference between the maximum and minimum values, normalized by the intensity.
- Value (V) is simply the maximum value among R, G, and B.

These are computed using:

$$V = \max(R, G, B)$$
$$S = \frac{V - \min(R, G, B)}{V}$$

$H =$ Based on the relative magnitudes of R, G, B

The inverse transformation is performed after enhancement (HSV back to RGB).

After applying the enhancements, the image is converted back from HSV to RGB, and the filtered image is saved in the specified format (JPEG, PNG, etc.).

3.3 The Proposed Algorithm

Input:

- $I \rightarrow$ Noisy RGB image
- axes $\rightarrow$ Number of gradient axes to compute seed points
- plot_filtering_info $\rightarrow$ Boolean flag for visualization

Output:

- $I_{enhanced} \rightarrow$ Enhanced image with noise removed

The algorithm's implementation sequentially integrates these chosen techniques, beginning with grayscale conversion and binarization to simplify initial image processing tasks. Morphological erosion further refines the image by removing isolated artifacts, creating an optimal condition for gradient-based seed point identification. Flood-fill is employed following seed detection as it effectively identifies connected regions based on gradient transitions, distinguishing meaningful structures from noise. DBSCAN clustering subsequently leverages flood-fill results, grouping areas based on density to further isolate and discard noise. Lastly, HSV color space enhancement employs statistical measures, specifically the mode, to adjust pixel values, thereby providing robust visual clarity by homogenizing noise-affected regions effectively while maintaining the texture of the original image.

Step 1: Convert Image to Grayscale: Given a noisy RGB image I, the algorithm first normalizes the image to the range [0, 1] and converts it to grayscale using the weighted sum. Otsu's thresholding is then applied to obtain a binary image $B(x, y)$.

- Normalize the RGB image to the range [0, 1].
- Convert to grayscale using the formula:

$$G(x, y) = 0.2989 R(x, y) + 0.5870 G(x, y) + 0.1140 B(x, y)$$

- Apply Otsu's thresholding to binarize the grayscale image:

$$B(x, y) = \begin{cases} 1, & G(x, y) \geq T^* \\ 0, & G(x, y) < T^* \end{cases}$$

Step 2: Morphological Erosion for Noise Removal: In order to retain segments of the relevant text, morphological erosion is performed iteratively using specifically designed structuring elements—a horizontal kernel to address horizontal noise and diagonal kernels for diagonal patterns. The erosion process refines the image, which is optionally visualized if the flag for filtering information is enabled.

- Define structuring elements:
- Horizontal Kernel: Detects horizontal noise.
- Diagonal Kernels: Detects diagonal noise patterns.
- Apply binary erosion iteratively to remove small-scale noise.

$$E(x, y) = \min_{(i,j) \in S} B(x + i, y + j)$$

- Visualize the results if plot_filtering_info = True.

Step 3: Compute Gradients and Detect Seed Points: Next, the algorithm evaluates the gradient transitions along 'n' equally spaced vertical axes ('n' 1-D arrays) where 'n' corresponds to the axes parameter. By detecting transitions in the gradient—from -1 to + 1—seed points are identified, which are subsequently classified as potential text or noise points.

- Divide the image into vertical slices based on axes.

- Compute image gradients:

$$G_x(x, y) = I(x + 1, y) - I(x, y)$$
$$G_y(x, y) = I(x, y + 1) - I(x, y)$$

- Identify transition points where the gradient changes from -1 to $+1$.
- Store seed points corresponding to meaningful regions (text) and noise.

Step 4: Apply Flood-Fill to Extract Connected Regions: A flood-fill algorithm is then applied starting from each seed point, resulting in connected regions whose areas are computed. The regions where flood-fill successfully connects pixels are considered likely to represent text.

- Initialize a flood mask and apply morphological flood-fill from seed points:

$$|I(x\prime, y\prime) - I(x, y)| \leq \tau$$

- Regions where the flood-fill succeeds are considered as relevant text/objects.

Step 5: Separate Relevant Data from Noise Using DBSCAN: To further separate noise from relevant text, the algorithm applies DBSCAN clustering to the areas derived from the flood-fill. This clustering groups seed points with similar flood-fill areas, where clusters corresponding to smaller areas are interpreted as noise and are discarded, while clusters with larger areas are retained as meaningful text. Histograms of the clustered areas can be visualized to validate this separation.

- Extract flood-filled regions and apply DBSCAN clustering:

$$N_\epsilon(p) = \{q \in P \mid d(p, q) \leq \epsilon\}$$

- Low-density clusters → Noise (discarded).
- High-density clusters → Retained as meaningful content.
- Visualize cluster separation with histograms.

Step 6: Apply Final Image Enhancement in HSV Color Space: In the final enhancement step, the image is converted from RGB to HSV color space. Here, rather than reapplying the flood-fill, the previously computed flood-fill mask is used to identify noise pixels. For these pixels, the intensity in the V-channel is replaced with the mode of the entire image (or, if refined further, a local mode could be considered), and hue and saturation are adjusted using additional statistical measures. Finally, the enhanced HSV image is converted back to RGB to yield the denoised, enhanced image.

- Convert image from RGB → HSV color space.
- For noise pixels, replace intensity with the mode of neighboring pixels:

$$V\prime(x, y) = \text{mode}(N(x, y))$$

- Adjust hue and saturation using statistical measures.
- Convert image back to RGB.

Step 7: Return Enhanced Image

- Output the filtered image I_{enhanced}.
- Optionally save and visualize the image at various stages.

Complexity Analysis

- Grayscale conversion: $O(N)$
- Otsu's thresholding: $O(N)$
- Morphological operations: $O(N)$
- Gradient computation: $O(N)$
- Flood-fill: $O(N)$
- DBSCAN clustering: $O(N \log N)$
- Final enhancement: $O(N)$
- Overall Complexity: $O(N \log N)$ due to DBSCAN.

4 Experimental Results and Discussion

The experimental dataset consisted of historical handwritten text documents with varying degrees of degradation and noise. Images were captured at high resolutions (300–600 dpi) to simulate real-world digitization scenarios. Since MODI script lacks an established OCR system, traditional OCR-based evaluation methods cannot be applied for performance assessment. Instead, we adopted a structured Likert-scale readability assessment, where independent human reviewers rated the clarity and legibility of restored text. This method ensures a qualitative yet systematic evaluation of the algorithm's impact on text readability. Conducting a structured readability evaluation for MODI script posed additional challenges due to the scarcity of individuals proficient in reading it. As a result, finding qualified reviewers was a difficult task, limiting the sample size for subjective assessments. Despite this, the experts provided consistent readability scores, ensuring a reliable qualitative evaluation of the proposed method. Subjective assessments were conducted by five independent reviewers, who evaluated readability improvements based on clarity and ease of text recognition on a 5-point Likert scale.

The proposed hybrid approach was evaluated specifically on handwritten and degraded document images, common in archival and digitization projects. The primary goal was to enhance readability by effectively removing noise and preserving crucial structural details of the text.

Initially, the input RGB images (Fig. 1) exhibited significant noise and degradation, hindering legibility. To address this, the images were converted to grayscale (Fig. 2), simplifying the data and facilitating subsequent adaptive binarization using Otsu's method. This binarization enhanced the contrast notably, especially in faded text regions, making handwriting clearer and more distinguishable, even under challenging noise conditions.

Subsequently, morphological erosion was applied using carefully selected structuring elements (Fig. 3). These included a horizontal kernel targeting horizontal noise patterns and diagonal kernels addressing diagonal noise.

The erosion successfully eliminated small-scale artifacts such as speckles and ink smudges. The resulting image (Fig. 4) demonstrated clearer separation between meaningful text and noise. Gradient magnitudes were analyzed (Fig. 5) to identify transitions and significant edges, crucial for seed point detection.

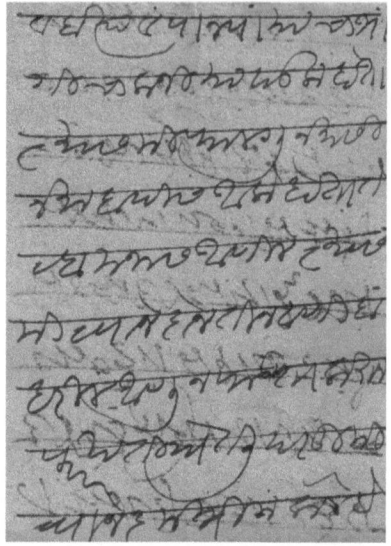
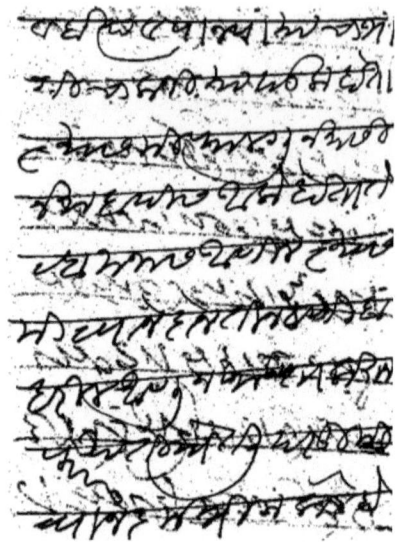

Fig. 1. Original Noisy RGB Image   **Fig. 2.** Grayscale Converted Image

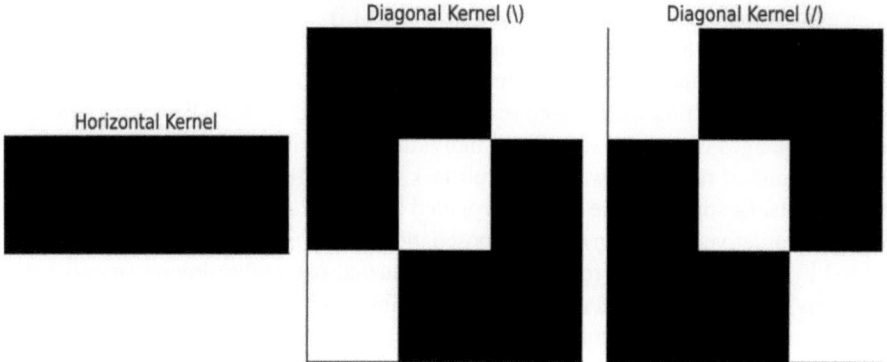

Fig. 3. Structuring Elements for Morphological Erosion

Figure 6 illustrates the identified seed points after gradient-based edge detection. These seed points represent significant intensity transitions in the image, corresponding to the potential locations of text regions or noise artifacts. By analyzing gradient magnitudes along multiple axes, the algorithm effectively pinpoints edges and transition regions, which serve as the basis for the subsequent flood-fill segmentation. The distribution of these seed points is crucial for distinguishing meaningful text from unwanted noise, as they guide the clustering and classification process.

Figure 7 displays the flood-fill mask generated using the detected seed points. The flood-fill algorithm expands from these seed points to identify connected regions based on intensity similarities. This process enables the separation of meaningful text structures from isolated noise artifacts. The flood-filled areas represent distinct clusters of text and

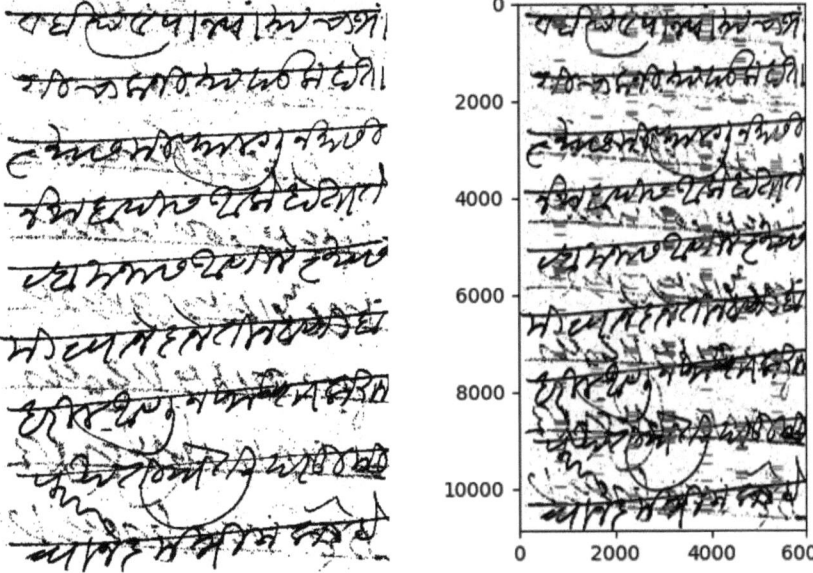

Fig. 4. Image after Morphological Erosion   **Fig. 5.** Gradient Magnitude Image

noise, forming the foundation for DBSCAN clustering. The effectiveness of this step ensures that text regions remain intact while suppressing noise, facilitating improved readability in the final enhanced output.

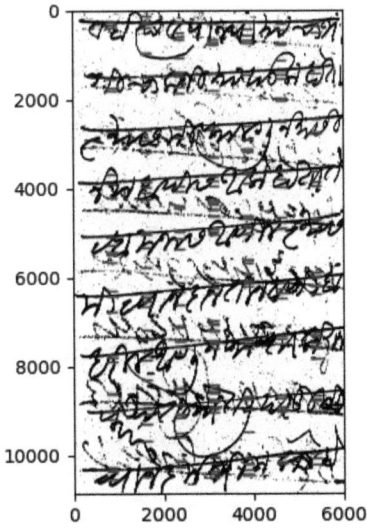
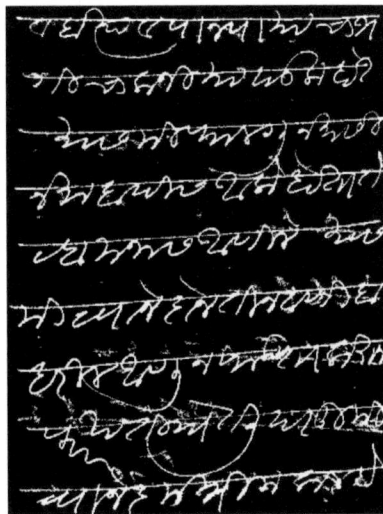

Fig. 6. Detected Seed Points   **Fig. 7.** Flood Fill mask

Figure 8 illustrates the distribution of flood-filled region areas originating from noise seed points. The histogram indicates that most noise-generated regions are relatively small, with the highest frequency around zero. This clearly confirms that noise points generally result in limited region expansion, validating the effectiveness of the proposed method in identifying and restricting the spread of noise.

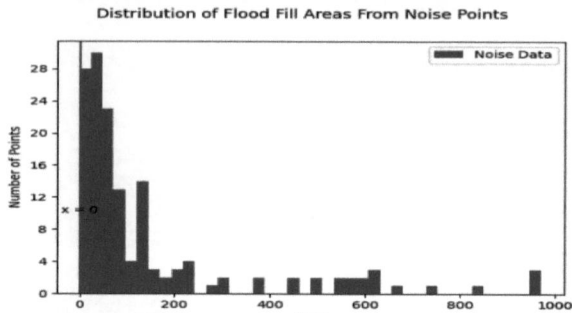

Fig. 8. Distribution of Flood-Filled Region Areas Originating from Noise Seed Points

Figure 9 demonstrates the distribution of flood-filled region areas originating from text seed points. Unlike noise-related regions, areas originating from text points typically exhibit larger connected components, evident from substantial occurrences at higher area values. This distinct contrast highlights the proposed algorithm's strength in accurately isolating meaningful textual content, significantly enhancing the readability and overall quality of processed documents.

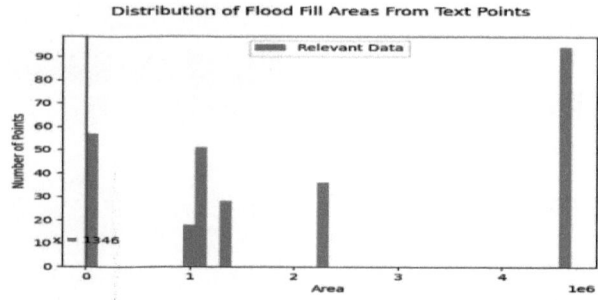

Fig. 9. Distribution of Flood-Filled Region Areas Originating from Text Seed Points

DBSCAN clustering was applied to further refine the separation of noise from text (Fig. 10).

The resulting image after flood-fill clearly delineated these areas from residual noise (Fig. 11). Dense clusters, identified as meaningful regions, were preserved, whereas sparse clusters labeled as noise were effectively discarded. For each seed point obtained from the gradient analysis, the connected region's area is computed using flood fill. Then, DBSCAN clustering is applied on these area measurements. This step groups seed points

Robust Image Denoising Using Gradient Seeds   237

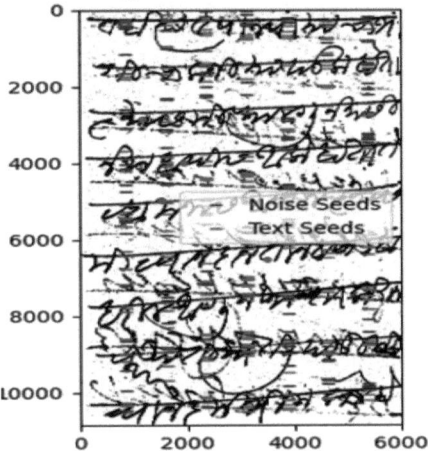

Fig. 10. Results after identifying noise and test seeds

with similar flood-fill areas. Seed points that form clusters with relatively small areas are interpreted as noise, while those in clusters with larger areas are assumed to correspond to relevant text. In this way, DBSCAN indirectly separates noise from text based on the intrinsic characteristics of their connected regions. Finally, image enhancement was conducted from HSV to RGB (Fig. 12), improving visual clarity and the readability of the final output.

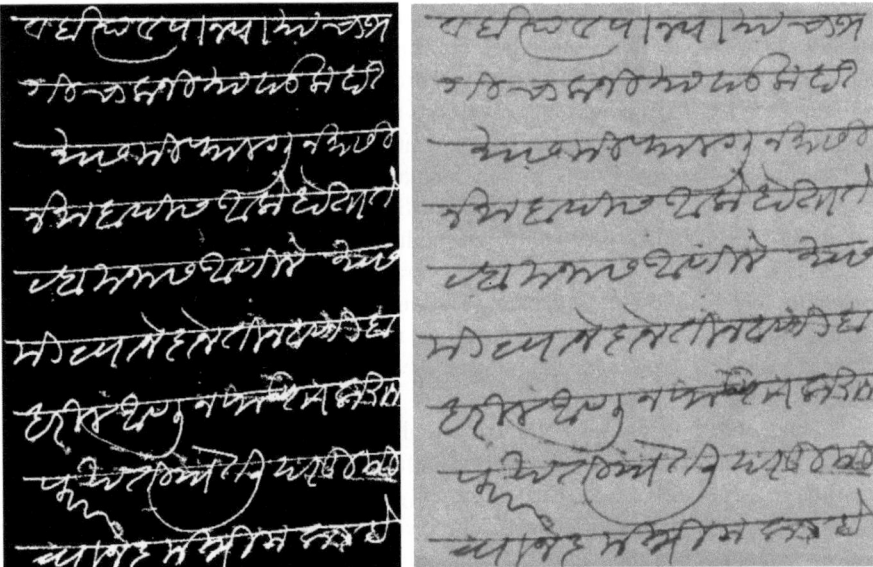

Fig. 11. Result after DBSCANS   **Fig. 12.** Enhanced Image

Subjective assessments from human reviewers confirmed significant improvements in image legibility. Subjective evaluation results showed improvement in readability, with average scores rising from 1.8 (pre-enhancement) to 4.5 (post-enhancement) out of 5 on the Likert scale. The experimental outcomes validate the effectiveness of the proposed hybrid approach in restoring historical degraded documents. The visual comparisons clearly demonstrate improved readability showing superior performance relative to conventional denoising techniques.

However, the algorithm's computational complexity remains a limitation, particularly for high-resolution documents or extensive digitization tasks. Future optimization, possibly involving GPU acceleration or parallel processing techniques, could significantly improve scalability.

Despite computational considerations, the approach offers considerable advantages in real-world scenarios, clearly addressing critical shortcomings of existing standalone methods.

5 Conclusion and Future Prospects

In this work, we presented a hybrid approach for enhancing handwritten and degraded document images, combining gradient-based seed detection, morphological processing, and DBSCAN clustering to improve the legibility of noisy and degraded text. The experimental results demonstrated that the proposed method effectively removed noise and enhanced contrast, leading to significant improvements in overall readability of the documents.

The experimental results demonstrate that the proposed hybrid method effectively reduces noise while preserving essential text structures in historical degraded documents. Notably, our approach with subjective readability assessments indicating substantial enhancement. By integrating morphological processing, gradient-based seed detection, and DBSCAN clustering, our method offers a robust solution to the challenges of text degradation and noise interference in document digitization projects.

Despite these advancements, computational complexity remains a limiting factor, particularly in high-resolution images. The DBSCAN clustering step, while effective, contributes significantly to processing time, highlighting the need for future optimization. Additionally, performance under extreme degradation scenarios—where text is barely distinguishable—still presents challenges requiring further refinement. While effective, our method struggles in extreme degradation cases where character shapes are severely distorted. A hybrid approach combining rule-based and learning-based methods could further improve restoration quality.

Looking ahead, there are several opportunities for further improving the proposed method. First, optimizing the computational efficiency of the algorithm is essential for real-time or large-scale applications, especially in the context of digitization projects. Exploring parallel processing techniques or incorporating GPU acceleration could help reduce the processing time without sacrificing quality.

One of the primary challenges in MODI script restoration is the absence of a standardized OCR system, which limits the feasibility of automated performance evaluation. Our approach circumvents this limitation by employing a structured human readability assessment. The limited number of MODI script readers not only complicates subjective evaluation but also highlights the urgent need for automated restoration and recognition techniques. Developing an OCR system for MODI script could significantly aid in preserving and accessing historical texts without relying on a small pool of human experts for validation. However, future research could explore the development of an OCR model tailored to MODI script, enabling automated text recognition and further enhancing restoration efforts.

To enhance computational efficiency, future work will focus on optimizing the algorithm through GPU acceleration and parallel processing, aiming to reduce runtime while maintaining performance. Further research could also explore the integration of deep learning models for text region segmentation, allowing more adaptive denoising strategies for severely degraded documents. Hybrid approaches combining deep learning with traditional morphological processing could provide enhanced adaptability while ensuring interpretability in noise removal tasks.

Additionally, further research could focus on improving the algorithm's performance in cases of extreme degradation, where portions of the text are nearly indistinguishable from the background. Integrating machine learning-based models for text recognition in conjunction with the current method may provide better recovery in such scenarios.

Future work could also explore the application of the hybrid approach to colored or multi-lingual document images, where noise and degradation may manifest differently across varying document types. By addressing these challenges, the proposed method could be refined and adapted to a wider range of document restoration and digitization tasks, contributing to the preservation of historical and archival materials.

Additionally, extending the method's applicability to colored and multilingual historical documents is a promising avenue. Many archival materials contain multi-hue backgrounds and non-Latin scripts, requiring specialized processing techniques. Investigating color-space transformations tailored to such cases, along with language-independent feature extraction methods, could significantly broaden the impact of this research in the field of document restoration.

References

1. Bovik, A.C.: Handbook of Image and Video Processing. Academic Press, Cambridge (2005)
2. Gonzalez, R.C., Woods, R.E.: Digital Image Processing, 4th edn. Pearson, Boston (2018)
3. Haralick, R.M., Sternberg, S.R., Zhuang, X.: Image analysis using mathematical morphology. IEEE Trans. Pattern Anal. Mach. Intell. **9**(4), 532–550 (1987)
4. Serra, J.: Image Analysis and Mathematical Morphology. Academic Press, London (1982)
5. Ester, M., Kriegel, H.-P., Sander, J., Xu, X.: A Density-Based Algorithm for Discovering Clusters in Large Spatial Databases with Noise. In: Simoudis, E., Han, J., Fayyad, U. (eds.) KDD 1996, pp. 226–231. AAAI Press, Portland (1996)
6. Han, J., Kamber, M., Pei, J.: Data Mining: Concepts and Techniques, 3rd edn. Morgan Kaufmann, San Francisco (2011)
7. Acharya, T., Ray, A.K.: Image Processing: Principles and Applications. Wiley, Hoboken (2005)
8. Jain, A.K.: Fundamentals of Digital Image Processing. Prentice Hall, Upper Saddle River (1989)

9. Pratt, W.K.: Digital Image Processing, 3rd edn. John Wiley & Sons, New York (2001)
10. Smith, A.R.: Color gamut transform pairs. In: Proceedings of the 5th Annual Conference on Computer Graphics and Interactive Techniques, pp. 12–19. ACM, New York (1978)
11. Gonzalez, R.C., Woods, R.E., Eddins, S.L.: Digital Image Processing Using MATLAB. 2nd edn. Pearson Prentice Hall, Upper Saddle River (2009)
12. Rajagopalan, A.N., Suryanarayanan, S., Mittal, S.: Adaptive morphological image filtering for improved noise reduction. J. Imaging Sci. Technol. **60**(4), 40401-1–40401-9 (2016)
13. Kumar, A., Kaur, J., Singh, R.: Optimized DBSCAN clustering for efficient noise removal in large-scale image datasets. Multimedia Tools Appl. **78**(14), 19545–19563 (2019)
14. Liu, W., Zhang, L., Yang, H.: Hybrid image enhancement using deep learning-based gradient estimation and morphological operations. IEEE Trans. Image Process. **29**, 5853–5865 (2020)
15. Chen, Y., Li, X., Wang, H.: Deep learning guided adaptive HSV image enhancement for noisy visual conditions. Neurocomputing **284**, 190–200 (2018)

Author Index

A
Adeliyi, Timothy   212
Ahmad, Muhammad Anwar   17
Arman, Muhamad Haikal   17
Assaf, Mansour H.   115
Atsango, C.   83

B
Barman, Dilip Kr.   45
Barve, Soham   170
Bezboruah, Tulshi   158
Bignotti, Alex   212
Boruah, Abhijit   45

C
Chand, Sarvesh   115

D
Das, Sonali   212
Datta, Sujoy   185

G
Gaber, Jaafar   72
Garima,   27
Gogate, Paritosh   170
Guleria, Aishvi   27

H
Hattingh, Marie   212
Hayden, Stephanie   224
Hazarika, Nityananda   158

I
Ismail, Ajune Wanis   17

J
Jindal, Shweta   27

K
Kaghazgaran, Mohammadreza   72

Kalita, Dushmanta M.   45
Kamble, Aparna   170

L
Lorenz, Pascal   72

M
Mala, T.   3
Mesrinejad, Faezeh   130
Moloo, Raj Kishen   59
Mtwenka, Sakhiwo   212

N
Nithish Kumar, V.   185

P
Pandey, Neel   95
Permessur, Shaeez   59
Praneeth Kumar, G.   185
Priyanka, D.   3

R
Ranwadkar, Shreeya   170
Roy, Ram Kishore   158

S
Sangeetha, S.   145
Shah, Vansh   197
Sharma, Bibhya   115
Sharma, Krishneel   115
Singh, Hidam Kumarjit   158
Sivaselvan, B.   185
Sonawane, Rohit   197
Sujatha, R.   145
Sultania, Saket   197

T
Tamhankar, Parag Anil   224
Tiwari, Harshvardhan   95

U
Uppada, Santosh Kumar   185

V
Vaidya, Hemanshu   170
van Deventer, J. P.   83

Varshney, Kamya   27
Vichare, Abhishek   197

W
Wani, Abid Hussain   130

MIX
Papier aus verantwortungsvollen Quellen
Paper from responsible sources
FSC® C105338

If you have any concerns about our products,
you can contact us on
ProductSafety@springernature.com

In case Publisher is established outside the EU,
the EU authorized representative is:
**Springer Nature Customer Service Center GmbH
Europaplatz 3, 69115 Heidelberg, Germany**

Printed by Libri Plureos GmbH
in Hamburg, Germany